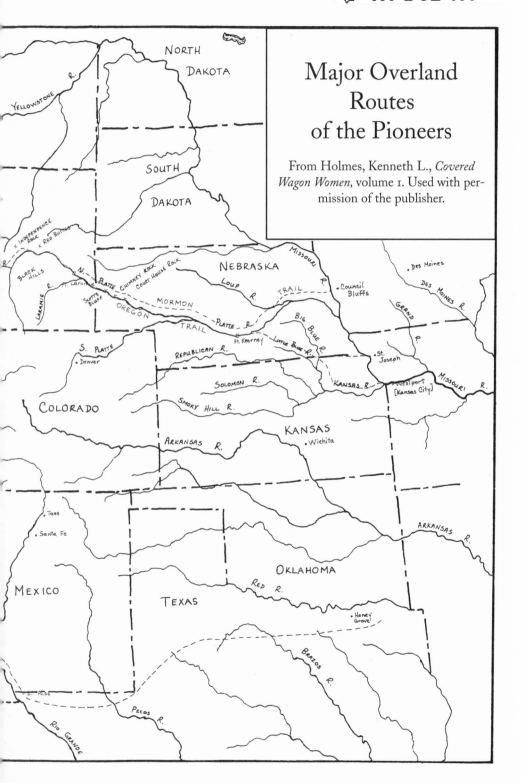

Major Overland Routes of the Pioneers

From Holmes, Kenneth L., *Covered Wagon Women*, volume 1. Used with permission of the publisher.

American Trails Series
XX

Harriet Hitchcock
From Holmes, Covered Wagon Women, *v. 8,*
and used with the permission of the publisher.

Children's Voices
from the
Trail

NARRATIVES OF THE
PLATTE RIVER ROAD

by
Rosemary Gudmundson Palmer

THE ARTHUR H. CLARK COMPANY
Spokane, Washington
2002

Arthur H. Clark Company
P.O. Box 14707
Spokane, WA 99214

LIBRARY OF CONGRESS CATALOG CARD NUMBER 2001047474
ISBN-0-87062-313-3

Palmer, Rosemary Gudmundson.
   Children's voices from the trail : narratives of the Platte River road / by Rosemary
Gudmundson Palmer.
      p. cm. —(American trails series: 20)
   Includes bibliographical references and index.
   ISBN 0-87062-313-3 (alk. paper)
      1. Pioneer children—West (U.S.)—Social conditions—19th century. 2. White
   children—West (U.S.)—Social conditions—19th century. 3. Pioneer children—West
   (U.S.)—Biography. 4. Frontier and pioneer life—West (U.S.) 5. Overland journeys to the
   Pacific. 6. West (U.S.)—Description and travel. 7. West (U.S.)—History—19th
   century—Sources. 8. West (U.S.)—Biography. 9. Trails—West (U.S.)—History—19th
   century. 10. Platte River Valley (Neb.)—Description and travel. I. Title

F596 .P35 2001
978'.02—dc21   2001047474

Contents

Illustrations

Aknowledgments

After making friends with hundreds of pioneer children who recorded their recollections, it is my turn to reminisce. I wish to express appreciation to those individuals who helped make my memories possible. I owe special thanks to professors in the College of Education at the University of Wyoming, to Dr. Phil Roberts in the history department, and to Joanna Orr and her colleagues at the University of Wyoming interlibrary loan and outreach programs who supplied the legwork for my Ph.D. dissertation, which is the forerunner of this book. To those who produced bibliographies of pioneers who crossed the plains, I extend my thanks. Among them are Mel Bashore and Linda Haslam, Davis Bitton, Kris White, and the late Merrill Mattes.

Special thanks go to those at the repositories listed in the bibliography who helped me access primary documents and illustrations, then allowed me to include these references in my writings. Other individuals also shared accounts of relatives who crossed the plains as children. For example, Tom Macaulay permitted me to use a photocopy of Eliza McAuley's diary, Frank Bender sent me a typescript of Flora Bender's diary, and both provided additional information about these young emigrants. I am especially indebted to Mel Bashore of the Church of Jesus Christ of Latter-day Saints Historical Department for his knowledge of Mormon pioneer companies and his willingness to share his expertise. To Bob Clark of the Arthur H. Clark Company, who accepted my book manuscript for publication and offered revision suggestions, and to Will Bagley who also read my manuscript and made suggestions, I offer my sincere appreciation.

I am grateful to family and friends who shared the joys and tribulations of my research and writing. My deepest appreciation goes to my husband Fred who tolerated, supported, and encouraged my scholarly endeavors. He also assisted in collecting primary documents and checked references during earlier drafts. My daughter Melanie spent hours in libraries and special collections helping me gather materials and make photocopies, although digging into archival documents was not her idea of fun. I am grateful to my son Chris whose support allowed me to achieve my research goals. Finally, I am grateful to my deceased parents who taught me to love pioneer stories and to nineteenth–century pioneer children who perpetuated their experiences on paper so that future generations can access their interpretation of this important moment in history.

Introduction

Bloomington, Indiana, Tuesday, March 20, 1849.—Our family, consisting of father, mother, two brothers and one sister, left this morning for that far and much talked of country, California. My father started our wagons one month in advance, to St. Joseph, Missouri, our starting point. . . . Our train numbered fifty wagons.[1]
                                                            —Sallie Hester, age 13

Between 1835 and 1869, approximately 350,000 pioneers followed the Platte River road from the Missouri River to South Pass, Wyoming, and then on to the Pacific Coast. Many other travelers made the trek part of the way to Utah, Colorado, or Montana. Men who desired free land, better health, economic or status improvement, or adventure made the decision to move to the West—and their wives and offspring often accompanied them. Families who joined The Church of Jesus Christ of Latter-day Saints (L.D.S. or Mormons) throughout the United States, the British Isles, Scandinavia, and other parts of Western Europe made the journey for religious reasons.[2] Ministers of other faiths took their wives and children west as well. Some of the emigrants kept a record of their three- to six-month trail experiences while they traveled; others wrote about them years later. Even children wrote. In fact, at no other time during the nineteenth century, except during the Civil

---

[1]Hester, "Diary," 234. For complete citations of footnote references, please refer to the Bibliography.

[2]Mattes, *Platte River*, 1–5. Mormon is a nickname for a member of The Church of Jesus Christ of Latter-day Saints. L.D.S. is an abbreviation frequently used when referring to this church or its members.

War, did Americans keep as many personal accounts of their lives. As a result, historians and other scholars have examined the mid-nineteenth century westward movement in considerable detail. These analyses, however, have primarily been from the viewpoint of adult emigrants. Although at least one-fifth of the overlanders were young people, their story is just beginning to be told.[3]

Contemporary historians and writers who have begun to consider the child's story include Lillian Schlissel, Sandra Myres, John Mack Faragher, and Julie Roy Jeffrey. As they described men and women emigrants, they mentioned youngsters, but only to connect young people's experiences to adult lives and not to deal with children themselves.[4] Elizabeth Hampsten discussed children growing up on the Great Plains, and Elliott West presented insights into children on the trail. West's focus, however, was young people in mining towns of the West and on farms and ranches in the Great Plains and Southwest. Emmy Werner described young California pioneers through their own writings as well as observations by adult travelers. John Baur discussed pioneer children going to California and their early life in the settlements.[5] In several journal articles Robert Munkres and Lillian Schlissel talked about women and girls on the road west, Howard Lamar focused on young men and their families, and Georgia Read elaborated on women and children on the trail. Articles by Ruth Moynihan, Elliott West, and Judy Allen dealt specifically with children crossing the plains.[6] Only a few authors, such as Susan Arrington Madsen, Jill Jacobsen Andros, and Violet Kimball, have investigated young Mormon emigrants.[7] But no one has

---

[3]Schlissel, *Women's Diaries*, 10; Faragher, *Women and Men*, 195–196; West, *Growing Up*, 13.

[4]See Schlissel, *Women's Diaries*; Schlissel, Gibbens, and Hampsten, *Far From Home*; Myres, *Westering Women*; Faragher, *Women and Men*; Jeffrey, *Frontier Women*.

[5]See Hampsten, *Settlers' Children*; West, *Growing Up*; Werner, *Pioneer Children*; Baur, *Growing Up*.

[6]Munkres, "Wives, Mothers," 191–224; Schlissel, "Mothers and Daughters," 29–33; Lamar, "Rites of Passage," 33–67; Read, "Women and Children," 1–23; Moynihan, "Children," 279–294; West, "Youngest Pioneers," 90–96; Allen, "Children," 2–11.

[7]Madsen, *I Walked*; Andros, "Are We There," 5–10; Kimball, *Stories*.

made an in-depth study of Mormon children crossing the plains, and no one has compared or contrasted them to young-sters going to the Pacific Coast. Also, there is a lack of research about children traveling on the California, Mormon, and Oregon trails. Most works deal with one or two trails but not all three, although Violet Kimball made an attempt in her book geared for early adolescent readers. Other books, such as those by Rebecca Stefoff, by Linda Peavy and Ursula Smith, or by Mary Barmeyer O'Brien, are being published for general or children's audiences and are not scholarly works.[8]

Writers who have described emigrant children have provided insights into youngsters and the westering experience, and they have suggested possibilities for further study. Besides the lack of research on young Mormon pioneers and children on the three trails, no one has attempted to analyze the child's perspective by distinguishing between contemporary accounts by young pioneers and reminiscences recorded years later. These primary documents are usually treated as the same, even though diaries and letters are more reliable in portraying the child's viewpoint. Most articles and books about children on the overland trail discuss common themes, such as animals, pleasure, curiosity, chores, fears, accidents, death, and Native Americans, without really seeing the event from "two or three feet off the ground."[9] In other words, they do not separate the child's vision from adult perceptions in reminiscences. While books and articles consider nostalgia and the remembered past, no one has connected them to young people crossing the plains.[10] By making these connections, perhaps the child's viewpoint may be more clearly understood.

This book examines the white child's perspective on the Platte River road's Oregon, California, and Mormon trails between 1841 and the 1869 completion of the transcontinen-

[8]Stefoff, *Children*; Peavy and Smith, *Frontier Children*; O'Brien, *Setting Sun*.
[9]West, *Growing Up*, xviii.
[10]For example, see Lowenthal, *The Past*; Milner, "Shared Memory," 2–13; and Milner, "View from Wisdom," 2–17.

tal railroad. After that year families still traveled to the West in covered wagons, but a more rapid means of transportation was available. To identify the child's perspective, I purposely chose first-person accounts which included twenty-three diaries, letters, and journals of young pioneers and 430 reminiscences of adults who made the trek as children. Arbitrarily, I chose the sixteenth birthday as the cut-off date for reminiscences but have included diaries and letters written by sixteen year olds since so few contemporary accounts by younger pioneers were available. All ages were calculated according to date of departure. The diaries, letters, and journals were written by children ten through sixteen, with almost all the authors being girls. This means that few male voices were heard and none from children younger than ten. While contemporary documents are difficult to obtain, hundreds of reminiscences are preserved in archives, special collections, and published sources. Even adults who were illiterate or chose not to write shared their stories, thanks to the Works Progress Administration (WPA) in Utah and Oregon and private interviewers, such as Fred Lockley, who created oral histories and thus reached a wider group of pioneers.[11]

Of 712 total documents, I selected 430 reminiscences and eliminated 259 memoirs which provided little or no information about the trek. Almost half of the emigrants who did not describe the journey were infants and toddlers or were born on the trail; the rest focused on other periods of their lives. In this book I refer to some accounts more than others, mainly because the writers developed their topics and experiences. All 712 documents belonged to white emigrants who crossed the plains as children or young adolescents. Almost all were born in the United States, Canada, the British Isles, Scandinavia, and Western Europe. Three-fourths of the young American pioneers had origins in the Midwest, and over 90

---

[11]For more detail on the selection and location of sources, refer to Bibliography herein. For information about oral interview sources, see Chapter 1

percent of foreign-born children came from Great Britain and Scandinavia. Tables I through IV in the Appendix provide a breakdown of state or country of origin, age and sex of children, and year of emigration. Some of these records have appeared in published sources; however, only 4 percent of the Mormon writers published their reminiscences while they were alive, while 24 percent of non-Mormons did. Many accounts were typescripts of manuscripts, and a limited number were original documents or microfilm copies of originals. If the account was not an original or photocopy of an original, it was difficult to ascertain if it was genuine. Also, it was hard to determine if these narratives provided a fair representation of all children who traveled on the California, Oregon, and Mormon trails. For instance, more records surfaced from the Oregon and Mormon trails than from the California Trail; however, fewer families traveled to the gold fields in the late 1840s and early 1850s. Other routes were available to the Pacific Coast, such as the Santa Fe and Southern trails, the Isthmus of Panama route, and sea voyages around Cape Hope. John Unruh noted that approximately two-thirds of Pacific Coast travelers went on these other routes.[12] Also, I located almost twice as many Mormon reminiscences as non-Mormon.

To critically analyze diaries, letters, journals, and reminiscences for the child's perspective, researchers should know about the historical moment in which the stories happened. By studying primary and secondary sources, historians may understand a time period better than those who lived in it. In addition to gathering information about the westward migration, researchers should gain insights into childhood, child development, and nineteenth-century American and Western European family life and culture. Many pioneers were influenced by the early and middle years of Queen Victoria's reign, for the British way of life affected its own nation and other countries, particularly the United States. Since emigrants sought

---

[12]Unruh, *Plains Across*, 401.

opportunities or religious freedom, not a new civilization, they carried their culture with them. The family was a critical social unit, and the trek westward was largely a family affair. The child's perspective on the overland route was somewhat different from an adult's, for children often saw what grown-ups missed. One must be cautious, however, about analyzing nineteenth-century children through today's eyes, habits, and behaviors. Not being grounded in the historical context might distort the perceptions of children of that period.[13] Yet history seen through the eyes of a nineteenth-century child can provide one more vision of the westward migration.

MID-NINETEENTH CENTURY SOCIETY

Unfortunately, a single image of mid-nineteenth century society cannot be neatly assembled like a jigsaw puzzle in which all the pieces join to form one picture. Individuals and families from different countries, social classes, and ethnic and racial backgrounds exhibited their own unique identities and behaviors. In the United States, for example, Native American and Spanish cultures coexisted with the British American Protestant way of life which exerted a type of hegemony during these years. Alternative viewpoints and lifestyles, such as those of American intellectuals like Whitman, Melville, and Poe, thrived as well. Furthermore, periods of economic boom and depression affected people's lifestyles. England prospered between 1848 and 1857, but from 1837 through 1842 and in the late 1850s Britain and America both suffered economic slumps. Moreover, mid-nineteenth century society did not emerge from a void but reflected trends from the previous century; for example, the Industrial Revolution helped create the dominant bourgeois Victorian culture.[14]

---

[13]Barzun and Graff, *Modern Researcher*, 122, 172.

[14]Coben, *Rebellion*, 27; Howe, *Victorian America*, 6, 8; McDannell, *Christian Home*, 9; Newsome, *Victorian World*, 25–26.

Between 1841 and 1869 as young pioneers crossed the plains, the Western world experienced a period of transition and turbulence. When eighteen-year-old Queen Victoria ascended the throne in 1837, the majority of Britons lived in rural communities. But industrialization, faster transportation, and increased communication and technology quickened the pace of life and loosened ties with the past. Great Britain's population grew rapidly, particularly in urban areas where factories and other industry offered opportunities for employment. Railways revolutionized freight transportation and domestic travel. During Victoria's early reign, Great Britain experienced economic difficulties, social discontent, and radical social reform. While the few amassed great wealth from the factory system, thousands lived in cellars or attics with open drains, poor sanitation, high mortality rates, and little education. Class tensions flared up in towns where workers were at the mercy of factory and property owners. From the onset of the Industrial Revolution in the late eighteenth century, women and children as young as five toiled long hours in factories and coal mines. Then in the 1830s, laws stipulated a maximum of ten-hour work days in factories and prohibited children under nine from working in textile mills and women and young children in underground mines. Before the repeal of the corn tariffs in the Hungry Forties, bread prices were exorbitant for the laboring classes, and the Irish potato famine caused thousands to die or flee to England and the United States.

The complex social stratification in Britain produced extremes in affluence and poverty. People of various classes lived in separate spheres, almost in worlds of their own. They observed different social customs and manners; their speech, clothing, education, food, and physical surroundings revealed their place in society. Few Britons owned land or dwellings. According to historian Sally Mitchell, "Victorians believed that each class had its own standards; and people were expected to conform to the rules for their class." The aristocracy and landed gentry basked in extravagance and leisure and, because of land inheritances and investments, did not work for money. The new and growing middle classes, which comprised 15 percent of the population in 1837, usually performed mental rather than physical labor. They hired domestic servants and tried to imitate the upper classes. The working classes, the bulk of the population, received minimal wages for physical, often dirty labor. Skilled artisans fared better than manual laborers who comprised three-fourths of the working classes.[15]

In the United States, class distinctions were less restrictive. Americans were a diverse, democratic, and independent people and did not adopt Great Britain's social stratification system. The American middle class was not rigidly defined by wealth, birth, or occupation, and men could achieve middle class status. As in England, the large and rising middle class began to imitate upper-class behavior. The nation grew rapidly from natural population growth, immigration, westward mobility, and new states in the Union. Industrialization, manufacturing, education, and faster means of transportation pushed the nation toward modernization. With the growth of textile factories in the North, many urban families found jobs in the mills; in the South plantation owners used slave labor. While the well-to-do built comfortable homes, others—such as slaves, some farmers, artisans, laborers, new immigrants, and urban poor—crowded into small one- or two-room dwellings. In the early Victorian years most American families lived on their own farmsteads. They believed in the work ethic and labored hard together for the good of the whole, a concept common to the young democratic republic.[16]

During the 1850s and 1860s, England increased in prosperity. Affluent females wore enormously wide skirts, males donned tall top hats and stuffy frock-coats, and the upper middle-class

---

[15]Harrison, *Early Victorians*, 1, 5, 18, 134, 151; Mitchell, *Daily Life*, xiii–xiv, 3, 5–7, 17–22, 44; Bartholomew, *Audacious Women*, 32.

[16]Larkin, *Reshaping*, 55, 148; MacLeod, *Moral Tale*, 143; McDannell, *Christian Home*, 6.

lifestyle became the model for the middle classes. Respectability and keeping up appearances became important. Middle-class families hired servants and emphasized refinement of manners and delicate language. The pompous, stereotypical image of Victorian life emerged during the mid-century, perhaps partly from the invention of daguerreotype photography which immortalized stiff visual representations of people and also from the didactic literature of the period. The Census of 1851 noted that over half of Britain's population was urban for the first time. Mass production made household goods available to more than the elite, and railroads transported newspapers, other printed materials, and perishable goods around the country. These decades were generally peaceful, although the Crimean War interrupted that peace for a time.[17]

America, too, generally prospered during the mid-Victorian years. This was an age of social, political, and economic opportunity. The drive for economic success and domestic comfort influenced many Americans. As incomes increased, individuals patterned their lives after the more affluent. Yet poverty spread in the growing cities. Industrialization, manufacturing, print, the telegraph, education, and improved transportation began to mesh the urban and rural, while rural and middle-class values moved across the plains to the West. Anti-slavery attitudes, problems of expansion and modernization, and sectional differences ultimately led to the Civil War in the 1860s. The war not only affected Americans in the East and Midwest, it also concerned pioneers who rode railroad cars through war-torn states to reach their jumping-off places for crossing the plains.[18]

During the 1840s, 1850s, and 1860s, Mormon converts in Europe left their homelands for the American West. More than 90 percent had roots in Britain and Scandinavia, with over half originating from the British Isles, specifically Eng-

[17]Mitchell, *Daily Life*, 71–74, 237; Sansom, *Victorian Life*, 9, 14, 19, 22, 29.
[18]Howe, *Victorian America*, 10–11; MacLeod, *Moral Tale*, 28, 111, 137, 142.

land, then Scotland and Wales. Of 289 accounts of foreign-born children which I analyzed, 50 percent of the writers came from England, 21 percent from Denmark, 8 percent from Scotland, 5 percent from Wales, and 5 percent from Sweden. As with Mormon converts from Europe, more than 90 percent of these 289 young pioneers came from Britain and Scandinavia. European Mormons gathered to "Zion" to join with those of their faith and to build a society based on their religion. Mormon leader Brigham Young noted that "they have so much of the spirit of gathering that they would go if they knew they would die as soon as they got there." Social, economic, and political changes in Great Britain and Scandinavia may have provided minor reasons for leaving their native lands. Approximately 11.5 percent of these European emigrants were middle class, although the percentage may have been slightly higher in Scotland. The rest were artisans, factory workers, miners, and other laborers. Many came from the industrial and mining areas of England, Scotland, and Wales. The first British Mormons left England in 1840 and continued to emigrate during the next several decades. Large groups sailed from Liverpool to the United States between 1853 and 1856 during the Crimean War and in the 1860s when times were economically tough for Britons.[19]

Industrialization and modernization also affected Scandinavia. In the 1850s and 1860s, Denmark, Sweden, and Norway experienced political and socio-economic troubles. Denmark encountered religious, economic, and social turmoil, although its agriculture prospered. Even with a new constitution which permitted religious freedom, Danish Mormons found themselves shunned by relatives and community. Most of these Mormon converts were farmers; artisans and unskilled laborers also joined the church. In the 1860s the convert pop-

---

[19]Olson, "Proselytism," 190, 191, 193; Taylor, "British Mormons," 250, 260–262; Church Educational System, *Church History*, 233; Bartholomew, *Audacious Women*, 26–30, 134–142; Buchanan, "Ebb and Flow," 316; Powell, *Utah Historical*, 54. See Table I in the Appendix.

ulation shifted from rural to urban. Danish Mormons first migrated to Utah in 1852, with peak years being 1862 and 1863 before war broke out with Prussia and Austria. Sweden and Norway belonged to the tight-ruling Swedish crown. Sweden did not allow religious freedom, so those who joined denominations other than the established church were often ostracized. Sweden grew economically and socially, but with an increase in population and decrease in food and jobs, large numbers of Swedes began leaving the country in 1867. The first company of Swedish Mormons emigrated to Utah in 1852. Like their Danish counterparts, most of the early Swedish pioneers had agricultural backgrounds, but in later years came from the cities.[20]

NINETEENTH-CENTURY CONVENTIONS

British attitudes spanned the Atlantic in the rapidly changing Western world. Many of Britain's middle and "respectable" working classes imitated the Royal Family's model of family life and moral values. Americans did too. Popular advice, etiquette, and self-help books encouraged British and American readers to internalize and refine these acceptable behaviors. Mid-nineteenth-century society adopted an elaborate code of conduct, etiquette, and thought. It included such conventions as separate gender roles and emotions, the sanctity of motherhood and family, piety and Christian worship, cleanliness and order, disdain for idleness, reticence in speaking about intimate matters and biological functions, sentimentalism, didacticism, and superiority of the white race. Although Queen Victoria did not discover many of these conventions, she gave them moral support. Americans may have supported these ideas more than did the masses in Great Britain, since its middle class comprised up to three-fourths of its population.

---

[20]Olson, "Proselytism," 194; Mulder, *Homeward*, 102, 110, 111; Mulder, "Scandinavian," 151–153; Mulder, "Utah's Ducklings," 234, 238; Powell, *Utah Historical*, 124–125, 537.

To what extent Victorian attitudes and behaviors influenced lower-class British and non-English speaking Mormon pioneers is difficult to ascertain. Some British Mormons were part of the "respectable" working class which adopted Victorian mores and hoped to rise socially. Laboring classes had less time for Victorian ways, for they struggled to survive. But they were obviously affected by the social norms of the day since the middle classes sought to conform the lifestyles and attitudes of laborers to a middle-class image. This was an era of Evangelical reform, Protestant education, moral responsibility, respectability, and independence. But conventions other than Victorian played a role in people's lives. Hard work, sobriety, piety, religion, conscientiousness, self-reliance, thrift, and duty reflected the Puritan past. These traits had been ingrained in the Western world for years and probably influenced people more than did some Victorian ideas. Other conventions, such as industry, punctuality, order, wise use of time, and loyalty to employers, reflected a contemporary industrial and manufacturing culture. Factory workers, miners, servants, and other laborers in Western Europe and America were acquiring these attributes before Victoria ascended the throne.[21]

GENDER

Whether in Western Europe or America, men and women traditionally performed different tasks. Men farmed or worked as artisans, fought wars, preached sermons, voted, and served in political positions. Women cooked, cleaned, sewed, gardened, pickled and preserved, delivered babies, cared for families, and nursed the sick. Children shared in chores from the time they were very young, with responsibility increasing with

---

[21]Cogan, *All-American Girl*, 16. For elaboration on nineteenth-century conventions, see Tompkins, *Sensational Designs*; Watson, "Cult of Domesticity"; Howe, *Victorian America*; Horton, "Victorian Era"; Minnegerode, *Fabulous Forties*; Coben, *Rebellion*; Mitchell, *Daily Life*; Harrison, *Early Victorians*; Reed, *Victorian Conventions*.

age. Boys assisted their fathers, girls helped their mothers and learned to manage the home, and everyone pitched in when farm or other seasonal labor required it. Sometimes circumstances forced one parent to fill the other's role when a spouse died or left home for extended periods of time.

During the nineteenth century, families in rural settings still performed traditional gender-related tasks. But the middle-class ideal attempted to define specific gender roles. Middle-class husbands left the family circle for employment, and wives stayed home and supervised the household and children, cultivated female friendships, engaged in philanthropically, and became consumers of goods and services. British boys needed an education, and girls prepared to be good wives and mothers by learning domestic tasks at home. Boys played more frequently than girls, and they learned traits of manliness, hard work, and physical fitness. In America, middle-class boys prepared for their future role of family provider. They developed "manly" characteristics like curbing emotions and engaging in active play and competition. Louisa May Alcott's *Little Women* portrayed how young ladies should act. They learned polite behavior and etiquette, such as walking in public with a chaperone, and tried to acquire feminine ways and engage in less active play. As Lydia Maria Child wrote in 1834, ". . . little girls should never forget that they are miniature ladies." Even with these social restrictions, middle-class American girls experienced more freedom and independence than did those of other cultures. In urban areas gender roles were also somewhat defined. Male workers were considered skilled while women and children were semi-skilled, and they labored in different areas of a factory. Some lower-class girls hired on as domestic servants or did needle work, while boys ran errands or performed jobs like street cleaning or chimney sweeping. Moreover, the women's rights movement, which began in 1848 in America, added another perspective to gender roles; this included Amelia Bloomer's bloomers which made their way across the plains.[22]

HOME AND FAMILY

In Puritan and Victorian times parents in Western Europe and America tried to provide a moral home environment for their families. Father ruled as the head of the house, and mother and children heeded his counsel. The patriarchal family was not unique to the Victorian period, however. Puritans and early nineteenth-century families also followed the biblical dictum of Paul from Ephesians 5:23: "For the husband is the head of the wife, as Christ is the head of the church." In addition, women were legally and economically dependent upon their husbands; they were taught to serve their spouses and children and suppress their own desires. Parents in turn disciplined their children and taught them to obey authority, be moral citizens, and acquire such virtues as selflessness, self-discipline, reverence, and gratitude to God and parents. Sometimes one or both parents died, and youngsters were raised by step-parents, aunts and uncles, or adult friends--or they made their own way in life. In large families parents sometimes bound out their older children in semi-dependent service to relatives, neighbors, or even strangers until the age of twenty-one.

During the Victorian era, the family, motherhood, and childhood became idealized and sentimentalized. Essays, religious sermons, novels, poems, and advice books philosophized on these topics and catered to middle-class audiences. The home was a haven from the world, a place to instill moral and religious values by mothers who, as the heart of the home, nurtured their little darlings. Bearing and rearing children had always been a woman's duty, but now motherhood and childhood were placed on pedestals. Advice writers and religious

---

[22]Mitchell, *Daily Life*, 41–66, 173–179, 265; Burstyn, *Victorian Education*, 18–19, 30–34; Coben, *Rebellion*, 13–23; Heninger, et.al., *Century*, 100–105; Child, *Girls' Own Book*, 108.

leaders reminded mothers about being their children's first teachers and instilling values and sound character traits in them. Many women heeded advice givers by increasing their efforts to nurture their little ones and mold their character. They often reflected upon their children's growth, development, and spiritual welfare in letters and diary entries.[23]

In reality many mid-nineteenth century homes did not follow the middle-class prototype of mother at home, father at work, and closely knit family. After the Industrial Revolution forced lower-class families into the workplace, the vast majority of British women worked away from home. While middle-class mothers focused more attention on their children and hired servants to perform household chores, mothers of the lower classes labored long hours in factories and often neglected house and family. Their youngsters experienced poverty and hunger and looked after themselves and younger children. Upper-class British parents expected nannies and governesses to care for their offspring, for aristocratic adults had their own agendas and pleasures. Their youngsters formed relationships with domestic servants in a separate part of the house. In contrast, in the United States with its large middle-class population many Americans considered home a refuge, a secure place to teach their children proper values. Although the British upper classes usually owned their own residences, many American and some Scandinavian families lived in their own homes, no matter how small. Mass production made household items more affordable, so the middle classes added carpets, curtains, furniture, and other furnishings to their dwellings. Few American families, except those in the South, employed servants as the English middle and upper classes did. When American parents needed assistance with never-ending chores, they enlisted their children. Or, some middle-class women hired young girls to help them. Since British and

---

[23]Minnigerode, *Fabulous Forties*, 74–75; Howe, *Victorian America*, 25–26; MacLeod, *Moral Tale*, 9, 29, 71, 73–74; Larkin, *Reshaping*, 50–53; Kett, *Rites of Passage*, 17–30.

American middle classes had spending money, book and magazine publishers catered to their cleaning and decorating whims.[24]

RELIGION

Christianity played a significant role in early and mid-nineteenth-century America and Western Europe. Even individuals who did not believe in God upheld the same moral and ethical standards as those who did. The "Second Great Awakening" in America in the 1830s and evangelical revivals in Western Europe revitalized religious worship. Church members in America proselytized and held camp meetings, and the American Tract Society passed out religious publications hoping to convert the nation to Protestant Christianity. Women their with natural endowments from the "heart" rather than the "head" flocked to church and instigated the "feminization" of churches during the nineteenth century. Home, neighborhood, and church functioned within the context of religious and moral principles. In Great Britain the Religious Census of 1851 noted that sixty percent of its population who were physically able to attend church services did. Britain's rural population had the highest attendance, and laborers in industrial cities had the lowest. Since working class families toiled six days a week, parents often sent their youngsters to Sunday School while they stayed home. When Tract and Bible Societies promoted religion among the lower classes, new parishes opened in some industrial areas. The "spirit of reform" pervaded Western Europe and America and prompted religious and social groups to support benevolent societies and movements such as temperance and anti-slavery. Charitable societies helped the poor. Churches and social groups formed networks

---

[24]Burnett, *Destiny Obscure*, 31, 37–38; Mitchell, *Daily Life*, 141–149; Burstyn, *Victorian Education*, 19, 30–31, 55–57; Cogan, *All-American Girl*, 23; Larkin; *Reshaping*, 10, 52–53, 134–138; McDannell, *Christian Home*, 7–9.

to control alcohol consumption, as drunkenness caused many family breakdowns, particularly among the poorer classes.

Many nineteenth-century families believed in a higher being and life after death. They worshipped a loving God who lightened their burdens. Since youngsters did not always grow to adulthood and adults often died prematurely, they prepared for death and a heavenly reunion with loved ones who had gone before them. Many families read the Bible, prayed, and attended church, and these experiences became an integral part of many childhood memories. Devout families kept the Sabbath Day holy by going to church, then at home they read the Bible and other religious books, prayed, sang hymns, and rested from weekday labors. Even children's books offered such counsel as, "Remember that God sees all your actions and all your thoughts. Be in the daily habit of prayer to him, and he will help you to cherish what is good, and drive away what is evil." Although secularism grew during this period and not everyone attended church, this was a value-laden age.[25]

EDUCATION

Many young Americans who crossed the plains had been taught the rudiments of reading and writing, for between 1850 and 1870 nearly half of America's children attended school to some extent. America was a rural nation, yet it surpassed much of Europe in literacy. By the early 1860s, the common school movement placed elementary schools in most of the states, and the McGuffey Readers educated many of the nation's children. America's educational system was based on Christian principles, morals, and sound character, for Thomas Jefferson and others of his time believed that "a democratic society ultimately depends upon the virtue and intelligence of the peo-

---

[25]Newsome, *Victorian World*, 194–197; Mitchell, *Daily Life*, 143–144, 239, 248, 256–258; Coben, *Rebellion*, 24–25; Howe, *Victorian America*, 21; Larkin, *Reshaping*, xv, 276–278, 300; McDannell, *Christian Home*, 16, 19; MacLeod, *Moral Tale*, 27–30; Child, *Girls' Own Book*, 284.

ple." Schooling was free and open to all, though the urban poor
and slaves lagged behind. Youngsters who toiled in factories
could attend Sunday School one day a week to learn reading,
writing, and religious values; they also had access to free Sunday School libraries. By 1870, 88.5 percent of America's white
children ten years old and older were considered literate. This
does not mean literate youngsters were scholarly readers, but
they could get by in their day.[26]

Before the 1860s, most Europeans could not read or write,
although Scandinavia and some German states had higher literacy rates. Danish children between the ages of seven and
fourteen received free schooling which was "provided by law
and sustained by taxation."[27] In 1845 in Great Britain, 51 percent of the females and 67 percent of the males were literate.
Children of the more prosperous classes acquired their education at home or in public, private, and boarding schools.
British working-class children obtained schooling from phil-
anthropic and religious organizations, but education was secondary to economic needs of the family. The Sunday School
movement, which originated in England, provided factory
children the basics in reading, writing, arithmetic, and religious instruction on the Sabbath. The Education Act of 1870
mandated government-supported schools, and every child in
England obtained the right to elementary education. By 1871,
literacy increased to 74 percent for females and 81 percent for
males.[28]

WRITING

The nineteenth century was an age of print. Magazines, nov-

---

[26]Larkin, *Reshaping*, 35, 53; Gutek, *American Education*, 57, 60, 66; Tompkins, *Sensational Designs*, 153, 157; MacLeod, *Moral Tale*, 21, 25; Hernandez, *America's Children*, 147.

[27]Jenson, *Autobiography*, 6; Gutek, *Western Educational*, 176. Other reminiscences of young Danish pioneers mentioned this type of education as well.

[28]Mitchell, *Daily Life*, 11, 166; Newsome, *Victorian World*, 146–147; Burnett, *Destiny Obscure*, 19, 129; Harrison, "Popular History," 10.

els, newspapers, religious tracts, school books, and children's fiction flourished, thanks to the steam-powered printing press and to mass transportation which distributed the materials. Women as well as men wrote articles and books during these years. Magazines like *The Saturday Evening Post* and *Godey's Lady's Book* formed a high percentage of reading material, particularly for women readers. Prescriptive writing, religious books, and poetry about nature, God, and deceased children became popular as well. Between 1820 and 1860, literature for children increased, partly as a result of the Sunday School movement which produced books, periodicals, tracts, and songs for all ages. Young people read stories which were sentimental, stilted, didactic, and moral. Even school books like the McGuffey Readers contained moralistic narratives and poems.

Nineteenth-century literature appealed to the "heart" as well as the "head." According to critics of the day, literature needed to benefit society, edify, and help readers practice what they already believed. Terms like aesthetic, didactic, serious, romantic, nostalgic, nationalistic, and sentimental described the writings of the period. "Romantic" described a style of art, music, and literature which was especially popular among the Victorian middle classes. The artistic work spoke to the sublime— to human feelings, the contemplation of the self, melody and harmony—rather than to science and reason. It reveled in nature's pristine form: rugged mountains, dense forests, clear lakes. Also during this period, romanticism "discreetly softened into sentimentalism." Writers of novels evoked sympathetic feelings by creating orphan and saintly women protagonists. Ethics rather than plot determined a novel's worth. Authors frequently made reference to the Bible and described deathbed scenes, for they considered mortality a probationary period for eternity. They wrote of such virtues as honesty, industry, chastity, and temperance partly from threats from political and social ills in a rapidly changing world. According to an 1848 *New York Herald* editorial, people also read sentimental, romantic, adventurous, trashy literature. This probably included American captivity tales about women and children stolen by Indians, which created preconceived notions about Native Americans in the minds of pioneers who made the trek west.[29]

THE TRAIL WEST

For the purpose of this work, several pioneering terms need to be defined. "Crossing the plains" was a phrase used by pioneers to mean not only the Nebraska prairie and Wyoming desert but also the entire distance to a destination in the West, including the Pacific Coast. The "jumping-off place" refers to small towns along the Missouri River between Independence and Council Bluffs where emigrants met to join wagon trains and prepare for the journey. As the railroad moved westward, so did the jumping-off place. Wyoming, Nebraska, became a popular starting point for Mormon pioneers in the 1860s, and when the railroad reached Laramie City and Benton, Wyoming, covered wagon travel decreased by several hundred miles.

"Platte River road" was a term used by emigrants for the central trail which followed the Platte River from the Missouri River through Nebraska to western Wyoming. There the trails divided for three major destinations—California, Oregon, and Utah—and other ending points in places like Colorado and Montana. "Platte River road," "Platte River route," "overland trail," and "overland route" are synonymous terms. Pioneers followed the Platte River through Nebraska and often mentioned Fort Kearny, Ash Hollow, Scotts Bluff, and Chimney Rock. In Wyoming they described Fort Laramie, Independence Rock, Devil's Gate, and South Pass. West of South

[29]Cranston, *Romantic*, 16–18, 59, 72–73, 138–140, 145, 149; Newsome, *Victorian World*, 10–12; Howe, *Victorian America*, 16–17, 23; Minnigerode, *Fabulous Forties*, 107, 115, 130–132; MacLeod, *Moral Tale*, 10, 15, 23; Reed, *Victorian Conventions*, 4, 7, 252.

Pass the trail divided, and emigrants either went southwest to Fort Bridger and Salt Lake City or northwest to Soda Springs and Fort Hall in present southeastern Idaho. California and Oregon travelers bid each other farewell in southern Idaho or northwestern Nevada, depending upon which road Oregon pioneers chose to take. Oregon-bound travelers either went north along the Snake River to the Cascade Mountains in Oregon or they followed the southern route through Nevada to Klamath Falls and the Rogue River Valley. California-bound pioneers often mentioned the Humboldt River, the forty-mile desert, and the Sierra Nevada Mountains. (See the map on endpapers.) There were cut-offs and variants in the trails as pioneers began searching for quicker routes to their destinations.

As the decades passed, the overland journey changed somewhat for young emigrants. The first white American women migrated to the Pacific Coast in 1836, and in the early 1840s families began making the journey. These pioneers contended with poorly marked trails, few supply stations, and inadequate information from word of mouth, newspaper accounts, guidebooks, and false advertising. In contrast to published warnings, they were usually met by friendly Native Americans who sometimes bartered, begged, or stole provisions but did not harm the travelers. In 1847, the Mormons left their winter camp near the Missouri River and started their exodus to Utah. Beginning in 1848, California gold fever turned the overland route into an international highway. Then cholera took the lives of many pioneers who journeyed west in the early 1850s.

Soon more affluent Americans began moving westward, and the trail became a commercial road for individuals intent on setting up businesses as well as farming. At the same time, poorer European Mormons relied on financial assistance from their church to get to Utah through a pay-back system called the Perpetual Emigrating Fund (PEF). Some walked the thousand miles pulling handcarts to make the trip more affordable. Eventually, travel time was lessened by steamboat, stagecoach, and railroad transportation. Between 1856 and 1869, trading posts, forts, stagecoach stations, and a few private ranches and settlements sprang up along the trail, making supplies and assistance more readily available. Pacific Coast emigrants were able to purchase goods in Salt Lake City. Freight moved back and forth from the Midwest to the West. By 1861, the telegraph enabled folks to send messages quickly from coast to coast. But Native Americans became a greater threat as white travelers intruded upon their lands, destroyed their means of survival, and killed them with guns or disease. Overlanders were afraid of attacks, but their fears were often groundless, especially if they were cautious and remained with large groups. By 1868, emigrants crossed the prairie by rail to Benton, Wyoming, and thus spent fewer weeks in covered wagons. These changes were obvious in the writings or reminiscences of children who crossed the plains.

Where did the trail begin for these young pioneers? Did it start when European Mormons left their homes in Denmark or at the ship dock in Liverpool? What about the voyage to America, the steamboat ride up the Mississippi, or the train ride to Council Bluffs? Unlike many children on the California and Oregon trails who had a rather uncomplicated first half of the journey but a more challenging last part, Midwestern Mormons in the late 1840s headed west unprepared after conflicts with neighbors caused them leave their homes prematurely. European Mormons often dealt with sickness and death as they struggled with a long and tedious voyage to America and journey to the jumping-off place. To limit this study, I have focused on the moment emigrants began the trek across the plains at or near the Missouri River and ended with the first major settlement at or near the final destination, for example, Salt Lake City instead of St. George in Utah, or Oregon

City instead of Portland. William Cronon noted that the place "one chooses to begin and end a story profoundly alters its shape and meaning."[30] One might understand a young pioneer's trail experience more clearly if his or her life in Denmark, voyage to America, journey to Nebraska, and first year in Utah had been included with the crossing-the-plains experience; nevertheless, a study must be manageable.

Choosing first-hand contemporary and reminiscent accounts by white Anglo-Saxons from America and Europe also altered the shape and meaning of the young pioneer experience for this study. So did allowing the documents to determine the direction of the inquiry and then letting young voices tell their story through quotes and recurring themes. I have attempted to identify the child's vision of the westward experience by looking at it from different angles of the same lens. First, I considered young people's diaries and letters. Then I analyzed children's relationships with parents and siblings, train members, and others on the trail. To focus on youngsters' perceptions, I used three means: actual documents written by children and young adolescents, the "I remember" context of oral and written reminiscences, and the "we remember" context of the same reminiscences. Finally, I analyzed what a few child pioneers included or left out of their writings by studying what other travelers said during the same emigration season. To retain the personality of the writer I copied quotes as they were written in the document, including grammatical and mechanical errors. Although footnote references are abbreviated in the text, complete citations can be found in the bibliography.

The mid-nineteenth century move to the American West is a valuable period to study for information about children's perspectives since so many primary documents, specifically reminiscences, are available about a common event. This book tells the story of crossing the plains from a child's view-

---

[30]Cronon, "A Place," 1364.

point, or at least as near as it can be told without the participants being present and speaking for themselves. In the past children were taught to be seen and not heard. Although these young pioneers can no longer be seen, except perhaps in old photographs, they now have a chance to be heard—and what insightful narratives they have to share.

CHAPTER I

When I Was A Child

When I was a child, I spake as a child, I understood as a child, I thought as a child: but when I became a man, I put away childish things.
—*1 Corinthians 13:11*

"All histories I have ever read of early days are mostly exaggerated bunk...They write what they know not of," said Mrs. Lee Whipple-Haslam who traveled the Platte River road to California in 1852 as a child and later wrote about it.[1] But when she wrote her reminiscence, did she record what she knew as a child or did she include "exaggerated bunk"? Some pioneers believed this was an important event in their lives and took time to write while they traveled; they kept diaries along the trail for a variety of reasons. Emigrants wrote letters home during or soon after the journey and many recorded their stories years later. Both men and women wrote their impressions of the trek. Sometimes they shared a common outlook of the trail experience; other times their masculine or feminine subjectivity influenced what they recorded. Single travelers, newlyweds, parents with children, and older couples voiced their attitudes about the journey.[2] What tales did children and young adolescents tell? What was their perspective in the crossing-the-plains experience?

Although it is impossible to study all children on the trail between 1841 and 1869, researchers can catch a glimpse of childhood by analyzing a representative sample of individual

---

[1]The Bible, 1 Cor. 13:11; Whipple-Haslam, *Early Days*, 3.
[2]Faragher, *Women and Men*, 12–15, 18.

records left by children. Judy Allen suggested that few young people wrote diaries, but this may be an assumption based on what historical documents are available today.[3] Children may have kept diaries but lost them, thrown them away as they got older, or embellished their original writings. Or, parents may have discarded the accounts. The only documents available for identifying the child's viewpoint are surviving diaries, letters, journals, and oral and written reminiscences. Adults who talked about children in their personal writings may have given impressions of childhood, but they did not see through a child's eyes.

In this chapter we will review the various types of accounts of children's travels on the trail, each with its own attributes and failings. Most writers who have studied young emigrants have examined contemporary and reminiscent documents through the same lens of credibility and reliability. Yet young pioneers who wrote diaries and letters processed the trail experience through juvenile feelings and perceptions. What could they realistically remember if they described their adventure years later? Did experience and memory blend with other tales of the trail? How much of a child's story was silenced or expanded when they "put away childish things"? What are the unique characteristics of diaries, letters, journals, and oral and written reminiscences?

For the purposes of this book, diaries are defined as daily or almost daily entries which young people wrote on the trail.[4] Letters are written communication sent to family or friends before or during the trek or soon after reaching the destination. A journal is an account written sometime after the journey's end and often taken from an individual's diary or field notes. Ada Millington's and Andrew Jenson's accounts are considered journals.[5] Both of these young people kept diaries while

---

[3]Allen, "Children," 2.

[4]Definitions of diaries, letters, journals, and reminiscences correspond to those in Mattes *Platte River*, 9, and Bitton, *Guide*, vi–vii.   [5]Millington, "Journal"; Jenson, "Journals," 68–90.

crossing the plains as teenagers, but Millington revised and embellished her diary six years after her arrival in California and Jenson rewrote his in 1895. A reminiscence is a series of rec-ollections written later in life. An interview is oral history con-ducted, recorded, and written by an interviewer of an informant. The interviewer may have used assigned questions, as in the case of the Utah Works Progress Administration (WPA) inter-views, or asked informal questions as did Fred Lockley. Often reminiscences and interviews were recorded more than fifty years after the event. To identify childhood memories and percep-tions instead of those remembered collectively by family or com-munity, the oral and written reminiscences in this book have been divided into "I remember" and "we remember" contexts.

AUDIENCE AND PURPOSE

In all of the documents, audience and purpose influenced what was said. Trail diaries were often written for public use—to be published in newspapers, sent home for family and friends to read, kept as logs for future emigrants—or for pri-vate perusal. When Tucker Scott assigned his two daughters to write the family diary, the girls probably knew it would be sent home for their grandfather to read. Tucker Scott also read the diary and occasionally added comments. According to Margo Culley, "many eighteenth- and nineteenth-century diaries were semi-public documents intended to be read by an audience." Harriet Blodgett noted an occasion in the nine-teenth century when an adult read a child's diary aloud to other adults and other instances when women read personal records of friends and relatives. Blodgett observed that a diarist who did not destroy her own writings knew they could be read someday. In her 1864 trail diary, thirteen-year-old Har-riet Hitchcock seemed to be writing for her own enjoyment. Her older sisters teased her about keeping a record, but she did not care. Yet when she said, "No one will ever see it only a thought now and then," she suggested that others might read her writing.[6]

Letters were usually sent home to family or friends to inform them of happenings on the trail. Margaret, Catharine, and Harriet Scott wrote to their grandparents during and after the journey to tell them about the trek and to reminisce about family back home. Elizabeth Keegan related her trip to her brother and sister and described her new life in California. Virginia Reed wrote to her "little cousin" from Independence Rock and again from California, for "I had promised to write to her before I left home and I was trying to keep my promise."[7] Sometimes authors downplayed fears or dangers, left things out, or added details depending upon who received or read the correspondence.

While diaries and letters were written during or soon after the journey, journals and reminiscences were recorded later to share with posterity, satisfy curious relatives, fulfill literary whims, or comply with requests from such organizations as the Oregon Pioneer Association[8] and Daughters of Utah Pioneers (DUP).[9] John Hyde Braley published his autobiogra-

---

[6]Scott, "Journal," 24–26; Culley, *A Day*, 3; Blodgett, *Centuries*, 14, 39, 58; Hitchcock, "Thoughts," 235.

[7]Scott Sisters, "Letters," 139–172; Keegan, "Teenager's Letter," 21–31; Murphy, "Letters to McGlashan," April 18, 1879.

[8]By 1873, adult pioneers who had migrated to Oregon in the 1840s were either elderly or dead, and unless the remainder did something to preserve their stories, "all memory of their westward journey and settlement would be lost forever." Therefore, the Oregon Pioneer Association was organized in 1873, with membership limited to pioneers who moved to Oregon Territory prior to January 1, 1855. Later, this date was changed to January 1, 1859. The first annual meeting of the association was held on November 11, 1873, with subsequent yearly meetings on June 15 "to promote social intercourse among its members." The association also urged members to record their personal experiences and preserve them in the association's archives. See "Collections," *Ore. Hist. Qtly.*, 247–248.

[9]The Daughters of Utah Pioneers (DUP) was organized in 1901 to remember pioneers who settled Utah territory before 1854 and to preserve old landmarks, collect personal manuscripts and other historical data, commemorate important dates, publish historical material, and teach pioneer descendants about their heritage. Later, the membership date was extended to 1858 and then to 1868 before the completion of the transcontinental railroad in 1869. Many Mormons kept personal records of their lives, and in some accounts the pioneer trek was only a small part of their history. See Winn and Olsen, "Daughters," 93–97.

phy "for my children and my children's children," and Mary Creighton kept an unpublished account of the trek west for her grandchildren. Elisha Brooks wrote to inform his posterity about his mother who died six years after they arrived in California. Friends of Emeline Fuller encouraged her to tell the tragic story of her train's massacre. Mrs. Lee Whipple-Haslam published a book dedicated "to the Pioneer Auxiliary," and Allene Taylor (Dunham) wrote for "children of today." William Robinson and Evan Stephens gave talks at DUP meetings. Susan Zimmerman (Terry) wrote a letter to the Mormon church assistant historian informing him about her wagon train and the people who traveled in it. Ruth May (Fox) shared her experience in a Mormon church periodical.[10] Some pioneers submitted reminiscences for preservation at the DUP Pioneer Memorial Museum in Salt Lake City, Utah.

INCLUSION/EXCLUSION IN ACCOUNTS

If audience and purpose can influence the content or tone of a personal document, what a writer chooses to include or leave out will also affect the piece of writing. There are spaces of silence in diaries, letters, journals, and reminiscences. For example, babies appeared out of nowhere. Rachel Taylor and Ada Millington recorded births in their trains without mentioning pregnancy. Martha Gay (Masterson) remembered her surprise at being awakened one morning by an infant's cry. "I asked mother whose baby was crying so. She said it was hers. I said not a word for some time," for Martha already had nine brothers and feared the infant was a boy.[11] Where was Martha during the birthing? Had the wagon pulled away from the train

[10]Braley, *Memory Pictures*, 7; Creighton, "To My Grandchildren," 1; Brooks, *Pioneer Mother*, title page, 34; Fuller, *Left By Indians*, 1; Whipple-Haslam, *Early Days*, dedication page; Dunham, *Across the Plains*, 1; Robinson, "Biographical Sketch,"188; Stephens, "A Talk," 1; Terry, "Garden Grove," 1851; Fox, "From England," 406–409, 450.
[11]Watson, "Laughing, Merry," 15–16; Taylor, "Overland Trip," 180; Millington, "Journal," 234; Barton, *One Woman's West*, 37.

as it did in Rachel Taylor's account? A crowded train made privacy difficult. Although Martha was almost fourteen years old and could have been present, mid-nineteenth-century reticent attitudes about personal matters may have prevented her from talking about it. At the journey's end several young pioneers wrote about new babies without mentioning that the women made the trek in their last months of pregnancy. They, too, observed the nineteenth-century convention about private or intimate matters. Even reminiscences ignored pregnancies. A few mentioned women who would soon become mothers, but most stated that a woman was sick during the journey, then later added that a baby was born.

In addition to not discussing pregnancy and birthing, pioneer accounts did not address sanitation and, in many cases, personal hygiene. In his diary, however, sixteen-year-old Thomas Cott Griggs mentioned bathing in the river. When asked later about toilet facilities, John Ray Young, a Mormon who emigrated in 1847 at the age of ten, remembered that in their organized companies "it was the custom to give the mothers and children the right side of the camp, and when traveling the right side of the train." Also, each family had one or two tents, and "before starting on the journey all were admonished that every family should have a good well covered (lid), slop pail, the tent and slop pail was a toilet for women and children." But no one explained what Mormon handcart emigrants did when twenty people slept in one large tent. Jeanne Watson suggested that diarists did not talk about toilet facilities because everyone knew what to do, and the subject did not intrigue pioneers as it does researchers today.[12]

Since children see, reason, and react differently from adults, diaries and letters written by young people during the journey or soon afterward paint the most authentic picture of a child's

---

[12]Griggs, "Crossing the Plains," 33, 35; Young, "John Ray," 1; Watson, "Traveling Traditions," 79. Watson noted that men mentioned bathing in rivers, but few women wrote about it. In this study a few female reminiscences talked about bathing, but no girls' diaries or letters did.

perspective. Looking at their writings can help readers today learn about the beliefs of a literate class who crossed the plains. Diaries and letters reveal the lifestyle and culture of a time period as well as the language of the writer. Researchers cannot always locate original documents, so they use what is available and, as a result, cannot accurately analyze the writer's personality. Published diaries and letters were sometimes edited for an audience different from the one intended, and often these changes were not explained. Before thirteen-year-old Virginia Reed's letter from California was printed in *The Illinois Journal*, it was edited by her step-father, James Reed, and then by the newspaper. For example, one section of Virginia's original document said, ". . . one of the men staid with us and the others went on with the cattel to water pa was a coming back to us with water and met the men & thay was about 10 miles from water." James Reed's additions and deletions were: "Walter Herron & Bailos[?] staid with us and the other boys Milt Elliott & J Smith went on with the cattel to water. papa was coming back to us with water and met the men & they was about 10 miles from water." Mr. Reed added specific names of individuals, changed "pa" to "papa," and made a few other minor corrections to his liking. The newspaper editor cleaned up many of Virginia's errors, but he also eliminated her personality: "Herren and Bayliss stayed with us, and the other boys, Milt Elliott and James Smith, went on with the cattle to water. Father was coming back to us with water, and met the men. They were then about ten miles from water."[13] Neither adult seemed to value the adolescent's writing as it was.

If diaries and letters remain intact, they can reveal a writer's everyday language--including slang--and mechanical errors. Such conventions also reflect the young person's perspective. Some youngsters had better writing skills than others, especially as they grew older, received additional schooling, or prac-

---

[13]Powell, "Nineteenth-century," 68–69; Donner and Reed, "Donner Party," 67; Murphy, "Virginia," Letter 2: 1; Reed, "Deeply Interesting Letter," Dec. 16, 1847.

ticed. For some writers, like Virginia Reed, this may have been a first attempt at composition. For others, the writing appeared quite polished. For example, in one diary entry fifteen-year-old Flora Bender said,

> We had good roads and tonight are camped in the woods. It is so pleasant and there is a nice spring of cold water, one of the best we have seen since we left home. We are two miles from Laramie, and I heard it was on the other side of the river—everything is over there. Such a lonely and beautiful evening this is. It does seem such a pity that we cannot spend it in any way but solitude.[14]

Either this young writer apparently composed other pieces, possibly while being educated through the nation's common school movement, or her published diary may have been a revision of the original.

CHARACTERISTICS OF TRAIL DOCUMENTS

Of all personal documents, diaries are the most reliable because they are written at the time of the event and reflect contemporary thoughts and feelings, even though much is consciously or unconsciously left out, whether it be taboo subjects or a writer's inner thoughts. William Matthews, author of an annotated bibliography of American diaries, stated that diaries are "the most immediate, truthful, and revealing documents available to the historian." Jacques Barzun and Henry Graff noted that "the value of a piece of testimony usually increases in proportion to the nearness in time and space between the witness and the events about which he testifies."[15]

While diaries may be the most reliable sources, they have strengths and weaknesses. Diaries describe immediate experiences, events, behavior, and impressions in a random, nonthematic way. They are fixed in time and space and, unlike memoirs, cannot be reconstructed after years of reflection. A diary of an

---

[14]Murphy, "Letters to McGlashan," April 18, 1879; Bender, Typescript, 5.

[15]Arskey, Pries, and Reed, *American Diaries*, xi; Barzun and Graff, *Modern Researcher*, 158; Culley, *A Day*, 23.

eight year old contains different information from that of a fifteen year old since age, interests, and developmental factors influence point of view. Judy Allen noted that young people's trail diaries reflected their youth and inexperience, and children were limited in their interpretation of events and the ramifications of the journey. But when examining the child's perspective, these are qualities that reveal personalities and perceptions of the experience. Allen also suggested that child diarists "exhibit little depth or insight in their chronicles." That depended on the child author. Some gave great insights, although their impressions were different from those of adult writers.[16]

Still, a diary entry is only one piece of an author's day. It may not portray the normal chaos of, for example, crossing the Platte River or being pelted by hail on the Sweetwater in Wyoming. Although diarists are on-the-spot witnesses, they may not see the reality before them. Instead, they may write about personal concerns and perceptions and ignore what might have lasting significance to certain historians. Again, when attempting to analyze a child's perspective, this can be a strength. A diary can catch a person's moods and private thoughts and preserve them at the age of writing.[17] Merrill Mattes pointed out a characteristic of childhood when he noted in *Platte River Road Narratives* that Flora Bender's diary was an "extraordinary diary of a fifteen-year-old, a fascinating footnote to history despite her adolescent poutings."[18] It was her "adolescent poutings" that made her writing valuable to my study. When Mattes assigned one or two stars instead of five to accounts by young people in his annotated bibliography of trail documents—although he gave four to Flora Bender—he was not searching for child insights but for historical and literary value from an adult viewpoint. Yet young people added their own views to the overland experience.

---

[16]Culley, *A Day*, 13; Allen, "Children," 2.
[17]For similar viewpoints see Lowenthal, *The Past*, 234; Faragher, *Women and Men*, 12; Schlissel, *Women's Diaries*, 12.   [18]Mattes, *Platte River*, 558.

Since diaries are always in process and the writer cannot see the future, they can be filled with surprise, mystery, and suspense for both author and reader. Private diaries may confuse today's reader because information obvious to the writer was omitted. Flora Bender talked about Nellie but never said who Nellie was. From a few entries one can infer that Nellie was Flora's sister. For example, Nellie wrote a letter to *Aunt* Cinda, and Clara (possibly another sister) told Flora and Nellie, "Hurry, girls, *Pa* is going to start in half an hour." From a Nevada newspaper account and from Flora Bender's short autobiography, we learn that Nellie and Clara were indeed her siblings. A few young diarists, though, identified individuals. Mary Warner named Celia as an aunt, and Harriet Hitchcock stated that Lucy was her oldest sister.[19]

Most bibliographical sources suggest that more American men than women kept diaries until the middle of the nineteenth century. In my research I located more trail diaries of girls than of boys. I found nine female diaries and one female journal in comparison with two male diaries, three male diary/journal combinations, and one male journal. Since two of the male diary/journal combinations contained nothing about the trek except in reminiscences, I analyzed three male diaries and one journal. The youngest diarist was a ten/eleven-year-old boy who wrote on the ship from England but not on the trail. The others were between twelve and sixteen. Younger authors with limited reading and writing skills would probably be coached by an adult. The female accounts discussed in this book were travel diaries, rather than spiritual diaries which they often were encouraged to keep, and usually contained a beginning, middle, and end.[20]

Letters can provide glimpses into a child's personality and,

[19]Bender, Typescript, 5, 6; Douglas, "Bender Family," 14; Bender, "Autobiography," 4; Warner, "Diary," 10; Hitchcock, "Thoughts," 236.

[20]See Culley, *A Day*, 3, and Bitton, *Guide*, for data about men writing and preserving more diaries than women. See Myres, *Westering Women*, xix, concerning girls keeping spiritual diaries.

like diarists, their authors were literate to some extent. All eight letter writers which I identified were girls. Children who wrote pre-travel letters showed feelings of anticipation as well as some knowledge of the trail. In 1853, Harriet Stewart and her siblings and step-siblings shared pre-travel thoughts with a cousin. Harriet, age fifteen, wrote, "I want to go to see the curiosities and git gold for sewing & to see the buffalo and hear the wolves howl." Her step-sister Margaret, also fifteen, was going "because the rest is a going and to meet my brother at the end of my journey." Sister Melissa, age thirteen, hoped "to go for the fun of travling and to ride a pony or an ox to drive cattle for my kind father, to help us get away from this sickly country." Margaret's eleven-year-old brother Franklin wanted "to go to see the Journeys & cross the rockey mountains and the cascade mountains and see the tall fir timber and smell the sea breese if I live to get there I will go to school some more." Perhaps Franklin had heard about deaths from cholera and other dangers on the way. His pre-travel fears emerged in this brief comment. In 1850, Susan Dudley, a fourteen-year-old Mormon, wrote to her aunt, "We are agoing to cross the river this morning we are twenty miles from our home we are going to the mountains where the temple shall be built . . . we will be three months on our journey it will be cold before we get there but we have got our winter clothes."[21] She, too, revealed feelings of anticipation and apprehension.

Letters from the trail had characteristics similar to diaries: suspense and mystery, immediate and personal concerns, and personality at the time of writing. But the writers may have been less inclined to reveal private thoughts because others would read them. From Independence Rock in present-day Wyoming, Virginia Reed of the Donner party wrote an upbeat letter to her cousin Mary Keyes about the Caw Indians preparing to fight the Crows, her father searching for wild game, and their company celebrating the Fourth of July with

---

[21]Sutton, "Travel Diary," 24; Dudley, "Dudley Family," July 1, 1850.

liquor and lemonade. The only sad part involved the death of
Grandmother Keyes. Virginia was not aware she would soon
be trapped by winter snow in the Sierra Nevada. Letter writers also considered their readers as they decided what to include
or leave out. William Hockett, who went to Oregon in 1847
at the age of nine, later analyzed his father's writings. "I have
been surprised in reading my father's letters to note how little he said about deaths of other members of the company other
than of us Salem people, but I suppose he thought our folks
here would not know anything about them."[22]

Letters composed soon after the journey revealed young people's thoughts, even though the beginning, middle, and end were
known. The writer could safely explain harrowing incidents, for
hindsight made them less frightening. Safe in California, Virginia Reed confided to her cousin, ". . . we met Pa with 13 men
going to the cabins o Mary you do not now how glad we was
to see him . . . O Mary I have not wrote you half of the truble
we have had but I hav Wrote you anuf to let you now that you
dont now what truble is." What thoughts might Virginia have
expressed in a diary during the ordeal? One can only speculate.
Shortly after reaching their destinations, Elizabeth Keegan,
Mary Murphy, and the Scott sisters also sent letters home.[23]
Though these letters were written after the journey, they still
portrayed teenage perspectives. Later as adults, Virginia Reed
and Catharine and Harriet Scott published recollections which
were quite different from their childhood letters.

Journals written from trail diaries are less authentic than
diaries and letters but more reliable than memories recorded
years later. But young writers' personalities and perspectives
cannot be ascertained without digging into the original documents. In 1866, Andrew Jenson kept a diary on his way to
Utah as a fifteen year old from Denmark but rewrote it in 1895.

---

[22]Murphy, "Virginia," Letter 1: 1-2; Hockett, "Experiences," 1.
[23]Murphy, "Virginia," Letter 2: 5-6; Keegan, "Teenager's Letter," 23-31; Murphy, "Three Letters"; Murphy, Letter TN; Scott Sisters, "Letters," 139-172.

Since I could not locate the original diary, I could not compare it to his journal.[24] Thirteen-year-old Ada Millington wrote her diary on the way to California in 1862. Six years later, she completed high school with literary ambitions, and she revised her trail writings. The result was an unpublished journal which can be studied today. An edited and slightly different version of this journal was later published, along with one page of the original diary. The same entries in her diary and unpublished journal can be analyzed for similarities and differences in personality, perceptions, and writing style. One of the diary entries began,

> Friday 18th [July 1862] started pretty early went over another mountain and went down into a kanyon where we passed a great many houses where we bought a great many vegetables stopped for dinner by a stream of good water close by a mountain from which we could see Salt Lake city[.]

The same entry in her unpublished journal said,

> Started early this morning. Bright and pleasant weather. Went over another mountain and down into a can[y]on in which we passed several dwelling houses and one saw mill. Whenever a house is to be seen every one commences looking first thing for the garden If there is one in sight three or four persons rush to the house to buy some vegetables. No one but a person who has "crossed the plains" knows how good it is to see signs of civilization once more. We passed a sheep-fold today in which there were some sixty sheep and they actually looked like old friends. We stopped for dinner near a clear stream of good mountain water. Had quite a feast with our vegetables, onions and lettuce principally. After dinner started on again, and after going about a mile, we could see Salt Lake City—by a sudden turn in the road.[25]

Ada at thirteen had not completed the journey and could not view the experience with the hindsight of Ada at nineteen. The sentence describing sheep that looked like old friends was not even alluded to in the original document. Did Ada Millington remember this detail six years later? Perhaps she

---

[24]Jenson, "Journals," 50; Jenson, *Autobiography*, preface.

[25]Clarke, "Journal Kept," 13–14, 23; Millington, "Journal," 243–244. Clarke edited Ada Millington's journal when he published it, so there are really three versions of Millington's writings: her original travel diary, an unpublished journal which is a later revision of the original diary, and Clarke's published version of the journal.

did, or perhaps she added it to paint a stronger picture of signs of civilization.

While diaries and letters more accurately show a child's perspective, they are difficult to find. Far more reminiscences have been preserved. Why might this be so? First, some pioneer children were limited in literacy skills, especially those from the British working classes, and by language if they left non-English-speaking countries. Second, adults do not always take a positive view of children's writings. In addition, child writers are usually supervised by adults, and parents rarely keep what they write or draw. If writings are preserved, child authors often discard them when they grow up. Sarah Hamilton scoffed at her own adolescent crossing-the-plains diary. Fifty years later she published it as poetry seen through adult eyes. In one verse she expressed her feelings about her childhood writings: "For childish fancies in this journal sleep That presence of an untaught wisdom shows." As already noted, Ada Millington and Andrew Jenson edited and embellished their teenage trail diaries, and Harriet Hitchcock's older sisters teased her for keeping a record of their trip. When the adult Virginia Reed (Murphy) learned that her sister found her teenage letter from California, Virginia told Charles McGlashan, author of a book on the Donner party, "I would not have you or any one else out of the family see that letter for all California, it was my first effort. . . . Please don't publish it, for it must be silly and foolish. What could a child wright at that age, not accustomed to writing either."[26] Although Virginia Reed referred to this letter as her first attempt to write, she had previously sent one from Independence Rock.

Since relatively few diaries and letters of young people are available, reminiscences can provide insights into a child's trail experience. Credibility, however, is lessened by the time span

---

[26]Hampsten, *Settlers' Children*, 6; Hamilton, *A Pioneer*, 8; Murphy, "Letters to McGlashan," April 18, 1879.

between the event and the writing and also by the circumstances under which the experience is remembered. Most of the reminiscences discussed in this book were written by older individuals, often fifty to eighty years after they made the journey as children. Perspective also influences what is recalled. Even people in the same wagon train may not have seen an occurrence exactly alike. Hence, childhood memories can be distorted. An author might have forgotten details or chosen to delete, add to, or embellish events depending upon audience and purpose. In her teenage letter, Virginia Reed did not mention that her step-father killed a man and was banished from the train. Years later, in a published reminiscence she included the incident to clear up false rumors. By comparing personal documents point by point and lining them up with historical facts, contradictions and interpretations can be accepted or discredited. Elliott West applied three standards to reminiscences: specificity, repetition, and congruence. He also stated the more exact a memory the better the accuracy, but he did not directly address collective and shared memory which can make recollections appear more exact. Longer memoirs can inform today's readers about the trek and sometimes about early settlement and pioneer lives. They provide details about the trail, weather, people, and happenings. Many reminiscences, though, are shorter documents which were written for posterity and limited circulation. According to Jay Mechling, historians who study childhood recollections should use the same cautions as those who analyze oral histories.[27] After all, reminiscences were oral history until they were put on paper.

The stories of many pioneers who did not write would have been forgotten had it not been for Fred Lockley and other oral historians. Lockley worked for the *Oregon Journal* for nearly twenty years in the early 1900s, and his column "Impres-

---

[27]Murphy, "Virginia," Letter 2; Murphy, *Across the Plains*, 17–19; West, *Growing Up*, xx–xxi; Mechling, "Oral Evidence," 580.

sions and Observations of the Journal Man" appeared daily in that newspaper. During his career, he interviewed more than 10,000 individuals, some of whom were children when they made the trek. Daughters of Cianda Davis (Pitman), Margaret Stout (Gibson), and James Gibson recorded their parents' trail experiences. *The Salt Lake Tribune* interviewed ninety-six-year-old Manomas Gibson (Andrus) who crossed the plains when she was five.[28]

In an attempt to pull the United States out of the Great Depression, President Franklin D. Roosevelt instigated the New Deal. As part of this program, Congress approved several relief and reform measures in 1935, one of which was the WPA and its Historical Records Survey. In Utah and Oregon the WPA conducted and transcribed interviews with pioneers and early settlers. For the Utah project, interviewers used seventy-eight standard questions. They asked about the pioneer's wagon train and incidents such as gathering berries, herding stock, and seeing buffalo and Native Americans. The interviewer was instructed to ask every question, record the answers, and "do not hesitate to add extra information which may pertain to the individual being interviewed."[29] Most, however, referred to the required questions. The quality of the interview depended upon the training of the interviewer; in spite of this drawback, oral interviews reached pioneers who crossed the plains as children and did not write about it.

How do people remember happenings of fifty years earlier? Did pioneers see the trail experience as children, or did they write with nostalgic, older eyes? People often cannot remember what they once believed, and time alienates them from feeling direct participation. Also, memories are continually being discarded and only a fraction of the past can be retrieved. So individuals fill in a memory or alert the reader with adult

---

[28]Helm, *Conversations*, 1; Cummins, "Crossing the Plains," 23, 25; "Jonathan Stout," 8; Gibson, "From Missouri," 1; Genealogical Society, *Utah Pioneer*, 3: 197.

[29]Hefner, *WPA Historical Records*, 5–6; Haskin, *Pioneer Stories*, 4: preface; Genealogical Society, *Utah Pioneer*, introduction to each volume.

vision or nostalgia. John Bond crossed the plains in 1856 at the age of twelve. His Mormon wagon train accompanied the Martin handcart company and experienced similar tragedies as a result of early blizzards in Wyoming. As an adult he wrote, "Alas! tender hearted mothers, carrying their nursing babies and giving them the bosom by the way, was a most shocking and cruel sight to behold by innocent and God-fearing people. A more heart rendering sight I have not witnessed in all my life." Twelve-year-old John would not have written with the same nostalgia and Victorian sentimentalism that the older John did. In an address to the Oregon Pioneer Association, J. C. Moreland, who emigrated as a child, included nineteenth-century hero worship in his remarks when he said that a pioneer's story "is so full of fascinating interest that it is richly worth repeating; and one never tires of hearing its recital. And it will live in song and story, history and legend, as long as the human race shall love to hear of and honor deeds of daring and heroism."[30] These philosophical comments were not made through children's eyes either. Children lived the journey's ups and downs, and the legend was created after pioneers reached their new home.

Other reminiscences, especially published ones, provide the reader with precise information about the trail, forts, and landmarks. They add rich detail and make the narration more interesting, but such facts could not have come from a child's mind. George Riddle traveled to Oregon at age eleven. In his published memoir he noted that Independence Rock "is situated on a plain and covers 25 or 30 acres. It is from 100 to 200 feet high." Devil's Gate "is about 6 miles from Independence Rock in what we would call a box canyon, with the precipitate rock walls several hundred feet high and the rocks having the appearance of having been split apart." Then he informed the reader that although he remembered the landmarks, "I have been aided in the

---

[30]Bond, "Handcarts West," 15; Moreland, "Annual Address," 26.

description by that given by Ezra Meeker," who re-traveled the Oregon Trail years later.[31]

ALTERING RECOLLECTIONS

Errors in dates and names may not mean an account is false. If children did not know the route when they made the trek and did not research it as adults, they probably recalled it the way they saw it as children. Marvin D. Jensen maintained that "the most authentic memoirs are those which admit some confusion of memory and distortion of perception." Harriet Zumwalt (Smith), who went to California at age twelve, seemed confused when she said, "I dont remember much about the country from Steamboat Springs for some distance. I do remember that it was a rough hilly road until we arrived at what was then called Sweet water or St. Marys River." The Sweetwater River is in central Wyoming and St. Mary's River, now known as the Humboldt, runs through Nevada. Louisa Sweetland admitted that "there are a great many things I can hardly remember, as I was not quite ten years old. However, I will mention a few that I can well remember." Almost four years old when he traveled to Utah, Charles Ross Howe later wrote his cousins, "Of course you cannot expect me to rember much of what occured traveling that long journey by wagon. I well remember about it but very few particulars."[32] Thus, the more accurate childhood reminiscences may not be ones that recalled events in precise detail.

Human memories are not like computer memories that are filed on disks for later retrieval in the same form. Instead, each time we recall an event we infuse it with new meaning. According to Steven Rose, there are two types of truth: one which actually happened and one which a person remembers hap-

---

[31]Riddle, *Early Days*, 12–13.
[32]Jensen, "Memoirs," 238; Smith, "My Trip Across," 12; Sweetland, "Across the Plains," 191; Howe, Letter, 2.

pened. A memory is not a reproduction of reality but a representation or reconstruction of it. Its pieces are reshaped, omitted, distorted, reorganized, and mixed with elements from the present and the past. As a person changes with life's experiences, so does memory. John Leo observed that "those who remember the past are condemned to revise it."[33]

How do we recall memories? Usually they are prompted by a chance remark, a name, a smell, an emotion, a photograph, notes from an experience, a parent reminding us that we should recall an incident. Some events we rehearse in our minds, discuss frequently with others, and say, "I was part of that historical trek across the plains." But pure memories are not influenced by outside reminders. Individual and private recollections can come unprompted, such as an earliest memory which is not linear or sequential or even makes sense but is seen through the eyes of a small child. Because "we are all exiles from our past," we remember this experience. An earliest memory, which often occurs between the ages of three and four, resembles a snapshot or a flash of light and is usually visual and intense. One scene remains indelible on the mind, while the rest of the recollection vanishes. This remembrance displays such emotions as fear, joy, anger, wonder and curiosity, sorrow and disappointment, shame and guilt—with fear and joy being most common.[34]

Elizabeth Brown (Needham) went to Utah when she was three years old, and she remembered "soldiers stopping us to look through our belongings. I tried very hard to protect my large doll which I had brought from my home in London." This memory was visual, brief, and involved the emotion of fear. Rachel Zimmerman (Samuels), not yet two when she went

---

[33]Rose, "Two Types of Truth," 26; Rose, *Making of Memory*, 2, 35; Leo, "Memory," 89.

[34]Hufford, Hunt, and Zeitlin, *Grand Generation*, 38–39, call sensory prompts which bring reminders from the past "touchstones." See also Neisser, *Memory Observed*, 47–48; Rose, *Making of Memory*, 2; Thelen, "Memory," 1120–1121; Huyghe, "Voices," 48–51; Dudycha and Dudycha, "Childhood Memories," 679; Waldvogel, "Childhood Memories," in Neisser, *Memory Observed*, 75, 78.

to California, remembered her uncle putting her "on a little black pony and as the train was rounding a curve he said, 'Look there at the wagons.'" Her recollection was visual and brief, photographic and pleasurable. Inez Adams (Parker) crossed to Oregon when she was nearly three. She recalled sleeping in a tent at Council Bluffs and hearing the wind make a "wild, eerie sound." She also visualized "a low valley where wild roses grew so tall as to almost meet over our heads . . . the lovely pink flowers, the fragrance of which lingers with me still." The fragrance may have come from subsequent memories of wild roses blooming in Oregon's Willamette Valley, but her recollection of flowers being as tall as she was belonged to a small child. An almost three-year-old probably would not remember the name of the place she heard the wind, but through family discussions she may have connected the sensory experience with their first camping spot. Inez Adams also mentioned stringing blue beads that "kept me absorbed for hours" but then added that her mother reminded her about this.[35]

"I Remember" vs. "We Remember"

As Inez Adams implied, the past we remember is both individual and collective, and many events related to us become part of our memory. By discussing events with an adult, children may unintentionally make the adult's recollection part of their "true" memory. Polly Claypool (Purcell) wrote about crossing the plains, "I was only three and one half years old, too young to remember . . . but having heard them so many times from my father and mother as well as my older brothers and sisters, at times I seem to be able to go over them with familiarity." Not yet a year old when he made the journey, Thomas Sprenger admitted, "Of course I remember nothing of that trip but I have heard some of the incidents mentioned many times over." James Swank recognized that part of his three-year-old memory was his own, but "I, myself, do not

---

[35]Carter, *Treasures*, 3:114; Samuels, "Early Humboldt," 18; Parker, "Early Recollections," 17–18.

positively know how much I remember of that trip. It seems as though I remember quite a little bit but perhaps a good deal of it is from hearing my parents speak of it so often." Charles Howe, not quite four, wrote, "Somethings my parents continued to discourse about after we arrived here I can fancy that I remember about." Mary Creighton only remembered that they "commenced the long westward journey" in the spring of 1849 "because I heard the older members of the family refer to that fact so many times." Sarah Palmer (Sharp), age ten, remembered some things, but others were told by her mother and "there will be many things which I have forgotten." Her memory was not perfect, but "it stands out plainly to me or I would not write it if I did not think it right."[36]

In other words, the stories we tell ourselves are ones we want to believe, and novel or unique events are those we remember best. The past can be a comfortable place to return to, especially with family members. Childhood memories often bear the stamp of family sharing, selecting, and editing and become shared memories for posterity. The family of Anna Bixby (Pence) gathered at Easter time to "spin tales of past history." Martha Gay's (Masterson) family frequently talked about earlier days. Martha was known as a storyteller and, according to a great niece, "When we went to visit, Aunt Mattie would take us out under a tree and tell us stories about crossing the plains and about Indians." At times family members relied on each other for confirmation of memory. Eighty-year-old Sarah Palmer (Sharp) depended on her older sister Eliza for details about the trek. "I can't remember, neither can Eliza, what we had to eat. We got our rations once in two weeks (I think). Flour, bacon, coffee, and Eliza thinks beans. Perhaps so. I can't remember."[37] Those who kept no written records encountered greater distortions in their recollections.

[36]Lowenthal, *The Past*, 194, 196; Purcell, *Autobiography*, 2; Haskin, *Pioneer Stories*, 5: 1; Howe, *Letter*, 2; Creighton, "To My Grandchildren," 1; Sharp, "Autobiography," 1, 5.
[37]Hall, "Early Memories," 493, 499, 502; Pence, "Pioneer Hardships," foreword; Barton, *One Woman's West*, xiii; Sharp, "Autobiography," 8.

Moreover, it is difficult to distinguish between primary and secondary memories—or even if they really happened. Child psychologist Jean Piaget discovered that his nurse had fabricated an event which he remembered about his early childhood. Because she repeated the fake story again and again, it became part of his memory. In contrast, some family experiences are not shared at all. Naomi Pike (Schenck) wrote to author McGlashan about the Donner party ordeal: "I was but three years old at that time and have no recollection of the suffering then endured. It was a subject always painful to my mother." Then she added, ". . . knowing that all the sorrow of her life was involved in that perilous journey I never allowed my curiosity to wound her and have not realized until reading your questions how little I really know of what is a part of my own life."[38]

Family recollections across generations create a shared memory and a group identity, but they can also expand to a broader audience of community members. Reminiscences are usually written later in life after being shared orally many times. If the listeners were pioneers, their stories intermingled within a community to develop collective memory. "In fact, we need other people's memories both to confirm our own and to give them endurance," said David Lowenthal. ". . . we revise personal components to fit the collectively remembered past, and gradually cease to distinguish between them" until collective memory results. We depend on others to help us decide what to forget, what to remember, and how to interpret the event.[39]

Pioneers did not carry a shared identity across the plains; they created it over the years by associating and conversing with each other. As Philura Vanderburg (Clinkinbeard) said, "New lands have strange tales to tell and the people in them are often great storytellers." Philura's published account described the trek, but she did not write it herself. Her daugh-

---

[38]Lowenthal, *The Past*, 196–197; Jensen, "Memoirs," 237; Schenck, "Letters to McGlashan," April 23, 1879.

[39]Lowenthal, *The Past*, 196; Thelen, "Memory," 1122.

ter "collected and arranged" Philura's experiences "in proper sequence, then wrote the story, reading it to her, page by page and story by story, for her criticism, writing and rewriting again and again until finally the tale was as she wished it to be." These childhood memories bore the stamp of sharing, selecting, and editing for posterity and for "boys and girls who can never hear my mother tell these stories." Although this account was written sixty-four years later in story form with dialogue and foreshadowing, the daughter promised that "each incident related is a true one, true in detail."[40]

In other words, even after reconstructing the past, people insist their recollections are unchanging and accurate. William Pleasants, who went to California in 1849 and again in 1856, said his published reminiscence was "a truthful narrative of his experiences . . . with a strict avoidance of anything pertaining to exaggeration or distortion." S. W. Campbell crossed to Colorado at the age of nine and, although he wrote sixty-nine years later, the introductory note assured the reader that "it contains no fiction, and every incident is true history just as he remembers it." Yet Catherine Scott (Coburn) who emigrated to Oregon at the age of twelve observed, "Much that is real in the history of these early struggles . . . is slipping from the prosaic domain of fact into the shadowy realm of romance; . . . Hence, to separate the real from the unreal is even now in many instances impossible."[41]

Memory is intertwined with the identities of individuals, groups, and cultures, including formal organizations like the Oregon Pioneer Association and Daughters of Utah Pioneers. Roger Launius observed how the Mormon History Association developed its group identity through shared memory. At yearly meetings he heard long-time members talk nostalgically about early gatherings and original members. These common experiences produced group memories and helped to define the

---

[40]Clinkinbeard, *Across the Plains*, dedication, foreword, 93.

[41]Thelen, "Memory," 1123; Pleasants, *Twice Across*, introduction; Campbell, "Oregon Trail," introduction; Coburn, "Old Pioneer Days," 16.

organization. Being part of a common past and understanding, it divided "us" from "them" and created identity. In the same way, meetings of the Daughters of Utah Pioneers, Oregon Pioneer Association, and Society of California Pioneers kept stories of the trail alive and helped build group identity. George Currey noted in an 1887 address to the Oregon Pioneer Association that he "never relished pioneer meetings from the fact there seems to be such an air about them, a sort of supplication for recognition, a dread that somebody is going to be forgotten." Yet in a 1907 address, George Himes reminded members they were meeting for the thirty-fifth year to share reminiscences and, in essence, build collective memory. Individuals who had not made the trek could not understand the experiences of those who did. "Even to many of those who made the arduous journey the events of the trip . . . seem like a series of dreams," and they asked themselves, "Did I really cross the plains?" Himes made the journey in 1853 in a covered wagon, and by the time he addressed the pioneer gathering, people were crossing the country in comfortable railroad cars.[42]

Sometimes first-person accounts submitted to pioneer organizations or publishers were not really first-hand recollections. Mary Ellen Todd's (Applegate) reminiscence was written and published after her death by her daughter. Adrietta Hixon heard her mother tell about the journey so many times that she wrote in first person and used her mother's expressions and phrases.[43] Susan Noble's (Grant) crossing-the-plains experience was written by a grandson who said, ". . . I

---

[42]Thelen, "Memory," 1127; Launius, "Mormon Memory," 3, 4, 18; Unruh, *Plains Across*, 382; Currey, "Occasional Address," 32; Himes, "Annual Address," 134–135.

[43]Hixon, *On to Oregon*, introduction. Since Mary Ellen Todd's account was written in first person, it may have confused some researchers of the westward trek. See for example Schlissel, *Women's Diaries*. On page 12 she noted that her book contained diaries, reminiscences, and letters, yet on page 84 she included Mary Ellen Todd's reconstructed account, then referred to Adrietta Hixon as another child pioneer when Hixon was Todd's daughter who authored her mother's story. Faragher and Stansell, "Women and Their Families," 157, 165, footnote 31; Faragher, *Women and Men*, 67, 68; and Mattes, *Platte River*, 393, also included Todd's second-hand story as a primary document. Perhaps some of my accounts were not primary documents either.

shall give you the first-hand story as she has many times told it to us children. . . . Grandmother died when I was about thirty years of age, so my information is not childish memory."[44] George Harrison's first-person account was submitted to the Daughters of Utah Pioneers for preservation and publication, but he was not the author. According to Lyndia Carter, Harrison's daughter and daughter-in-law wrote it after hearing his story many times. One wonders how many accounts submitted to pioneer organizations were actually written by the emigrant. By the time the Daughters of Utah Pioneers began collecting histories, the second generation usually submitted them when the organization urged daughters to record their mothers' stories.[45]

The Editor's Hand

Occasionally personal histories like William McDonald's were printed verbatim in DUP volumes, such as *Heart Throbs of the West* and *Our Pioneer Heritage*.[46] But many of the histories were edited for publication. Before being published by the Daughters of Utah Pioneers, Lucy Canfield's diary was altered considerably. Editor Kate Carter deleted several entries and shortened some of the girl's already brief writings. One section of Carter's abridged version read,

> Sept. 1st. Made 17 miles and camped opposite Chimney Rock. 'Tis a wild but pretty country around here. There is a stage station near it. 4th. Traveled about 9 miles. Roasted a duck for our supper.

The unabridged account to which Carter referred said,

<u>September 1 – Monday</u> – made 17 miles and camped opposite Chim-

[44]Grant, "Robbed By Wolves," 357. Susan Arrington Madsen studied journals and personal histories by young emigrants for her book *I Walked*, vii–viii. Susan Noble Grant's story was written in first-person but was not her personal history.

[45]Carter, *Treasures*, 2: 105–114. Lyndia McDowell Carter, author of a book in press about the Martin handcart company, telephone conversation with author, 18 January 1997; Winn and Olsen, "Daughters," 97.

[46]Carter, *Pioneer Heritage*, 11: 189–196. Carter's *Heart Throbs, Pioneer Heritage*, and *Treasures* were printed volumes of pioneer stories submitted to the Daughters of Utah Pioneers and used as lesson material for the various camps' monthly meetings.

ney Rock. Tis a wild but pretty country around here. there is a stage station near it, the first house we've seen for a long time.

September 2 – Tuesday. Mr. mcfarlin broke a single tree. Drove 14 miles and camped near Scott's Bluffs, a pretty place.

September 3 – Wednesday –

Travelled about 8 miles & camped for dinner.

About 5 o'clock went on two or three miles. Rose and I had a short horse back ride.

September 4 – Thursday.

Travelled about 9 miles. Began raining. We stopped for night. Roasted a duck we got on the plains for our supper.[47]

What little personality Lucy Canfield revealed in her diary was basically eliminated when the editor got hold of it. Another problem surfaced with Lucy's diary. The unabridged version was not her own; it had been copied and submitted to DUP by someone else. What changes were made by the woman who transcribed the account by hand and donated it to the DUP? Two other transcripts of Lucy's diary are available for study, and they are slightly different from the one Carter used.[48] Which are Canfield's real words? These are problems researchers must face when dealing with documents which are not the originals.

Author Embellishment

Sometimes the authors themselves embellished their reminiscences. George Currey, a teenage emigrant to Oregon, suggested that "every genuine old pioneer is in honor bound to have had the hardest time on the plains of any other person living or dead." With nineteenth-century sentimentalism Octavius Pringle recalled his trip in 1846 when the southern route to Oregon's Willamette Valley was not even a trail.

---

[47]Carter, *Pioneer Heritage*, 6: 28; Canfield, Diary, Sept. 1–4.

[48]In 1961, Marian Mitchell Barron made a handwritten copy of Lucy Canfield's diary and submitted it to the DUP, then Kate Carter edited and published parts of this account. See Canfield, Diary, and Carter, *Pioneer Heritage*, 6:27–30. Another typescript from Julia Carver of Salt Lake City, Utah, is in the author's possession. See Canfield, "My Journal." Also, Lucy B. Roach of Ventura, California, submitted a handwritten copy of Lucy's diary in 1960, which apparently was written by Lucy Canfield Margetts as an older woman. See Margetts, "My Journal."

Although only fourteen, he was designated to make a three-day journey to a depot for provisions, then return with a relief party. He wrote,

> You may well imagine the disappointment and dreadful fear... when it was known that his return trip must be made alone, and that through a wild country uninhabited save by wild beasts and possibly wild Indians. But with undaunted courage and many misgivings he resolved to show no cowardice and thinking of parents, brothers and sisters who might be suffering for food resolved to make the attempt.

Pringle described his arrival back in camp with adult embellishment:

> ... embraced in the arms of a loving mother and smothered with sobs and kisses of gratitude and thankfulness for the return of her boy, his mother declared ... that the vision of her boy being torn by wild beasts or tortured by savages would startle her in her sleep and distort her dreams.[49]

Daniel Pendleton, not yet six when he went to Utah, sentimentally colored his recollection as well. "Our trip by ox-teams was tiresome as all such were. I was too young to feel the fear and dread with which my elders regarded every coming swell and every hidden turn of the road before and behind us, for we must be constantly on the alert for savage foes." Had he been exposed to nineteenth-century captivity novels? Elisha Brooks entertained audiences in California before publishing his trail experiences at age eighty-one. After so many retellings, even his humor seemed rehearsed. ". . . I remember those dried apples. From my experience I can recommend dried apples as an economical diet; you need but one meal a day; you can eat dried apples for breakfast, drink water for dinner and swell for supper."[50]

Other pioneers described the trek as a great adventure. Evan Stephens' trip to Utah "was such an experience of pleasure to me, that I found it difficult to sympathize with the pioneers

[49]Currey, "Occasional Address," 39; Pringle, *Magic River*, 3, 6.
[50]Pendleton, "Autobiography," 1; Brooks, *Pioneer Mother*, 11.

who thought it a hardship." Ruth May (Fox) was "too young to think about trials and hardships" of the journey at age thirteen, "but I am quite sure that travel and romance were appealing to my nature." Mary Creighton went to California at age six or seven and "had a perfectly splendid time." Many children did have a positive trail experience, but instead of being nostalgic, Mary wrote, "Perhaps the perfect confidence I always had in my father's ability to manage just right everything he had any connection with together with a sense of my mother's watchful care had a good deal to do with my freedom from the tribulations of grown ups."[51]

Other Influences on Reminiscences

Published memoirs and other resources influenced pioneer writers and helped create shared and collective memory. William Hockett used his father's letters from the trail as springboards for his own recollections. "Anyone reading this may know that it is strictly true, as my father's letters show plainly that there is no coloring or exaggeration used, and even now after the expiration of over 66 years, I cannot read these letters without feeling a horror or [sic] what my parents, sister and uncle must have endured." How much of what the family suffered did nine-year-old William comprehend at the time? Through his father's letters, William the adult expanded his childhood images. Sarah Zaring (Howard) jogged her thoughts by reading *The Covered Wagon* by Emerson Hough. "Many places he mentions and happenings he records bring fresh to my mind the names of places I had forgotten, and to my mind similar incidents to the ones recorded." What memories had she already internalized from family and community before reading the novel? George Riddle used *Vitor's History of Indian Wars of Oregon* for facts about the Modoc Indians. Howard R. Egan wrote his own reminiscence after

---

[51]Stephens, "A Talk," 1; Fox, "From England," 406; Creighton, "To My Grandchildren," 1.

copying his father's diary for publication. Pauline Wonderly must have referred to another record because she noted specific dates in her account. Since William Pleasants made two trips across the plains, he may have acquired details for his memoir by visiting the trail more than once.[52]

When working with reminiscences, researchers need to be aware that individuals reshape the past to fit present needs through their cultural expectations and traditions. Like historians, we subjectively and selectively rewrite our personal experiences by filtering them through the historical moment in which we live. Hindsight provides greater knowledge of the past because we know the outcome, but it also limits our ability to relive an event. All written history is a combination of past and present. Nineteenth-century pioneers internalized certain values and prejudices just as we do today. When we analyze their lives, we ascribe our cultural idiosyncrasies to them. In the forward to Martha Gay's (Masterson) account published in 1986, the editor stated that the pioneer was a product of her social and cultural world and she wrote with the racial biases and language of her time. But the editor was looking at Martha's peculiarities through her own late twentieth-century eyes.[53]

According to the new historicism point of view, written history can be seen from three vantage points: mine as a reader/researcher today, the pioneer's at the time of writing a reminiscence, and the child who actually crossed the plains in the mid-nineteenth century. In 1922, Mrs. Lee Whipple-Haslam wrote her childhood recollections. "I smile," she said, "when I see the present generation trying to imitate the primitive '49 dress. They are just about as near the mark as are the histories one reads." Yet she in her late seventies was looking

---

[52]Hockett, "Experiences," introduction; Howard, "Crossing the Plains," 1; Riddle, *Early Days*, 24; Egan, *Pioneering*, 5; Wonderly, *Reminiscences*, 4–12; Pleasants, *Twice Across*, introduction.
[53]Lowenthal, *The Past*, 207, 217; Thelen, "Memory," 1121; Lowenthal, "Timeless Past," 1264–1268; Barton, *One Woman's West*, xv.

back through 1920 binoculars. Which set of eyes were seeing what she said next? "And in crossing the plains we encountered many obstacles . . . But always nature has some compensation. After the storm the rainbow. After the desert clear streams of pure cold water." Her reminiscence also included themes of Manifest Destiny and wilderness conquest: "But filled with the spirit of adventure, the pioneers entered that phase of human endeavor to conquer the wilderness and, as ordained by God, to civilize the Pacific slope." These binoculars belonged to an adult, not a child crossing the plains. Even so, Mrs. Whipple-Haslam included childhood memories of her first spanking, too much buffalo meat, and "an overgrown dutch oven."[54]

Influences on Oral Histories

Individuals who wrote reminiscences were, of course, literate. Some dictated memories orally and, as a result, did not demonstrate writing ability. Rebecca Moore (Tanner) related her overland experiences to her daughter, a member of DUP, who possibly recorded them for preservation with the organization. Six-year-old Harry Payne traveled from England to Utah and later told his stories to a scribe after sharing them with his "children and grandchildren as they cluster around my knees." Although Mary Larsen (Price) had learned to read and write in Denmark, she dictated her experiences to her son and said nothing about her ability to write in English.[55] Many individuals left no records because they were illiterate or chose not to write. Native American children watched trains pass through their lands. Black youngsters crossed the plains to the West. Where are their voices? Too often historians rely on "literate elites . . . a small but influential minority," to provide a record

---

[54]Veeser, *New Historicism*; Thomas, *New Historicism*, 206–212; Whipple-Haslam, *Early Days*, 4, 6–8, 10.

[55]Lesson Committee, *Enduring Legacy*, 11: 365; Payne, *Payne Family*, 25, 29; Carter, *Pioneer Heritage*, 4: 208.

of the past. Dictated reminiscences and oral histories can help us hear from a segment of society that is usually voiceless.[56]

Oral history is personal information related by a literate or illiterate person to an interviewer who records what is said. Interviews may be informal conversations or, as in the case of the Utah WPA project, more formal sessions with specific questions. Sometimes assigned questions slant an interview and limit or eliminate personal sharing. A good interview will allow the memorist time to construct a story and share feelings about it.[57] Seventy-eight questions fired rapidly at informants may not permit reflection and elaboration. Some of the Utah WPA transcriptions were extremely brief, perhaps because the interviews were conducted that way. Also, the questions had no order. They jumped from mode of travel to the pioneer's first home and the way bricks were made. Some questions required a hodgepodge of responses:

> Relate some of the interesting incidents of early days. Tell about coming to your state in a covered wagon. Tell of some of your childhood impressions. Describe activities such as gathering wild berries, herding stock, working in the fields, yoking oxen, etc. Tell of some of the early day quilting bees, corn husking parties. . . . Describe farm life of forty, fifty, or sixty years ago. Compare it with today.[58]

This format for conducting oral histories may have been confusing and even overwhelming to some informants.

Elisha Wilbur was five when he crossed the plains and ninety-one when interviewed by the Utah WPA. The assigned questions determined the direction of the conversation, and the transcription patterned what was asked. For example,

> 13. [Elisha Wilber's arrival in Utah] In October 1852.
> 14. J. C. Little was leader of the company.
> 15. Came by Oxteam. Had three oxen and a cow to pull the wagon
> . . . .

---

[56]Lowenthal, *The Past*, xxvi.
[57]Grele, "Using Oral History," 570–571.
[58]Utah WPA Survey, "Pioneer Questionnaire," and each of the 44 volumes of Genealogical Society, *Utah Pioneer*.

31. Mr. Wilbur saw plenty of buffalo crossing the plains. The Indians killed the buffalo and traded the skins to the emigrants for food stuffs. His father killed antelope in Utah.[59]

James Tegan, a nine-year-old emigrant to Utah, responded to the WPA questions at age eighty-one. Because the interviewer asked, "Do you recall seeing any buffalo or hunting any wild game," Tegan recalled seeing many buffalo and wild horses. When queried about his first contact with Native Americans, he said, "The first Indians I ever saw was at the crossing of the Platt[e] River in 1868. I remember two of them were drunk and as a boy I enjoyed watching them very much." Had he been allowed to reflect and tell his own story, he may have recalled other happenings—and also had more to say.

In contrast, informal interviews which allowed for contemplation produced greater insights into pioneer experiences. One of Margaret West Irvin's daughters wanted her mother's trail experiences recorded before she died, so an interviewer visited the eighty-one-year old woman more as "a neighbor and friend than as a reporter." The friend "encouraged her to talk freely and informally." During one visit, Margaret "brought out the old family Bible and leather-covered Methodist Hymnbook to show me the warped covers and the water stains on their leaves as a result of the wetting the books received while the wagons were fording the Platte River." Later, the interviewer asked if they sang as they traveled. "Without any hesitancy she sang some of the songs for me, and one by one I took down the words and music, playing the tunes over on the piano till I was sure I had the melody, then I filled in the harmony later."[60] Oral history such as this can enlarge the view of children on the trail, for much of what pioneers remembered was never recorded.

Before the advent of audio and videotaping, interviewers took notes, then put them in words as near as possible to what

---

[59]Genealogical Society, *Utah Pioneer*, 30: 6–7.
[60]Federal Writers Project, "James Tegan," 4, 6; Adams, "Covered Wagon," 1, 10, 17.

the informant said. Depending upon training, oral history guidelines, and accuracy of notes, some interviewers may have embellished their transcriptions with their own bits of wisdom. After asking the WPA questions to Nicholas Gourley (Teeples), the interviewer probably filled in gaps with her own knowledge about the Willie and Martin handcart companies. She described the rescue of the stranded emigrants from a rescuer's point of view, not a pioneer's, and added inaccurate data.

While oral history is a way of recalling the past, traditional historians have frowned upon it because its form is not fixed, its chronology may be faulty, and its information may be unsupported by historical evidence. But this type of record can provide a wider perspective on a culture and time. Memory may be limited and older informants may not accurately remember how they acted, interacted, or thought in earlier days, but they can remember childhood images. Rarely will one person recall all the details of an event, though when many are interviewed, patterns unfold and historians can discern common threads.[61]

In a newspaper interview ninety-two-year-old Catherine Pilling said, "I'm afraid I cannot tell my story interesting enough .... You will have to 'elevate' it somewhat, most likely." It is true that pioneers, their descendants, and other individuals have elevated the overland experience until it has acquired a nostalgic and "mythic place in our cultural heritage .... Lost in this vision, all too often, is the reality of the experience."[62] Lost also is the perspective of the child who made the journey with adults. Was it a pleasure trip? Who or what did young people write about? How did diaries and letters differ from reminiscences?

Most writers who have discussed children on the trail have lumped diaries, letters, journals, written reminiscences, and

---

[61]Genealogical Society, *Utah Pioneer*, 28: 92, 99; Allen and Montell, *From Memory*, 3, 15.
[62]Skov, "From Handcart," April 4, 1931; Holmes, *Covered Wagon Women*, 11: 8.

oral histories together without distinguishing between contemporary and later documents. Some, like Elliott West, Judy Allen, and Emmy Werner, noted the difference but treated the accounts the same when they discussed childhood experiences and themes. Other authors, such as Ruth Moynihan, Georgia Read, and Violet Kimball, viewed all records alike.[63] Writers have also failed to consider shared and collective memories in reminiscences, except perhaps to recognize them. In this book twenty-three diaries and letters written before, during, or soon after the overland trek are key sources for identifying a child's perspective and are reality checks for oral and written reminiscences. What do contemporary and later accounts say about the trail experience and human relationships? How are they alike and different? How do children's writings compare to adult diaries? Since the twenty-three diaries and letters were written by older youngsters, a small child's perspective cannot presently be determined. Still, youngsters' perceptions of the overland journey can be analyzed in contemporary and reminiscence accounts if scholars and readers are aware of the strengths and weaknesses of the various types of documents.

---

[63]West, *Growing Up*; West, "Youngest Pioneers," 90–96; Werner, *Pioneer Children*; Moynihan, "Children," 279–294; Read, "Women and Children," 1-23; Kimball, *Stories*.

CHAPTER II

Words From the Trail:
Young Pioneers' Diaries and Letters

"Thoughts by the way. And why not! . . . And what is the harm in simply penning a few thoughts now and then by the way side or by the side of the way, for it is a new and strange way that we are going to travel. . . . And as thought is ever busy I will make my hands help a little by scratching them down on paper, for my diary is too small for the purpose, and memory too short. Of course it ise'nt a Journal and no one will ever see it only a thought now and then."[1]

Thirteen-year-old Harriet Hitchcock was traveling to the Colorado gold mines in 1864 with her parents and two sisters when she recorded her "thoughts by the way." Diaries and letters written by young pioneers on the trail or soon after arrival at the destination can reveal pieces of who they were and what they thought. Writing style, elaboration or lack of it, opinions and feelings, and topics they discussed all contribute to learning about their attitudes and perceptions of the trail experience. Since such a small number of writings have been found, they cannot represent all children on the trail; however, they do show personality and perspective more accurately than reminiscences because youngsters actually wrote them. Diaries and letters belong to the

---

[1]Hitchcock, "Thoughts," 235. See also, Webb, *Family History*, 66–84, for another typescript of Harriet Hitchcock's diary and photocopy of the first page of her handwritten account.

historical moment in which they were written; reminiscences cover a broader time frame.

Twenty-three young diary, letter, and journal writers expressed their thoughts about the journey to Oregon, Utah, California, Nevada, and Colorado. A few wrote letters before leaving for the West; some started diaries before reaching the jumping-off place; others began writing on the trail. All twenty-three writers were white, literate to some extent, and between ten and sixteen years of age. (See Table 1.) Girls wrote nine diaries, fifteen letters, and one journal. Margaret Scott wrote letters and parts of the family diary, so I counted her twice. Boys contributed two diaries, three diary/journal combinations, and one journal. Diary/journal combinations were written as diaries but had journal or reminiscences added to them. Susan Dudley, Harriet Stewart, William Freshwater, and Christian Neilsen wrote contemporary accounts before but not during the trek across the plains. Their writings reveal the young pre-overlander's personality and perspective. Some young pioneers, like Mary Murphy, did not write until after they reached their destination.

Although I identified fewer total documents from the California Trail—67 compared to 157 from Oregon and 465 from Utah—the California Trail produced ten diary and letter writers, the Oregon Trail five, and the Mormon Trail seven.[2] Another diarist followed the Platte River road to Colorado. Why were more diaries and letters available from the California Trail, especially when fewer families journeyed there than to Oregon and Utah? It is difficult to know how many young pioneers actually wrote because either their accounts were not preserved or they are hidden in private collections which are not accessible to researchers. Almost all of the diaries and letters referred to in this book came from published sources, such as the *Covered Wagon Women* series, and archive

---

[2]These totals do not include twenty-three documents from other destinations, such as Montana, Colorado, and Idaho.

Table I. Diaries, Letters, and Journals

Year	Age	M/F	Name	Origin	Destin.	Type of Writing
1846-47	12-13	F	Virginia Reed	IL	CA	Letters, 1846 and 1847
1847	13	F	Mary Murphy	TN	CA	Letter
	15	M	William Pace	TN	UT/NE	Diary/journal combination
1849	13 1/2	F	Sallie Hester	IN	CA	Diary
1850	14	F	Susan Dudley	NH	UT	Pre-letter, letter*
1852	12	F	Elizabeth Keegan	MO?	CA	Letter
	16	F	Eliza Ann McAuley	NY	CA	Diary
	15 1/2	F	Margaret Scott	IL	OR	Parts of diary, five letters
	12 1/2	F	Catharine Scott	IL	OR	Letter
	11	F	Harriet Scott	IL	OR	Two letters
1853	14-15	F	Rachel Taylor	IL	OR	Diary
1854	15-16	M	Patrick Murphy	MO	CA	Diary
	15	F	Harriet Stewart	IL	OR	Pre-letter with siblings*
	14 1/2	M	Christian Neilsen	Denmark	UT	Diary/journal combination*
1861	16	F	Edith Lockhart	?	CA	Diary
	15-16	M	Thomas Griggs	England	UT	Diary
1862	12-13	F	Ada Millington	IA	CA	Journal (revised diary)
	15 1/2	F	Lucy Canfield	NY	UT	Diary
1863	15	F	Flora Bender	OH	NV	Diary
	10-11	M	William Freshwater	England	UT	Diary/journal combination*
1864	15	F	Mary Eliza Warner	WI	CA	Diary
	13	F	Harriet Hitchcock	PA	CO	Diary
1866	15 1/2	M	Andrew Jenson	Denmark	UT	Journal (revised diary)

* These young people wrote diaries and letters before the actual trek.

or library collections.[3] It appears that more descendants of California Trail travelers saved their records or made them available to the public.

How were the California Trail accounts preserved? Virginia Reed's step-father kept her 1847 letter in a trunk, and her sister discovered it three decades later. A relative returned the 1846 letter to Virginia fifty-two years later. Eventually the let-

---

[3]To locate additional documents for his series, Kenneth Holmes, the editor of the *Covered Wagon Women* series, wrote newspaper columns, talked on radio shows, and visited with private groups and individuals. As a result, he obtained some of the best diaries and letters of young people. This suggests that other contemporary accounts might be tucked away in some dresser drawer or attic waiting to be discovered. See Holmes, *Covered Wagon Women*, 1: 23.

ters found a home in a California library, as did a typescript of Mary Eliza Warner's diary.[4] Mary Murphy's 1847 letter is housed in a Tennessee archive. I borrowed a photocopy of Eliza Ann McAuley's original diary from Thomas Macaulay, a descendant of Eliza's brother, and typescripts can be found in California repositories.[5] Patrick Murphy's daughter, Edith Lockhart's granddaughter, and Elizabeth Keegan's great-granddaughter made typescripts of the original documents and deposited them in libraries or historical societies.[6] A California periodical published Sallie Hester's diary in 1925, and Ada Millington's daughter loaned her journal to Charles Clarke who edited and published it in a California magazine. The unpublished journal is on microfilm in a California library. The Nevada Historical Society obtained Flora Bender's writings from two of her nieces and published them. Frank Bender, a descendant of Flora's brother, sent me a typescript of her diary.[7]

The Oregon and Colorado accounts appeared as a result of research for the *Covered Wagon Women* series. David Duniway, co-editor of one volume in the series, made the Scott diary and letters available for publication. His grandmother Abigail, her sister Margaret, and their father wrote the diary; and sisters Margaret, Catharine, and Harriet composed the letters I analyzed. A family member provided Harriet Augusta Stewart's letter for publication. Rachel Taylor's diary came from a descendant who saw a newspaper notice about the covered wagon volumes. Catherine Webb, a relative of Harriet Hitchcock, obtained her Colorado diary and printed it in a family book, then heard about the series and offered it for publication. According to Webb, Harriet had two diaries. "One is very

---

[4]Murphy, "Letters to McGlashan," April 18, 1879; Donner and Reed, "Donner Party," 66; Murphy, "Virginia," Letter 1, note; Warner, "Diary."

[5]Murphy, Letter TN, 1-2; McAuley, Diary, 1-88; McAuley, "Iowa," 35.

[6] Murphy, "Across the Plains Diary"; Humphrey, "Original Diary"; Keegan, "Teenager's Letter," 21.

[7]Hester, "Diary," 231; Clarke, "Journal Kept," 13–14; Millington, "Journal"; Bender, "Notes," note page; Bender, Typescript, 1–18.

brief and sometimes only has one word to describe the weather
. . . . It also goes until they arrive home on March 9th. The
expanded version ends on January 30th." But Webb did not
say if one was a lengthy revision of the other or if Harriet
Hitchcock kept two diaries near the same time.[8]

How were the Mormon Trail diaries and letters obtained?
Brigham Young University (BYU) typed a copy of William B.
Pace's diary, and BYU's special collections department received
typescripts of Susan Dudley's correspondence. Thomas Cott
Griggs's diary and Andrew Jenson's journal are on microfilm
in the L.D.S. Church Archives in Salt Lake City. A granddaughter of Christian Emil Neilsen submitted a typescript of
his writings to the Daughters of Utah Pioneers (DUP) with
the note, "Each year I hear you asking for Autobiographies of
pioneers which hve [sic] never before been printed. . . . I would
be so happy to have you use it in one of your Pioneer Books."
A family member submitted a typescript of William Henry
Freshwater's diary to the DUP, and the organization published
it. Two slightly different accounts of Lucy Canfield's diary can
be found in the L.D.S. Church Archives, and I received
another transcript from a relative of Lucy Canfield.[9]

Mormons have always been encouraged to keep personal
records because of their belief in the eternal nature of the family. Ancestors and descendants are part of a family unit, and
church members are counseled to share their life experiences,
values, and faith with their posterity. When the church was
organized, a scriptural directive admonished its leaders to keep
records. Individual members heeded this advice as well. Philip
Taylor noted that Mormons were "conscious of their own historical importance, and therefore much addicted to the keeping of records." Even fourteen-year-old Christian Neilsen from

---

[8]Scott, "Journal," 26–27; Scott Sisters, "Letters," 139–140; Sutton, "Travel Diary," 23; Taylor, "Overland Trip," 149; Hitchcock, "Thoughts," 234–235; Webb, *Family History*, 65.

[9]Pace, "Diary"; Dudley, "Dudley Family"; Griggs, "Crossing the Plains"; Jenson, "Journals";
Neilsen, "Autobiography"; Carter, *Pioneer Heritage*, 7: 248–252; Canfield, Diary; Margetts,
"My Journal"; Canfield, "My Journal."

Denmark felt compelled to finish his father's diary the day he died on the Mississippi River. Christian wrote, "Now I will begin to write what transpires at this time. Great sorrow rests on my mind. I am now both Father and Motherless. Today 1 o'clock died my Father, calm and peasefull." Andrew Jenson began a journal at the age of thirteen "through the influence of some of the L.D.S. missionaries who visited at our house."[10] Jenson was a prolific writer and as an adult became assistant historian for the L.D.S. Church. Ten-year-old William Freshwater wrote on his way to America but not on the trek to Utah. Perhaps he grew disinterested because of his age, or the excitement of trail travel precluded time to make a diary record. Like Andrew Jenson, adults may have encouraged him to write. Yet diaries and letters of Mormon children are difficult to find.

CALIFORNIA TRAIL ACCOUNTS

Who were these young people who wrote about their trip to the West? Twelve-year-old Virginia Reed left Springfield, Illinois, in 1846 with her mother and step-father, three half-siblings—eight-year-old Martha (Patty), six-year-old James, and three-year-old Thomas—and her elderly Grandmother Keyes. Although the older woman suffered from consumption, she wanted to go west to see a son who was there. Virginia's father died when she was small, and James Frazier Reed married her mother and raised the child as his own. Reed acquired considerable wealth from a furniture-making business in Springfield and decided to take his family to California, partly to see if his wife could get rid of her "sick headaches." Accompanying the family and their three wagons were a domestic servant and her half-brother as well as several hired men. The Donner brothers joined them near Springfield. Thirteen-year-old Mary Murphy was part of that company with

---

[10]Doctrine and Covenants, 21: 1; Ludlow, *Encyclopedia*, 770; Taylor, "British Mormons," 249; Neilsen, "Autobiography," 6; Jenson, *Autobiography*, 10.

her widowed mother, four brothers, two married sisters, their husbands, and three small children. Lovina Murphy, Mary's mother, left Tennessee with her children and met a married daughter in Missouri. With two wagons the family of thirteen joined the Donner train. Both Virginia Reed and Mary Murphy wrote letters to relatives describing their harrowing experiences on the way to California.[11]

During the 1849 gold rush, fourteen-year-old Sallie Hester accompanied her parents, two brothers, a younger sister, and a Methodist missionary train to California "in search of health, not gold," as she explained in her diary. Sallie's father was a successful lawyer in Indiana when he decided to move west. He became the wagon master of 50 wagons, 134 men, and an undetermined number of women and children. Reverend Isaac Owen and several other ministers went with the company as missionaries. Members of this religious train agreed to certain stipulations: ". . . mutual aid will be given to each other. Godd [good] moral character will be required of all wishing to join the company, with satisfactory assurances that the Sabbath will be observed when practicable." Bylaws decried gambling, card-playing, profanity, and drunkenness.[12]

Sixteen-year-old Eliza Ann McAuley left Iowa for California in 1852 with her brother Tom, age twenty-two, sister Margaret, age twenty-eight, and a herd of dairy cows. Their father had been a dairy farmer in Iowa, but he went to the gold fields a few years earlier while his family remained with the dairy. Ezra Meeker, his wife, baby, and several young men joined the McAuley train, and Tom was chosen as leader and scout of the party. The traveling companions were in their teens and twenties, with Tom and Margaret being the old-

---

[11]Morgan, *Overland in 1846*, 1: 248–251; McGlashan, *History*, 13–14, 20–22; Murphy, *Across the Plains*, 1, 37. For a list of families who traveled in the Donner train, see Murphy, *Across the Plains*, 36–37. Murphy listed the ages of Patty and Thomas as eight and three, but Morgan noted their birth dates which made them nine and four.

[12]Hester, "Diary," 231–235; Purdy, "Isaac Owen," 47–49.

est. Along the way Eliza McAuley kept a diary of her adventures.[13]

Also in 1852, twelve-year-old Elizabeth Keegan went to California with her mother, a servant girl named Kate, and a hired man. After she arrived, the young pioneer wrote a letter to her brother and sister in St. Louis describing her trip and life in the West. Patrick Murphy was raised in St. Louis where he received a common school education. In 1854 when he was nearly sixteen, he hired on with Wiles and Company's stock train with 21 men, 525 head of cattle, 35 horses, and 4 wagons bound for California. Along the way he kept a diary. Sixteen-year-old Edith Lockhart left Harlem, Missouri, in 1861 with her mother and three men. At Omaha they joined a larger company bound for California, and Edith Lockhart recorded the journey in her diary.[14]

Ada Millington, who turned thirteen on the trail, wrote her diary in an old account book on the way to California in 1862 with her parents, older half-brother Ira, and younger siblings: Grace (11), Olivia (9), James (Bucky, 6), Seth (3), and George (1). An uncle, aunt, cousin Fred, and several hired hands joined them. Ada's father was a lawyer and owner of a newspaper in Keosauqua, Iowa, when he decided to move to a healthier climate to heal wounds he received in the Mexican War. Fifteen-year-old Flora Bender, her parents, sisters Nellie and Clara, and brother Charles left eastern Nebraska for Virginia City, Nevada, in 1863 to meet two older brothers who were employed in a telegraph office. Flora's maternal aunt and uncle who lived in the West helped convince the family to emigrate. If the typescript of Flora Bender's diary is accurate and not an embellished revision, this record is one of the most prolific of all the adolescent writings I have found. Fifteen-year-old Mary Warner kept a diary

---

[13]McAuley, "Iowa," 33–34; Smith, Letter, Oct. 3, 1999.

[14]Keegan, "Teenager's Letter," 21; Murphy, "Across the Plains Diary," 1, biography 1; Humphrey, "Original Diary," 1.

in 1864 while accompanying her mother, three younger siblings, and other relatives to meet her father in California. Mary's father and Uncle Chester had previously taken bands of horses across the plains and established a cattle ranch in the Sierra Nevada. Uncle Chester returned to Illinois, married, and headed for California again with his bride, his sister Celia, and Mary's mother and her four children, ages fifteen, thirteen, eleven, and three.[15]

Oregon Trail Accounts

Of the six Oregon Trail accounts, four belonged to one family. In 1852, Margaret Scott, age fifteen, helped her seventeen-year-old sister Abigail write the family diary while going west with her parents, siblings, and relatives in a larger train. Her father Tucker Scott caught "Oregon fever" but was detained from going for more than a decade. After his brother was killed, Scott had to assume half the debts, which bankrupted him. His wife's relatives went west in 1851, so he prepared for an 1852 migration. Scott took his invalid wife, who died near Fort Laramie, and children Mary Francis (19), Abigail (17), Margaret (15), Harvey (14), Catharine (12), Harriet (11), John (8), Sarah (5), and William (3), who died on the trail in Oregon. Uncles, aunts, and cousins joined their train, along with others from Illinois. Besides assisting with the diary, Margaret Scott sent five letters home to grandparents. Her sister Catharine wrote one letter and Harriet sent two describing the journey and life in Oregon.[16]

Almost fifteen when she left Illinois for Oregon in 1853, Rachel Taylor celebrated her birthday near Independence Rock in Wyoming. She kept a diary while traveling with her parents, older siblings, and an uncle, aunt, and their four daugh-

---

[15]Clarke, *"Journal Kept,"* 13, 16–17; Douglas, "Bender Family," 14; Warner, "Diary," foreword.
[16]Scott, "Journal," 23–24, 32–38; Scott Sisters, "Letters," 139–172.

ters, ages two to ten. They joined a preacher's wagon train consisting of Reverend Royal, his wife, their minister sons and families, their twenty-year-old daughter Mary, the Burt family, and approximately twenty men and two hundred cattle. In 1853 before leaving Illinois, fifteen-year-old Harriet Augusta Stewart sent a letter to a cousin in which she and her siblings and half-siblings volunteered reasons for wanting to go to Oregon.[17]

MORMON TRAIL ACCOUNTS

Seven young Mormons wrote about crossing the plains to Utah. William Pace moved from Tennessee to Nauvoo, Illinois, with his Mormon family, and at the age of ten became captain of a company of boys in the Nauvoo Legion. ". . . my father, being an expert drill master, soon initiated me into all the mysteries of drill and command." In 1846, Pace's family went to Council Bluffs, Iowa, with other church members. "Then came the requisition from the President of the United States for five hundred men to form a Battalion" to fight in the Mexican War. "Brigham Young called upon my father and others to volunteer." Pace's father enrolled as an officer, and his fifteen-year-old son became his servant "as I was too young to enlist." The Battalion marched to California on the southern route, then some of the men returned to Nebraska in 1847 when they finished their duty. Pace kept a diary the whole time. On the return journey, he witnessed the first pioneers building homes and preparing for winter in the Salt Lake Valley.[18]

In 1850, fourteen-year-old Susan Dudley wrote a letter to her aunt before leaving Nebraska, then another in Utah without describing the trek. Christian Neilsen was born to Danish parents in Middlefart, Denmark. His father was a clog maker, and "my earlyest recolection are Father making the wooden part and Mother making the Leather tops. They used

[17]Taylor, "Overland Trip," 149–152; "Letters of S. H. Taylor," 124; Sutton, "Travel Diary," 23–25.
[18]Lesson Committee, *Chronicles*, 7: 170–171; Pace, "Diary," 31.

to work until Midnight and early in the morning until they got money enough to buy a farm." The family learned about the Mormon religion and were baptized, then at the age of fourteen, Christian Neilsen left Denmark with his family. After his parents and two sisters died on the Mississippi River, the boy finished his father's record and went to Utah in 1854 with his surviving siblings in a Mormon train. On the way Christian Neilsen nearly died from the measles and, as a result, did not write during the journey.[19]

Born in Dover, England, Thomas Griggs lost his father at the age of nine. Two years later his mother and he joined the Mormon Church and sailed to Boston, where the youth worked in a dry goods store for more than four years. Members of their small church group organized a brass band, and Thomas enthusiastically joined. Two months after the Civil War commenced, Griggs, his mother, his brother, several relatives, and church members started for Zion. The adolescent kept a diary from Boston to St, Joseph, Missouri, where he turned sixteen without noting it, then on the way to Utah in a company of Saints. Fifteen-year-old Lucy Canfield spent her early years with her parents and her paternal grandparents in a New York farming community; several cousins also lived nearby. Lucy's mother and grandfather died when she was small, and the girl and her father remained with his mother until they left for Utah in 1862. While crossing the plains with her father and cousin Rose, Lucy wrote almost daily in her diary. William Freshwater accompanied his parents and sister from England to America in 1862, then crossed the plains in 1863. The ten-year-old boy made diary entries in England and on the voyage, but it appears he recorded his crossing-the-plains experience later in Utah. I have included his England and ship account for its writing style and personality.[20]

---

[19]Dudley, "Dudley Family," July 1, 1850, and Sept. 30, 1851; Neilsen, "Autobiography," 1, 6–7.
[20]Griggs, "Crossing the Plains," 1–2, 18–20; Jenson, *Biographical Encyclopedia*, 1:711; Canfield, Diary;
    Margetts, "My Journal"; Carter, *Pioneer Heritage*, 6:26–27; Carter, *Pioneer Heritage*, 7:248–251.

Andrew Jenson was born in Damgren, Denmark, in 1850. His parents joined the Mormon Church in 1854, and as Andrew grew, he became interested in scriptural history. "Before I knew that such a thing as a Bible chronology existed, I made one myself." The village schoolmaster treated the Mormon boys badly, so the Jensons home-schooled their two sons. At the age of twelve Andrew and his year-older brother Jens attended the village school with a "fair-minded" teacher and were "permitted to study those branches of education we desired." Andrew successfully passed the examination and received a certificate that excused him from school, but since his brother needed another year, Andrew went too. "In the early part of 1864 I finished my education so far as the public schools of Denmark were concerned." When Andrew turned fourteen, "which in Denmark is considered the age when peasant boys can take care of themselves," he became a salesman to the peasants and saved money to go to Zion. His father tucked away enough to take himself, his wife, and their four-year-old son. Andrew promised Jens he would work in Utah and send for his brother, which he did. Andrew recorded his journey in a diary he had begun several years earlier.[21]

THE TRAIL TO COLORADO

One young diarist did not go to Utah or the Pacific Coast. She followed the Platte River road to Colorado in 1864. Thirteen-year-old Harriet Hitchcock lived in Pennsylvania "in a beautiful tract of country with a long range of hills onto the south, and the clear blue waters of one of our Great Lakes on the north." Her father joined the gold rush, so "my two elder sisters and myself concluded to accompany Pa on his annual trip to Colorado." The writer did not say when his "annual" trips began. Harriet traveled with her parents, two sisters—

[21]Jenson, *Autobiography*, 4–13; Jenson, "Journals," 68–90.

Eliza Ann McAuley, shown here with
her husband, Robert Egbert.
Courtesy of Thomas Macaulay, Reno, Nevada.

Flora Isabelle Bender.
Courtesy of Frank Bender.

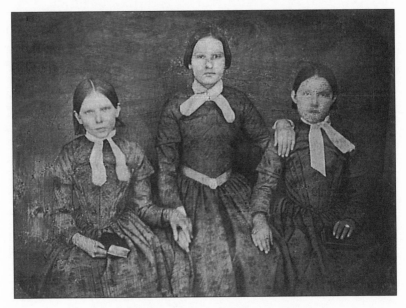

Harriet, Margaret, and Catharine Scott.
*From a daguerreotype, 1852–1853, provided by David Duniway,
for use in Holmes,* Covered Wagon Women, *v. 5, and used
with the permission of the publisher.*

Lucy and Bell—and two hired men. She kept two diaries, with
the published version describing the trip to Colorado, her stay
there, and the journey home. Since I did not locate either of
the original records, I have used the published version although
it may be a revision.[22]

Harriet went west because her parents did, and so did most
pioneer children. But two sixteen-year-old diarists chose to
make their trek to California without parents. Eliza McAuley
accompanied a brother and sister, and Patrick Murphy joined
a stock train. It is interesting that each kept a diary enroute.
Patrick had obtained a common school education, and Eliza's

---

[22]Hitchcock, "Thoughts," 233–236. If Harriet Hitchcock's larger diary is a revision of the orig-
    inal, it should be revisited and studied as I did with Ada Millington's journal and diary.

penmanship and writing ability indicate a literate background. She valued her record keeping enough to make ink from plants when she ran out along the trail. Although travel accounts were popular in the nineteenth century, these young diarists may have written because they were excited about going to a new land, impressed by "history in the making," or intrigued with the idea of being on their own as adults.

LITERACY ON THE TRAIL

Some of the young writers commented about literacy, and four mentioned school experiences. Before leaving for California, Sallie Hester waved goodbye to "the old Academy" and "kind teachers and schoolmates." Since her father was a successful lawyer in Indiana, she probably came from a middle-class home that valued education. The daughter of a "comparatively poor" tailor and farmer, Flora Bender attended school in Indiana and Nebraska, thanks to America's common school movement. "Two weeks ago today," she wrote, "I was sitting in the little School House at Bell Creek [Nebraska], surrounded by all my friends." Ada Millington and other children had "spelling school" on the trail during a rainstorm. Ada was raised in a middle-class environment with a lawyer/newspaperman father. After reaching Oregon, Harriet Scott continued her education and said, "I like the school very well."[23]

Young writers displayed literacy skills through the diaries they kept en route, but many of them also sent letters to relatives and friends. Flora Bender and her sister Nellie sat by some trees and composed several letters, then the next evening Flora reported, "We have seven to mail at Laramie." When Eliza McAuley "met an Express to 'the States,'" she sent a letter with the returning travelers. Rachel Taylor's "two letters to far off friends" went with Californians going eastward. Young

---

[23]Hester, "Diary," 235. Bender, "Autobiography," 1–2; Bender, Typescript, 3; Millingon, "Journal," 208; Scott Sisters, "Letters," 160.

emigrants also anticipated receiving mail but sometimes were disappointed. Lucy Canfield and Mary Warner each found three letters waiting at Fort Laramie. Near Fort Hall Margaret Scott wrote to family but did not receive "a single sylable from any of you," and after two months in California, Elizabeth Keegan complained to siblings back home, "I have written so many times that I have almost despaired of getting an answer."[24]

Besides mail they received on the trail, a few young travelers mentioned other reading materials they took with them or obtained along the way. One afternoon Flora Bender passed the time reading, "for we brought a good supply of papers and magazines along." Later, when they "laid by," she read again. This prolific young writer was the only one who mentioned taking such materials on the trail. Edith Lockhart spent a day in "reading, conversation & so forth." It is unfortunate that neither adolescent identified what she read. At times Rachel Taylor and Eliza McAuley consulted guidebooks, and Eliza "met a returning Californian with papers for sale. We bought a copy of 'The El Dorado News' for 50 cts." While camping on the Platte, Mary Warner noted "some poetry found and read before the company describing Charlie Chapman which created considerable fun." Later, they "came to a guide board, but there were two hand-writings on it so we could not tell anything by it--in one place it said there was a spring two miles off, and in another place it contradicted it, so we didn't know whether there was any spring or not."[25]

PENMANSHIP, MECHANICS, AND WORDING

Since some young emigrants produced their own diaries and letters, their perspective, personality, and writing style should

---

[24]Bender, Typescript, 5; McAuley, Diary, 32; Taylor, "Overland Trip," 166; Margetts, "My Journal," Sept. 7; Warner, "Diary," 9; Scott Sisters, "Letters, 162; Keegan, "Teenager's Letter," 30.

[25]Bender, Typescript, 2–3; Humphrey, "Original Diary," 2; Taylor, "Overland Trip,"166; McAuley, Diary, 37, 42–43, 59; Warner, "Diary," 8, 28.

appear in the pages. However, only four of the accounts which I found can be examined for precise wording, mechanics, and penmanship since published works are often edited. I obtained photocopies of original diaries by Thomas Griggs and Eliza McAuley, letters by Virginia Reed and Mary Murphy, and one page of Ada Millington's original diary which was included with her published journal.

What was the literacy background of these five young writers? According to family tradition, Eliza McAuley's family spent long winter evenings telling stories, reading, and engaging in discussions. Her brother attended Howe's Academy in Iowa, and Eliza's diary entries suggest that she, too, was educated. Thomas Griggs may have acquired some schooling in Boston, but his writing was not as mature as Eliza's. Both were sixteen years old. Of the thirteen-year-old writers—Ada Millington, Virginia Reed, and Mary Murphy—Ada Millington appeared the most skilled. Perhaps her family emphasized literacy more than the others since her father graduated from college, practiced law, and owned and edited a newspaper. Although Virginia Reed's step-father ran a profitable business, writing may not have been a family priority, for Virginia later admitted that these letters were her first attempts. I have no information about Mary Murphy's educational or socioeconomic background, only that her mother was a widow from Tennessee.[26]

What do the original documents reveal about penmanship, mechanics, and wording? The writers wrote legibly and in cursive, although Virginia Reed's tiny handwriting in her second letter was somewhat difficult to read. The five writers appeared fluent in thought, for they seldom deleted or altered words. Eliza McAuley filled 88 pages during her five-month journey, and Thomas Griggs completed 62 pages in three months. Virginia Reed wrote nearly two pages in one letter and six and a half in a second; Mary Murphy's letter filled one and one-half pages.

[26]Macaulay, Letter, Sept. 22, 1999: 2; Clarke, "Journal Kept," 16; Thrapp, *Encyclopedia*, 2: 1034–1035 and 3: 1199–1200.

Of the five writers Eliza McAuley exhibited the most competence in writing skills. Her spelling and grammar were excellent, but she needed help with commas and paragraphing. Sometimes she made logical use of commas; other times she inserted them at will: "Here we ferried the wagons, and swam the cattle across. This evening, we came to settlement, again. Bought some corn at 20 cts per bushel, and potatoes at 60 cts." Thomas Griggs produced a few spelling and grammatical errors, and his punctuation and capitalization were sporadic: ". . . he told her on the Cars starting that there was a lot of 'Mormons' on board and to take care of her Baggage for the mormons where dreadful theives." Ada Millington left out periods, commas, and capital letters in her one-page example: "[S]topped for dinner by a stream of good water close by a mountain from which we could see Salt Lake city we went on and got there about the middle of the afternoon a while before we got there it rained pretty hard & hailed some we had hardly stopped before . . ." Virginia Reed lacked skills in capitalization, punctuation, grammar, and spelling: "[P]aw goes a bufalo hunting most every day and kils 2 or 3 buffalo every day paw shot a elk som of our compean saw a grisly bear W hve the thermometer. . ." Mary Murphy also needed assistance with grammar and mechanics: "We Was then about 2 hundred miles from the settlements that evening it comenced snowing in three days We got to the devideing ridge of the sirenavada." Mary spelled her sister's name "Hariete" or "Hariette" instead of "Harriet."[27]

These original documents contained the writer's precise wording. Ada Millington "went by Brighams [Young] house there was a high stone wall around it higher than a man's head over the gate was an eagle monnted on a beehive cut out stone and over the door was a lion cut of stone. . ." Virginia Reed's grandmother "bee came spechless the day before she died We

[27]McAuley, Diary, 16; Griggs, "Crossing the Plains," 3–4; Clarke, "Journal Kept," 23; Murphy, "Virginia," Letter 1: 1; Murphy, Letter TN, 1–2.

We stopped at noon fed and watered from the store in our wagons, and drove again till night, when we fed and watered again, and rested until 10.30. We then started and drove the rest of the night, passing the boiling springs about midnight. These springs boil up with a great noise, emitting a very nauseous smell, but as it was dark we could not examine them very closely. We hear that a woman and child have got scalded very badly by stepping into one of them.

Sunday Sept 31st

Made our breakfast on bread and milk, having no wood to cook with, and one of the cows stole all the water we had so we are obliged to put up with light diet. We are now seven miles from the Truckee River, but the road here becomes very heavy and sandy. After traveling three miles the teams

began to give out so we had to unhitch them from the wagons and send them on to grass and water. The boys went on with the cattle, leaving Mr Daugherty, Margaret and myself with the wagons. After resting awhile, M and I started on taking with us a cow that had given out, and been left behind. We took a bucket a short distance before her, and the poor thing thinking there was water in it, would get up and struggle on a few steps, and then fall exhausted. After resting a few minutes we would get her on again a few steps. In this way we had gained about a mile, when we met Thomas returning with a canteen of water. We took a drink and gave the rest to the poor cow, which revived her so that she was able to get to the river. Thomas said that when the cattle were three miles from the river they smelled the water and lifting their heads started on a run for the river and never stopped until they

A page from Eliza Ann McAuley's diary. *Courtesy of Thomas Macaulay, Reno, Nevada.*

In camp Thursday Aug 8th 1861
I started this a.m. in company with bros Page and Paxman and our Charley (Griggs) to visit Chimney rock which seemed about 2 miles from the river but found it nearly 5 miles. We clambered to the top of the ledge and carved our names on the rock and gather some wild flowers, with 3 cheers for Brigham and the pioneers and a narrow escape from tumbling rocks, we started for and came up with the camp at Noon halt. This p.m. bro Paxman shot a rattle snake lying in the road. Passed Reeds' Independent company and

camped having made 19 miles Thunder and Lightning storm in the evening

In camp Friday Aug 9th
Passed opposite Scotts' Bluff this a.m and also a half breeds hut. Thunder storm this p.m. Made 18 miles

Saturday Augt 10th/61
Came in sight of Laramie peak which loomed up in the distance like a cloud. We now commenced to get wood again for our fires, having for the past 2 weeks been without it. Thunder and lightning, as usual this p.m.

Sunday Aug 11th/61
To day we crossed a creek with

Thomas Cott Grigg's diary entries Aug. 8–10, 1861.
Courtesy L.D.S. Church Archives, Salt Lake City, Utah.

The first page of Virginia Reed's 1847 letter.
Courtesy of Bancroft Library, University of California, Berkeley, Calif.

California Teritory May the 25 1847
Dear Uncles aunts and cousins i take
my pen in hand to say a few words to
you all i will give you a small sketch
of our travels after we [left] there we went
on to St Louis and Foster and Swrth came
with us and then we came on to Independance
and there we wrote to you and then we left
the United States and in about six hundred
miles from there to the Sweetwater river and
there wrote again and then crost the Rocky
mountains and took Hastings new rout by
the big salt lake and had to make our road
which left us behind about two or three
weeks and we got out of provisions and had
to kill our oxens there was about 85 persons in
our company My Foster was going to go ahead
and some back provisions but in loading
this rifle shot it went of and shot Mr Pike
in the back he died in about one half hour
and in that time he suffered more than
tongue can tell it was on the last day of
october we was there about 2 hundred miles
from the settlements that evening it commenced
snowing in three days we got to the dividin
ridge of the sirenavada or snowy range of
the california mountains it was snowing so
that we could not find the road and we
stoped by the mountain lake it snowed 2
weeks it was then beyond hope almost for us to
go Father so we killed what few catle we
had left we made several attempts to go on foot
but the snow was soft and we could almost
sink to our necks after we had been there 2-3
months a company of ten men and five women
went over on snow shoes Foster Swrth Harriette
and Lemuel was in this company they were
thirty days coming 100 miles they starved till
ware so weak that they could not stand and
then lived on there dead friends that were
dying every day lemuel died among the rest
there was but 2 men got through Foster was
one that got through all the women got
through and a company went out after the
rest that were in the mountains when they
got there half the company starved to death
Company ha[d]

The first page of Mary Murphy's 1847 letter.
Courtesy of Bancroft Library, University of California, Berkeley, Calif.

Ada Millington's diary pages, July 18 and 19, 1862.
Courtesy of the Historical Society of Southern California, Los Angeles, Calif.

buried her verry decent We made a nete coffin and buried her under a tree we had a head stone and had her name cutonit and the date and yere verry nice, and at the head of the grave was a tree we cut some letters on it the young men soded it all ofer and put Flores on it[.]" Mary Murphy "made several atempts to go on foot but the snow was soft and we would almost sink to our necks." Thomas Griggs "almost got blowed over by the hurricane." Eliza McAuley's writing demonstrated fluency in description and clarity of thought. In a previous analysis I made of her published diary, I assumed she quoted from a guidebook when she described "The Ancient Bluff Ruins." But after reading the actual diary, I discovered that Eliza McAuley did not mention a guidebook as often as the published account did, and her original diary exhibited clear penmanship and competent writing skills. Eliza could easily have penned these thoughts without a guidebook:

> This forenoon we passed "The Ancient Bluff Ruins", a picturesque mass of rocks resembling castles, fortifications &c in ruins. Here, a crumbling turret, there a bastion, and in other places, portions of a wall with portholes, making the illusion complete.
> Near this we find wild southern-wood rue, tansy, and several other garden herbs in their wild state, also some beautiful carnations and roses.[28]

WRITING STYLE AND PERSONALITY

While original works best reveal the writer, typescripts can disclose perspective, personality, and writing style if they are accurate representations of the originals. Still, researchers must work with what is available. In his study of published and unpublished documents, John Mack Faragher noticed that adult women diarists wrote more intimately in first person, while men used the impersonal "we." This was not necessarily true with the young pioneer writings I studied. Of nine girl diarists, only

[28]Clarke, "Journal Kept," 23; Murphy, "Virginia," Letter 1: 1; Murphy, Letter TN, 1; Griggs, "Crossing the Plains," 30; Mc Auley, "Iowa," 54; McAuley, Diary, 33–34; Palmer, "Voices," 62. The guidebook which Eliza McAuley used has not yet been located.

Flora Bender, Mary Warner, and Harriet Hitchcock used "I" extensively. Others implied "I," referred to "we" as the traveling group, or combined "we" and "I" in their entries. In the Scott family diary, Margaret Scott usually used "we," possibly because she was representing others. Yet her own letters contained the more personal "I." In one letter she said, "I looked back as long as I could see any thing of Old Illinois and it was with many tears that I left the boat to see my native land no more." Of the five male writers, four used the impersonal "we." Patrick Murphy and Thomas Griggs occasionally stuck in an "I" without elaboration, and in his only entry Christian Neilsen shared his feelings about the death of family members. "I am now both Father and Motherless. . . . O God protect me and my brothers and sisters."[29]

Faragher noted that women diarists tended to elaborate, describe, embellish, and explain, while men usually made terse, unadorned, and hastily written entries and neglected to record dates. Yet my three young male diarists meticulously kept track of each day traveled. Faragher also observed that women talked about people and emotions while men hid feelings and did not expound on individuals. The diaries I analyzed generally followed this pattern. Nineteenth-century culture prepared children for separate gender roles, which may explain the similarity in gender writings. Girls were encouraged to keep spiritual diaries, which were often introspective. In addition, social and cultural expectations of the period may have helped females be more reflective in their writings.[30] Most of the girl diarists wrote fluently, and a few revealed personality, opinions, and feelings. If the published accounts mirror the original diaries, Flora Bender and Harriet Hitchcock wrote as though they were sharing secrets with best friends. In Nebraska, Flora Bender said:

[May 7, 1863] Today we commenced our long-talked-of trip across the

---

[29]Faragher, *Women and Men*, 129; Scott Sisters, "Letters," 141; Neilsen, "Autobiography," 6.
[30]Faragher, *Women and Men*, 130–133; Stearns, "Girls, Boys," 37; Myres, *Westering Women*, xix.

plains, and . . . camped for the first time near Clark's Ranch. There are some people opposite us and I plainly see that we shall not want company. Clark's girls came over this evening and invited us over to their house to have a dance. . . . But that dance was a splendid affair - a very select crowd, indeed - so select that we couldn't stand it and came home immediately, and so ends our first night on the road to Nevada.

Near Fort Kearny, Flora provided a personal definition of crossing the plains. "We are camped tonight on the barren prairie, no wood, no water fit to drink—surely this is crossing the plains." She allowed the reader to jump into her mind and learn some of her thoughts. Definitely not meek and reserved, her entries portrayed her as talkative and spunky. One day she complained, "The roads today were as bad as yesterday - sand, sand, sand. Will we ever get through it?" Later she grumbled,

All the curiosities are on the other side of the river. Sometimes I wish we had went that way. It is so lonely here tonight. No girls but Nellie and I – how I wish Mary Marvin was here. We could amuse ourselves in some manner. This is a beautiful moonlight evening – I should enjoy a dance tonight.[31]

Like Flora Bender, Harriet Hitchcock confided in her reader.

Well here we are on the 2nd day of June 1864 in this great state of Kansas, ten miles from St Joseph, doing as all other travellers are doing, camping out. . . . Lucy my oldest sister is cooking our supper for the first time on our new stove in the open air. This new mode of life seems very strange and I can hardly realize that we are here. . .[32]

Mary Warner and Rachel Taylor wrote pragmatically without heavy elaboration. Some of Mary Warner's entries were short and to the point, while others included explanation and personal attachment:

Monday, May 23 [1864] . . . We did not stop at noon; but not long before we camped, we passed a telegraph office where there was a good dwelling house and chain fence around it. It was as neat a looking place as we have passed since we left Kearney. After crossing Hinn's Fork we . . . camped on Black Fork, about two o'clock, after going twenty two miles.

---

[31]Bender, Typescript, 1, 3, 5.
[32]Hitchcock, "Thoughts," 236.

> Mrs. Dunwell, Aunt Celia and I tried to fish but we finally concluded that there were no fish in the river.[33]

Rachel Taylor wrote conversationally without expecting to impress a reader. Some of her entries were brief; others described and explained:

> Aug. 9th [1853] We had to ascend a very long steep hill, but after reaching the summit, we had good roads for several miles. Our course lay through lovely glades, and beautiful groves of fir, and then again more mountains. Thus we proceeded until a late hour of night and then had to encamp without suitable feed for our jaded teams.

Occasionally Rachel Taylor revealed her personality. She noted that Pella, Iowa, was "a settlement composed almost entirely of Holland Dutch" who "look comical enough, stumping about with their wooden shoes."[34]

Edith Lockhart usually wrote short, often incomplete sentences which, according to a typed transcript of her diary, she punctuated with dashes: "Very pleasant---Travelled 19 miles, camped by Green river---A mule train camped near us---[.]" In many diary entries Edith Lockhart and Lucy Canfield made terse and unembellished comments, but the content included female concerns about people. A few times Lucy Canfield shared feelings and opinions. Once she "crossed wood river and had an awful night with the miskeetoes. got up a bout midnight and slept on the ground. Dont like wood river muskeetoes much."[35]

Sallie Hester made succinct remarks in her diary, but she also included personal involvement and nineteenth-century romantic embellishment:

> Our journey through the [Nevada] desert was from Monday, three o'clock in the afternoon, until Thursday morning at sunrise, September 6. The weary journey last night, the mooing of the cattle for water, their exhausted condition, with the cry of "Another ox down," the stopping of train to unyoke the poor dying brute, to let him follow at will

---

[33]Warner, "Diary," 15.

[34]Taylor, "Overland Trip," 157, 173–174.

[35]Humphrey, "Original Diary," 10; Margetts, "My Journal," Aug. 12.

or stop by the wayside and die, and the weary, weary tramp of men and beasts, worn out with heat and famished for water, will never be erased from my memory.[36]

Margaret Scott adorned her writings with nineteenth-century sentimentalism, as did her seventeen-year-old sister Abigail, who recorded most of the family diary. Both girls embroidered scenery descriptions and added the word "romantic," an adjective which reflected the artistic style and culture of the time. In one place Abigail said,

> [June 3, 1852] . . . I ascended on horseback to the top of highest one [bluff] that we could see from the road, and there saw, indeed a romantic spectacle.; The Platte below me flowing on in peaceful music, intersected with numerous islands covered with timber, when when no other timber could be seen, The emigrants wagons cattle and horses on the road in either direction as far as the eye could reach. . .

In a later entry Margaret wrote,

> About noon we stopped nearly opposite the "Scott bluffs" sometimes called capital hills These hills have a truly grand romantic appearance calculated to fill the mind with indescribeble amazement approaching almost to sublimity. There are numerous cedars growing uppon them, which gives them a still more grand appearance.[37]

Was Margaret imitating her older sister's writing style? Probably not. Her trail letters also contained nineteenth-century embellishment. To her grandfather she wrote, ". . . a thought of home will send a thrill of sorrow to my heart time and things may change and fine spun theories may glare arround me but you will remain inscribed uppon my memory for time and eternity."[38]

Like adult male diarists, the young men usually made short, unadorned, and quickly drafted entries. William Pace especially reflected this style. He did not share feelings or per-

---

[36]Hester, "Diary," 240–241. In my dissertation, I noted that Sallie Hester was a pragmatic writer without heavy elaboration. See Palmer, "Voices," 60. As I studied her diary again, I realized that Sallie Hester, like Margaret Scott, was influenced by ninteenth-century sentimentalism.

[37]Scott, "Journal," 60, 66. Lucy Canfield, Flora Bender, Rachel Taylor, Sallie Hester, and Ada Millington also used the term "romantic" in their writings. See Coben, *Rebellion*, 161, footnote #5.

[38]Scott Sisters, "Letters," 146.

sonality; in fact, his account provided no indication he was a young writer. However, in one entry in California he revealed a hint of personality: "Inspection at nine oclock & in the afternoon had A Dress perade wich Capt Hunt acted as Colonel & he done things up Bungling i'l assure you[.]" Thomas Griggs discussed personal activities while Pace only mentioned the group. In one entry Griggs wrote,

> In camp Thursday Aug 8th 1861 I started this a.m. in company with bros. Page and Paxman and our Charley (Griggs) to visit Chimney rock which seemed about 2 miles from the river but found it nearly 5 miles. We clambered to the top of the ledge and carved our names on the rock and gather some wild flowers, with 3 cheers for Brigham [Young] and the pioneers and a narrow escape from tumbling rocks, we started for and came up with the camp at Noon halt.[39]

Patrick Murphy varied terse entries with complete sentences, explanation, and occasional feelings. His diary began, "On April 11, 1854 – I bid adieu to St. Louis and departed for California, thinking that the pleasant time I would have on the plains, killing game and riding after the herds of buffalo, would over-come all suffering and hardships which I might be compelled to endure."[40] William Freshwater wrote maturely for a ten year old if his account was published verbatim. On the voyage to America he wrote,

> [June 8, 1863] In the morning, wind very fair but during the day it increased until the sailors had to tie ropes about the ship to hold themselves on. They spiked all the hatchways down and would not let any of the passengers go on deck at all. The captain told us it was the worst storm he had ever witnessed although he had made many trips across the ocean.

When he noted that "a child of three years died on board this morning of consumption," one wonders what ten-year-old Freshwater was thinking.[41] His writings only offered a glimpse into his young personality.

Another factor that influenced how and what young peo-

---

[39]Pace, "Diary," 11; Griggs, "Crossing the Plains," 44.

[40]Murphy, "Across the Plains Diary," 1.

[41]Carter, *Pioneer Heritage,* 7: 249. Kate Carter may have altered the wording and corrected the mechanical errors before publishing this young boy's account. I could not find the original.

ple wrote was what occurred on the trail. William Pace kept a diary until he reached the Sweetwater River in Wyoming, then snowstorms and lack of firewood, grass, and provisions probably forced him to stop writing. Years later he described the last part of this trek to Nebraska. On the way to Colorado, Harriet Hitchcock discussed events, people, and places in unique ways and made her diary delightful to read. But on the return trip her entries stated facts, used third person almost exclusively, and contained little personality, which may have implied she was afraid. On November 29, 1864, the Sand Creek Massacre occurred in Colorado. Under the direction of Colonel John M. Chivington, the American military slaughtered between one hundred and eight hundred Native Americans, including women, children, and old men. The military rode victoriously into the streets of Denver with scalps of many victims. On January 15, Harriet's family returned East with a train of 150 wagons, 600 men, and a military escort.[42]

One quality that barely crept into diary entries was humor. Patrick Murphy was the only male to make a witty remark. Their "horses had fasted so long that they were thinking of eating the wagons; consequently grass was welcome." A few young ladies expressed clever thoughts. Eliza McAuley's brother "made me practice target shooting with his pistol. I was very expert at missing the mark, but managed to hit the tree three times out of five[.]" Rachel Taylor observed two horses "hitched behind our wagon, and after traveling awhile, they evidently concluded to go the other way, and commenced pulling backwards. The result of this strategm was the pulling in two of the wagon cover." Flora Bender hoped to find "good grass, but it isn't here. There are two grasshoppers to one spear of grass."[43] Harriet Hitchcock made several clever comments. Near a stage station she saw a man

---

[42]Pace, "Diary," 33–36; Hitchcock, "Thoughts," 261–264. See also Utley, "Indian-United States," 4: 168; Hoig, *Sand Creek Massacre*; and Scott, *Blood at Sand Creek*.

[43]Murphy, "Across the Plains Diary," 6; McAuley, Diary, 7; Taylor, "Overland Trip," 154; Bender, Typescript, 9.

... sitting on the top of the house watching his horses while they are feeding on the plains three or four miles away. Saw some bipeds resembling birds that are called Snipes and I think they are rightly named for they look as though the wind had blown here from some distant clime They do not sing at all perhaps the wind has blown the music all out of them.

Another time Harriet complained about pesky insects. Traveling during the Civil War most likely helped her coin her mosquito analogy.

This part of the world abounds with Musquitoes of an enormous size some nights the air is filled with them. Our Musquitos bars are the blue skies I should think that all of the musquitoes in the world had got inside of the bars and were awaiting further orders, if I was Colonel of their regiment I would drive them into the river on double quick.[44]

Except for a few of these diarists, the letter writers exhibited more personality and feeling, perhaps because they addressed real audiences. In two letters to her cousin, Virginia Reed used "I," "we," and long passages of personal conversation. Unlike Margaret Scott's flowery expressions, Virginia's writing probably reflected how she talked. Since her original letters are available for study, readers can analyze her everyday language. In the first letter her positive mood and speech patterns appear: "I am a going to send this letter by a man coming from oregon by his self he is a going to take his family to oregon We are all doing Well and in hye sperits so I must close yur leter. you are for erer my affecionate couzen." In her letter from California Virginia Reed poignantly discussed her Donner party experiences as though her cousin were present. "... I frose one of my feet verry bad that same night thare was the worst storme we had that winter & if we had not come back that night we would never got back we had nothing to eat but ox hides o Mary I would cry and wish I had what you all wasted."[45]

---

[44]Hitchcock, "Thoughts," 240, 242-243.
[45]Murphy, "Virginia," Letter 1: 2; Murphy, "Virginia," Letter 2: 4.

Like Virginia Reed, Mary Murphy corresponded with relatives after arriving in California. She, too, explained this tragic
experience with deep feeling. "... i have nothing to live for
a poor orphan Fatherless and motherless and almost Friend-
less.... i hope i shall not live long for i am tiard of this troublesome world." At the beginning of her letter the lengthy
run-on sentences may suggest how Mary Murphy spoke:

> ... i will give you a small sketch of our travels after we left there we
> went on to St Louis and Foster and Sarah came with us and then we
> came on to Independance and there we wrote to you and then we left
> the United States and in about six hundred miles from there to the
> sweetwater river and thare wrote again and then crost the Rocky moun-
> tains and took Hastings new rout by the big salt lake and had to make
> our road which kept us behind about two or three weeks and we got
> out of provisions and had to kill our oxen there was about 85 persons
> in our company[.][46]

Harriet Stewart and Susan Dudley wrote letters before
going west, and they spoke conversationally as they might have
talked. After Elizabeth Keegan reached California, she sent
her sister and brother a little book which she tried to fill with
her thoughts. Her tone was chatty, she used "I" and "we," and
she voiced opinions:

> We are in sight of the snowy peaks of the Sierra Nevada mountains
> visible all the time.... Little did I think when I was learning and pos-
> ing those mountains that I would ever behold them. I also seen Fre-
> monts Peak down from whose snowy top runs the sweet water river it
> has the coldest water in it I have ever tasted. The only curiosity I thought
> worthy of note was singularity of hot and cold water almost within reach
> of each other There was some of them so hot that they make coffee
> in a few minutes.[47]

Margaret Scott's letters were conversational, but with orna-
mentation and sentimentalism. In the first of five letters to
her grandparents, she stated, "... it was a hard trial to bid adieu
to Illinois forever and to submit ourselves to be caried from

---

[46]Murphy, Letter TN, 1–2. The typescript of Mary Murphy's letter from the California repos-
   itory is slightly different from the original handwritten account in the Tennessee archives.
[47]Keegan, "Teenager's Letter," 29–30.

our loved native land and to launch ourselves uppon the unruffled bosom of the 'Great father of waters.'" Most likely this
was not Margaret's everyday speech. Was she trying to impress
her grandparents? Had she been influenced by the popular novels or poetry of her day? In two letters she included several
stanzas of poetry, most likely her own.[48]

In contrast to Margaret Scott's writing, her younger sister
Catharine described the journey without embellishment. She
wrote long passages and referred to what "we" did: "[W]e had
to travel sometimes 15 (*miles*) & upwards without water when
we got to it it was not like the water at home but so warm
that we could hardly drink it." Only at the beginning of her
grandfather's letter did she refer to "I" when she informed him,
"I have went through a great manny changes and difficulties,
since I last saw you."

Eleven year old Harriet Scott used "I," shared opinions, and
discussed what was important to her at the time of writing.
Interestingly, she used the same phrase as Catharine who wrote
the same day. Perhaps she copied from her older sister, or
maybe both girls heard the phrase from family members about
that part of the trip. Harriet wrote, "[T]here are in some places
sand and dust which are hot enough to roast eggs and is very
ennoying indeed," and Catharine said, ". . . the dust was in
some places knee deep and sand hot enough to roast eggs."
With the two letters Harriet wrote on the same day, she voiced
different opinions of Oregon and, thus, illustrated the importance of audience. To her grandfather she said,

> [E]very thing here is new and strange to me and does not seem like
> home. I cannot be runing about in the grass lot and pasture and rolling
> down the Corn (*in*) the crib I cannot be a running to Grandfathers
> with the news papers as I used to do nothing seems like home here to

---

[48]Scott Sisters, "Letters," 141, 142, 148. For information on the types of novels and poetry and
style of writing to which Margaret Scott might have been exposed, see Minnigerode's *Fabulous Forties*, 105–139, and Tompkins, *Sensational Designs*, 122–146. Margaret probably was
influenced by the moral tales written for the children of her time as well. See MacLeod,
Moral Tale, and Kett, *Rites of Passage*, 113–114.

me it keeps a continiual rain here in the winters and is very dull and gloomy[.]

Harriet's attitude was more positive with her cousin: "I like Oregon what I have seen of it very well but it does not seem like home."[49]

CULTURE AND MORALS

Several letter writers used similar introductions which were probably common to mid-nineteenth-century America. Mary Murphy began her letter with, ". . . i take my pen in hand to say a few words to you all." Susan Dudley wrote, "I take my pen in hand to let you know that we are all [well] at present." Harriet Scott said, ". . . it is with a high degree of pleasure that I take my pen in hand to let you know that we are all well at present." Margaret Scott concealed the same phrase within her characteristic embellishment. "In compliance with your request and very agreeable to my feelings I this beautiful Sabbath morning take my pen i[n]to my trembling hand to adress a few lines to you."[50]

Just as letter introductions suggested nineteenth-century culture, so did the values young pioneers expressed. Eliza McAuley noted that a steer was bitten by a snake, but "an application of tobacco and whiskey soon relieved him." She quickly added, "That is the only use any of our party makes of those articles." Mary Warner and her aunt "played Chess, which Mrs. Lord thought was the first step toward gambling." In Rachel Taylor's train Fletcher Royal "upset his wagon with the family in it but no one was injured." This occurred a month before his wife gave birth, and Rachel did not mention that the woman was pregnant or even inside the wagon. Later, she reported, "Mrs Fletcher Royal has a fine boy, so we learn from

---

[49]Scott Sisters, "Letters," 157–160.
[50]Murphy, Letter TN, 1; Dudley, "Dudley Family," July 1, 1850; Scott Sisters, "Letters," 145–146, 160.

the Doctor who went back to their encampment." Margaret Scott fretted about burying emigrants "in this uninhabited country inhabited only by the red man of the forest." Flora Bender called the Snake Indians a "hostile and a dirty looking savage race" and concluded that the River Jordan in Utah was "only fit for Mormons to drink." Two soldiers invited Flora Bender and Nellie to a dance, "but we would not go, because all were strangers to us, and Mrs. Holland could not go" most likely as a chaperone.[51] Flora and Nellie conformed to the etiquette of the day in which young ladies should not be unaccompanied in public. Harriet Hitchcock received a letter from an aunt with middle-class ideals who

> imagines me as "hoopless and shoeless standing with arms akimbo, mouth extended, tongue protruding, nose contracted, surveying the wonders of this wonderfully wonderful world." Just as though I couldent cross the plains without looking like a squaw. And then to cap the climax she says My Dear Niece Eda do be careful and now swallow a live Buffalo. Dear me I suppose she thinks that I belong to the Arabs by this time but never mind she will see when I get home that I am the same light hearted Eda that I ever was.[52]

Several of Margaret Scott's letters contained religious and sentimental poetry. One verse said,

> We'ev had a tedious journey
> And tiresome it is true
> But lo! thus far through dangers
> The Lord has brought us through[.]

The girl added a pious plea. "O! my dear Grandfather will you pray for me that I may be delivered from temptation." A nineteenth-century middle-class woman epitomized piety, submissiveness, purity, and spiritual strength, and Margaret Scott reflected the female attitude of her day.[53]

---

[51]McAuley, Diary, 12; Warner, "Diary," 21; Taylor, "Overland Trip," 177, 180; Scott, "Journal," 67; Bender, Typescript, 10, 12, 14.

[52]Hitchcock, "Thoughts," 242.

[53]Scott Sisters, "Letters," 142. See Welter, "Cult of True," 225; Wishy, *Child and Republic*, 30; Kett, *Rites of Passage*, 75–78; and Cott, *Bonds*, 126–137.

Another characteristic of nineteenth-century culture was Sabbath observance. By studying emigrant accounts, Winton Solberg suggested that today's readers can discover nineteenth-century attitudes about Sunday. John Mack Faragher noted that women as "society's moral guardians" wanted to keep the day holy by resting and worshipping, yet even all-men trains disputed over Sabbath travel. Wayfarers who stopped on Sunday still had chores to do. As they moved along the trail with provisions dwindling and the seasonal clock pointing toward winter, emigrants often became divided between practicality and values. Many relinquished religious desires for physical safety.[54]

What did young writers say about the Sabbath Day? All of my female diarists commented about it at least once. Sallie Hester and Rachel Taylor talked about Sunday stops and preaching, but both belonged to religious trains. Several girls engaged in acceptable Sabbath activities: Sallie Hester caught up on diary entries, Margaret Scott and Flora Bender wrote letters, and Rachel Taylor described singing practices. Rachel also noted that "the Sacrament of the Lords Supper was administered probably for the first time between the Missouri River and the settlements of Oregon." She included Biblical references, such as "the winds blew and the rains fell, and as our cloth house was founded upon the sand of course it fell." Harriet Hitchcock referred to the Bible when she compared covered wagon travel to the railroad. "The manner of raising the steam is by the use of a whip about twenty feet long with the voice raised an octave higher than when Moses sounded the trumpet to lead the children of Isreal out of the wilderness."[55] Flora Bender complained about the lack of Sabbath observance on the trail. "We have to do everything on the plains Sunday as weekdays." She also shared personal views about the Sabbath.

... Fannie's uncle tried to get us to go fishing. But I was stubborn and

---

[54]Solberg, "The Sabbath," 21, 25, 26; Faragher, *Women and Men*, 95–97.

[55]Hester, "Diary," 236; Scott Sisters, "Letters," 141, 145; Bender, Typescript, 5; Taylor, "Overland Trip," 168, 172, 176; Hitchcock, "Thoughts," 239.

would not go, and consequently kept the rest back. If any one else had been leading and it had not been Sunday, I would have gone willingly. But I'll not do anything on Sunday if it can possibly be helped.

In Salt Lake City Flora Bender attended a Mormon church service and voiced her opinion.

We bolted into the walls of the Bowery, where service was held. A large congregation were assembled. The sermon was Mormonism – music splendid. . . . Some old ladies looked quite suspicious at us when we laughed at some of Heeber Kimbal's outrageous expressions. How can people be fooled by that nonsense is a myster[y] to me.

To Patrick Murphy the Sabbath was just another day. In Nevada, "all of the boys are busy climbing the mountains and prospecting for gold through the ravines."[56]

Surprisingly, adolescent Mormon diarists spent little time elaborating on Sabbath observance or other forms of worship, like prayer, even though the purpose of their journey was religious and reverencing the Lord's holy day was part of their belief. The only time William Pace commented about Sunday worship was at Salt Lake City on his way back to Nebraska. Thomas Griggs noted a few church meetings, and at the jumping-off place a large drum called the train together for prayers. Lucy Canfield barely mentioned worship services on the trail, yet Andrew Jenson stated in his journal that public prayers and remarks were offered every night. He also shared religious feelings, but whether he wrote them as an adolescent or later as an adult cannot be ascertained. Perhaps Mormon children crossing the plains had more exciting things to discuss than church, especially if it was a normal part of the trek. Christian Neilsen's one entry after losing family members revealed the depth of his belief in God.[57] Tragedies and lack of security may have caused young writers to talk about their faith, while a safe journey allowed for other topics of discussion.

---

[56]Bender, Typescript, 5, 7, 11; Murphy, "Across the Plains Diary," 13.
[57]Pace, "Diary," 31; Griggs, "Crossing the Plains," 28, 31, 54; Margetts, "My Journal," Aug. 3, Oct. 18, 19; Jenson, "Journals," 74; Neilsen, "Autobiography," 6.

Practical Matters

Although John Mack Faragher noted obvious differences between male and female trail diaries, he also observed that adults shared three topics: health and safety, practical aspects of the trail, and landscape. Young writers mentioned these also. Health and safety issues are considered in later chapters. What practical matters did young pioneers describe? All recorded dates, usually places, and sometimes miles traveled. Keeping track of place and time might have been important to them as they moved through unfamiliar territory to new destinations. Thomas Griggs was specific about the time of day since he carried a watch. In contrast, Margaret Scott and Harriet Hitchcock appeared unconcerned about miles traveled. "We traveled I suppose about 18 miles," Margaret said, and Harriet only mentioned miles once, and that was on the return trip.[58]

All young writers noted road conditions and the three essentials for crossing the plains--grass, fuel, and water. Some referred to guidebooks for identifying landmarks or receiving direction. Rachel Taylor crossed a creek "which is called in the Guide Book, Wood River." Eliza McAuley wrote, "As our guide-book crosses to the south side of the river at Fort Laramie, and we keep up the north side, we are following the trail without knowing what is ahead of us." Somewhat relieved, she added several days later, "The trail crosses here, and we now have the use of our guide again."[59]

Almost all diarists mentioned the weather. On the California Trail William Pace made numerous entries about pleasant, rainy, cold or frosty conditions, and "a large snow storm." Eliza McAuley reported excessive heat and a storm which "broke in all its fury." She fell asleep "in the tent, and when I

---

[58]Faragher, *Women and Men*, 14; Griggs, "Crossing the Plains," 27; Scott, "Journal," 66; Hitchcock, "Thoughts," 263. Thomas Griggs' watch was probably a pocket watch instead of a wrist watch which I mentioned in my dissertation. The historical moment in which I wrote influenced what I said, and this is an excellent example of the new historicism thinking. See Palmer, "Voices," 75.

[59]Taylor, "Overland Trip," 163; McAuley, Diary, 37, 39.

woke up the bed was nearly afloat, and two of the boys were trying to hold the tent up." She complained about wind in Wyoming and Nevada and cold mornings in the Sierra Nevada. So did Patrick Murphy. He reported "a heavy storm came up in the night and blew down the tent and wet everything." Mary Warner also grumbled about the wind: ". . . it was very disagreeable getting supper and eating it for our victuals were well seasoned with sand." Edith Lockhart commented almost daily about the weather.[60]

Margaret Scott displayed anxiety when "clouds gathered thick upon the mountains" in Oregon "and a strong south wind, warned us, of an approaching storm;--we were therefore afraid to start in the mountains." The next day "our apprehesions [sic] of a storm could no longer be a matter of doubt, and at nine o'clock, rain comenced slowlly falling, and continued falling at intervals until noon when the clouds broke away." The snow on Mt. Hood's summit created quite a spectacle. Was Margaret Scott frightened? She did not reveal her personal feelings. Rachel Taylor declared that it rained so hard "that the men on guard left the cattle to themselves and came into camp." The next day she added that "the horses had become frightened by the heavy thunder of the preceding night and had strayed away." But Rachel did not admit that storms bothered her, even though emigrants that year witnessed more than ample moisture.[61]

In addition to weather, young overlanders talked about provisions, sleeping conditions, "home and hearth," and chores. Sallie Hester's family carried "a cooking stove made of sheet iron, a portable table, tin plates and cups, cheap knives and forks (best ones packed away), camp stools, etc. We sleep in our wagons on feather beds." Eliza McAuley and her siblings

---

[60]Pace, "Diary," 24–33; McAuley, Diary, 29; Murphy, "Across the Plains Diary," 3, 12; Warner, "Diary," 9.

[61]Scott , "Journal," 131; Taylor, "Overland Trip," 161. Rachel Taylor's uncle, S. H. Taylor, wrote a letter home stating that "the season has been wetter than any that has preceded it for many years." See "Letters of S. H. Taylor," 121.

took a tent and "a sheet-iron camp stove which we can set up inside, and be warm and dry." Later, she kept a "home and hearth" tradition: "We have settled down to regular house-keeping, and this being Monday, it is of course washday."[62] Other chores are discussed in the next two chapters.

THE WESTERN LANDSCAPE

While adult diarists often saw the aesthetic beauty of the landscape as "God's artistic masterpiece," most young writers did not. They interpreted each new scene through a literal lens, and their first impressions were sensory. Edith Lockhart was the only diarist who attributed nature's beauty to Deity. "The Scenery to-day," she wrote about the Black Hills, "was indeed grand! We were surrounded by Mountains which showed the Power of the Almighty." Margaret Scott was the only letter writer to agree. ". . . I went to the river and gazed awhile . . . as I stood there I unvoluntarialy exclaimed who would not admire nature and adore nature's God."[63] The landscape of the West was unlike anything children had known in other parts of the United States or Western Europe. This arid country with tall sagebrush, strange rock formations, broad horizons, and few trees was as foreign to them as the moon. Youngsters walked several miles to climb Courthouse Rock, and they inscribed their names on Register Cliff. They shivered under immense skies with only their wagons to protect them from the elements. Nearer the Pacific Coast youngsters struggled through the dense forests and steep, rocky grades of the rugged Cascade Mountains or Sierra Nevada. The landscape had a profound influence on their trail experience.

Young male diarists made practical observations about the western scene. William Pace "crost some lofty mountains and through some very heavy Pine timber." At Soda Springs in

---

[62]Hester, "Diary," 237; McAuley, Diary, 1, 54.
[63]Faragher, *Women and Men*, 14; Humphrey, "Original Diary," 7: Scott Sisters, "Letters," 147.

present-day Idaho, Patrick Murphy wrote that the springs "are situated on a flat piece of land and where the water boils up, it forms a crust, like on the inside of a tea kettle, which in time closes up; then the water breaks out in another place." Thomas Griggs "came in sight of Laramie peak which loomed up in the distance like a cloud." Historian Elliott West observed that young pioneers were literalists who used their senses and compared the landscape with objects familiar to them. These diary entries agree with his conclusions.[64] Similes like crusty tea kettles and clouds emerged from young people's life experiences.

Although most of the young writers mentioned scenery, girl diarists described it more frequently and with adjectives common to the nineteenth century like "romantic" and "beautiful." They, too, used their senses. Sallie Hester watched springs "puff and blow and throw the water high in the air. The springs are in the midst of a grove of trees, a beautiful and romantic spot." Eliza McAuley reported "a very singular looking mountain. At first it appeared like a sugar-loaf," a familiar cooking item. In Echo Canyon, Utah, Mary Warner "saw some of the most beautiful scenery . . . This Canyon is a narrow valley about as wide as a city street, and on both sides are higher rocks of the same kind as Needle Rock, some of which project nearly to the road." A few girls wrote creatively about the landscape. "Just back of us Independence Rock stands out in bold relief, and in front of us yawns the Devils Gate," wrote Rachel Taylor. Edith Lockhart passed "an amphitheatre formed by the Bluffs," and "some little pointed Bluffs" which "should be called the six Sisters." Harriet Hitchcock described the Platte as "a very wide river but shallow and singular in its appearance being filled with islands of sand. . . . It is navigable for mules only their ears are serving for sails."[65]

---

[64]Pace, "Diary," 25; Murphy, "Across the Plains Diary," 7; Griggs, "Crossing the Plains," 45; West, *Growing Up*, 27, 30–31.

[65]Hester, "Diary," 239; McAuley, Diary, 52; Warner, "Diary," 16; Taylor, "Overland Trip," 170; Humphrey, "Original Diary," 6; Hitchcock, "Thoughts," 237.

Several young writers described the same place on the trail. Three diarists approximately the same age mentioned Pyramid Circle, or City of Rocks, in southern Idaho. Patrick Murphy saw this feature as "a collection of rocks formed like pyramids; is about two hundred feet high; there are two columns standing together and to the spectators it looks like a king and queen." To Rachel Taylor "the Pyramids resemble more than anything else petrified hay stacks." Eliza McAuley thought the scene was

> one of the greatest curiosities on the road. In some places a pillar rises to the height of 150 ft, with smaller ones piled on the top and sides, looking as though a breath of air would hurl them down. These pyramids are of various colors; the sides have been washed by the rains into all manner of fantastic shapes, giving the place a most romantic and picturesque appearance.

All three painted visual pictures, particularly Rachel Taylor with her "petrified hay stacks."[66]

Of all the writers, Margaret Scott sometimes tried too hard with description. Hills at Scott's Bluff "have a truly grand romantic appearance calculated to fill the mind with indescribeble amazement approaching almost to sublimity. There are numerous cedars growing uppon them, which gives them a still more grand appearance." In contrast, Flora Bender described scenes as she saw them. "This Platte water is perfectly abominable, so warm." Courthouse Rock resembled "an old court-house gone to ruins," and she "never saw anything equal to" Independence Rock. "They say it covers 100 acres of ground. (But that, I don't believe) - is of solid rock and just as smooth as can be."[67]

Female letter writers recalled the landscape in more general terms. Virginia Reed "went over great hye mountain as strait as stair steps in snow up to our knees." Harriet Scott saw "a great many curiosities on the road it was a very grand

---

[66]Murphy, "Across the Plains Diary," 8; Taylor, "Overland Trip," 176; McAuley, Diary, 63-64.
[67]Scott, "Journal," 66; Bender, Typescript, 2, 5, 8.

sight indeed for any person that is not used to it." Margaret Scott gave two rivers an "unruffled bosom," and Elizabeth Keegan wrote that the first part of the journey was

> beautiful and the scenery surpassing anything of the kind I have ever seen large rolling praries stretching as far as your eye can carry you covered with verdure. The grass so green and flowers of every discription from violets to geraniums of the richest hue.[68]

CONCLUSION

Just as young emigrants saw the landscape from different perspectives, their writings portrayed individual attitudes and personalities as well. At least twenty-three diaries, letters, and journals are available for today's readers to catch a glimpse into the thoughts and actions of mid-nineteenth century pioneer children, most of whom were in their early teens.[69] These writings indicate that social, religious, and cultural conventions accompanied them on the trail. Children lived in a social context with codes of conduct, etiquette, and customs. They learned mores from family, community, and print such as etiquette books, magazines, newspapers, and sentimental novels. Young writers followed the conventions and restrictions of their time. For having relatively little formal schooling, they were surprisingly literate and fluent in written expression. They recorded their thoughts clearly, and their grammar and word choice reflected their oral expression.

How are young emigrant writings different from adult diaries and letters? What did these twenty-three young writers add to the trail experience? They offered opinions, perceptions, and personality through less experienced eyes. Some youngsters displayed "adolescent poutings," impressions,

---

[68]Murphy, "Virginia," Letter 2: 5; Scott Sisters, "Letters," 141, 147, 159; Keegan, "Teenager's Letter," 24.

[69]Lillian Schlissel called her seventeen young writers "diarists," yet almost all of these accounts were reminiscences, not diaries. See Schlissel, *Women's Diaries*, 150, and Tables beginning on 233.

descriptions, and poignant feelings. Ten writers allowed readers to enter their minds long enough to share adolescent
thoughts. But of these ten, we can only be certain about the
contents of the original writings. Flora Bender and Harriet
Hitchcock projected adolescent thoughts better than any
other young diarist—if their published accounts are accurate.
In original letters Virginia Reed and Mary Murphy offered
tender feelings. Other writers shared descriptions and topics
unique to their adolescent years; for example, adults probably
would not write about attempting to flood a prairie dog out
of its burrow. However, to compare or contrast youth and adult
contributions to the trail experience, one must carefully study
the contemporary writings of both and determine what children and adults added, deleted, or emphasized. Did women
write more introspectively than girls? Were young writers more
open to discussing personal opinions about individuals in their
train? Did adults flavor their writings with expressions like
"drowned rats"?

An analysis of greater numbers of contemporary documents
by young people would increase our understanding of the pioneer child's personality and point of view. Still, the available
accounts provide a taste of young pioneers' perceptions of the
westward trek, especially when penmanship, word choice,
grammar, and mechanics can be critiqued in original documents.
Hopefully, additional diaries and letters of young pioneers will
surface, especially those written by smaller children.[70] Unless
their writings can be found, reminiscence may be the only way
small overlanders can share their views of the trail experience,
but their perceptions and personality at the time of travel will
remain obscure. Still, we have heard voices, although in whis-
pers, of young pioneers on the Platte River road.

---

[70]After I completed most of the writing for this book, I discovered Ellen Burt's published diary.
 She traveled in Rachel Taylor's train and, according to one source, was thirteen years old.
 I could not document her actual birth date, so I did not add her diary. See Mumford, *Royal
 Way West*, vol. II, beginning on page 22.

CHAPTER III

"My Family and I":
Diaries, Letters, Journals, Reminiscences

We are now seven miles from the Truckee River . . . . After resting awhile, M [Margaret] and I started on, taking with us a cow that had given out, and been left behind. We took a bucket a short distance before her, and the poor thing thinking there was water in it, would get up and struggle on a few steps, and then fall exhausted. After resting a few minutes we would get her on again a few steps. In this way we had gained about a mile, when we met Thomas returning with a canteen of water. We took a drink and gave the rest to the poor cow, which revived her so that she was able to get to the river.[1]

As the above diary entry suggests, sixteen-year-old Eliza McAuley knew that cooperation with her family was essential for crossing the plains successfully. She and two older siblings worked together to transport themselves and their animals safely to their father's home in California. The westward migration was a family affair, and children usually accompanied one or both parents and siblings. Many adults on the California and Oregon trails had uprooted earlier and knew the challenges of traveling in covered wagons and starting over in unfamiliar regions. Families who left Midwestern farms or small towns carried their skills and equipment with them on the trail. This was not the case with Mormon families from Europe. Most lacked experience with camping out and driving oxen. Being unfamiliar with the distance across

---

[1]McAuley, *Diary*, 76–77.

the American continent and the rigors of the journey handicapped foreign emigrants, particularly handcart pioneers. Britons who read Frederick Piercy's illustrated guide for travelers learned little about the realities of the trail. As Wallace Stegner noted, Piercy romanticized his drawings and made the trek appear "softer than it was." He failed to depict "the stark western earth, bare or stony or prickly with weeds and bunch grass," the changeable weather, and other unpleasant details. After arriving in the Utah Zion, L.D.S. members sent letters home to Europe encouraging their families to come. These Europeans heard about trials on the trail, but they learned the ways of the pioneer through experience.[2]

Whether pioneers left from Europe or America, the westward migration involved families. Elliott West estimated that children made up 20% of the emigrants, but data suggest that Mormon companies contained a higher percentage of children. In a demographic study of the 1,300 pioneers who arrived in Utah in 1847, 44% were seventeen or younger. Half of these were between three and eleven years old.[3] These children played an important role in a family's trail experience. What did young overlanders say about their relationships with parents and siblings in diaries, letters, journals, and oral and written reminiscences? Since diaries, letters, and to an extent journals are reality checks for reminiscences, they need to be considered first; then childhood memories can be analyzed.

FAMILY RELATIONSHIPS IN DIARIES, LETTERS, AND JOURNALS

Of the twenty-three diaries, journals, and letters which I studied, thirteen writers emigrated with both parents or step-

---

[2]Schlissel, *Women's Diaries*, 27–28; West, *Growing Up*, 8–9; Faragher, *Women and Men*, 16; Linforth, *Route from Liverpool*; Stegner, *Gathering of Zion*, 218. For details about British emigrants, see Taylor, "British Mormons," 260, 262, and Buchanan, "Imperial Zion," 65. For information on Scandinavian Mormons, see Mulder, "Scandinavian Saga," 145, 151–152, and Olson, "Proselytism," 194–195.

[3]West, *Growing Up*, 13; *Deseret News Church Almanac*, 103–104.

parents, five went with mothers, two with fathers, two with siblings, and one with no family. Those who wrote about family members referred most often to these themes: responsibilities, pleasure, sensory and curiosity experiences, illness/death, animals, literacy, fear, and values/religion. This small sample cannot be representative of what all young people thought and wrote about family members on the trail, but it does reveal a few of their immediate and individual concerns and perceptions.

None of the male diaries or journals which I examined elaborated on family relationships. William Pace mentioned Lieutenant Pace in the Mormon Battalion company but never acknowledged the man as his father. Later in an adult reminiscence, Pace filled in a few holes from his diary. He accompanied his father to California and back to Nebraska with his father directing the return journey, yet the boy did not talk about him. Perhaps the fifteen-year-old kept the company diary and, therefore, remained impersonal. Patrick Murphy traveled as a hired hand in a male stock train with co-workers as his only support. Thomas Griggs mentioned his mother at the beginning and end of the trek, and he visited Chimney Rock with Charley Griggs but did not identify him as a brother. When Thomas became ill and rode in a sick wagon for two days, was his mother concerned? Andrew Jenson left Denmark with his parents and a younger brother. In eastern Nebraska he talked about his family, but he said nothing more about them until they reached Utah. Surely his mother nursed him when he was "violently sick, being attacked by a sort of cholera" for almost a week. These four writers followed the pattern John Mack Faragher noted about male emigrant diarists disregarding relationships, but many more young male diaries need to be analyzed to ascertain how—or if—they discussed parents and siblings.[4]

[4]Pace, "Diary," 13, 15, 16; Lesson Committee, *Chronicles* 7:171–173; Murphy, "Across the Plains Diary," 1; Griggs, "Crossing the Plains," 25–27, 44, 61; Jenson, "Journals," 49, 69–71, 80–81; Faragher, *Women and Men*, 128–133.

All of the female diary and letter writers mentioned their families at least once. Like two of the male writers, Sallie Hester, Lucy Canfield, and Edith Lockhart noted them before and after the journey. Sallie's and Lucy's fathers, however, led their trains and probably ignored their daughters much of the time. Rachel Taylor hardly noticed her mother and sister, but she frequently discussed her father and brothers. One night her father searched for a camping spot and did not return. "We then began to be afraid that he was still behind us, and came to a halt . . . . Still Father came not." The next day he found them after taking the wrong road, getting ahead of the train, and spending the night with a Methodist preacher. Although Mary Warner briefly mentioned her mother, she said nothing about three younger siblings, including three-year-old Cora who surely needed tending. Since older daughters helped raise little ones, did Mary assist with Cora? After their father joined them in Salt Lake City, Mary added him to her diary. In one entry he and Uncle Chester had a friendly argument "until nearly midnight, and when they stopped they did not agree any more than when they commenced."[5]

Harriet Hitchcock neglected writing about her mother but talked about her father and older sisters. She even inferred sibling rivalry when she began keeping a diary:

> Lucy will think me a thoughtless silly girl for she always remembers every thing and in her quiet way, will in future years convince us that her memory is sufficient for any emergency, and Bell who always speaks her thoughts before she thinks them will undoubtedly advise me to admire the beauties of nature as she is doing and even now she is telling me that I had better note down where we came from and where we are going lest I should forget. Which I will now do.

Harriet composed a hymn to a mother bird "who sat perched over my head," but forgot part of it when she wrote it down. "I wont let Bell know it and I can have the good of thinking that I did compose a long hymn." Hymn singing was common to nineteenth-century Christian culture, but Harriet the

---

[5]Taylor, "Overland Trip," 171–172; Warner, "Diary," 31.

author went one step further and created her own. Later, she forgot sibling contention when she shared adventures with her sisters. One day they tried to oust a prairie dog from its hole by dumping water inside. Lucy "jumped and screamed as a large animal came rushing out with glaring eyeballs looking fiercely at us." The young people were "frightened and the animal seemed no less so as he slowly walked away the water dripping from his sides, probably he had never received such treatment from girls before." In reality, the prairie dog was a badger, "a very savage animal when attacked."[6]

Throughout her diary Eliza McAuley expressed a close relationship with her sister and brother. Growing up on a dairy farm with their father often absent due to poor health, the siblings worked together to keep the dairy running. Since Eliza and her siblings already relied on each other, going west in a small company probably accented this relationship. Eliza and sister Margaret made the journey in stylish short dresses with bloomers and calf-skinned topboots on their feet. They washed clothes and cooked, made leather shoes for their cattle, and found an antelope that became "a great pet in camp, and is equally fond of Margaret and me. She bleats and cries if either one is away from her." When their brother Tom left camp to search for a mare, Eliza noted it; she also described the family's struggles through the Nevada desert. When their father joined them on the trail, Eliza discussed him as well. After climbing a snowy Sierra Nevada peak, their sixty-year-old father showed the girls how to descend. He went "but a few steps when his feet flew from under him, and he went sailing down the mountain side with feet and hands in the air. After a moment of horrified silence we saw him land, and begin to pick himself up, when we gave way to peals of laughter."[7]

Like Eliza McAuley, Flora Bender included her family in

---

[6]Hitchcock, "Thoughts," 235–237, 240–241.

[7]Smith, Letter, 1; McAuley, Diary, 2, 33, 84–85. The entry about descending the snow-capped mountain was embellished in the published diary. See McAuley, "Iowa," 79–80, and Palmer, "Voices," 95.

her writings. She noted gender-specific tasks which her father performed, such as searching for lost animals and picking up mail at Fort Kearny. Her mother called on lady friends without her daughters, but she involved them when she washed clothes and attended a Mormon church service. During the nineteenth century, women participated in religious worship more frequently and in greater numbers than men. Flora did not say whether or not her father accompanied them to church. But at the Platte Bridge in Wyoming, the family "went over the river" where "Pa had to get the tire of a wagon wheel set," and they found "quite a town." Flora briefly mentioned two younger siblings, Charlie and Clara, and she frequently talked about Nellie, a sister two years older. The girls wrote letters, went to a dance, telegraphed brothers in Virginia City, and called on female friends. One of their friendly visits appeared less than cordial: "Nellie and I went to Mrs. Hopsons' tent – she was as pleasant as a basket of chips on a cold day." Flora seemed concerned when Nellie and their mother became ill and the family waited at a stage station for several days. Nellie "could not stand it to ride, however soft the bed, so we had to stop. The merchant there kindly gave us one of his rooms to stay as long as we pleased."[8]

Ada Millington also discussed her family, although she may have added details when she revised her diary. Her middle-class parents hired five young men to assist with the animals and chores, thus lessening the family's trail responsibilities. "Pa" bought and sold animals and purchased items, and Ada recorded the cost. "Ma" was in the first trimester of pregnancy with twins, but Ada said nothing about her mother not feeling well. Sometimes Ada referred to "we girls," which probably included her two younger sisters. Waiting to cross the Green River, "we children amused ourselves" by naming one island "Long Island, another No. 10, others Grand, Rock, Aristocratic Islands." The "we children" most likely meant Ada, her siblings—Grace, Ollie,

[8]Bender, Typescript, 6, 8, 11, 15.

Bucky, Seth, baby George—and cousin Fred. In Nevada when Bucky and George became seriously ill, Ada carefully recorded this, but she did not say if she helped nurse them. Bucky recovered, but George did not. "Ma thinks if we had been at home he needn't have died." A hired man took the baby's body to Carson City for burial, and when the family arrived, they visited the cemetery plot. "Pa cut 20 notches on each rail near the head of the grave, for his age 20 months." Their mother took the boys back to camp while "Pa and we three girls went on to look at the town." On the trail again Bucky celebrated his sixth birthday with "Ma" cooking ginger cakes. Carrying on family traditions like this may have provided a sense of home, especially after the death of a loved one. When they crossed into California, the family acquired additional chores because "so many of the men have left us." Ma drove the mule wagon, Pa and Ada's half-brother worked with the ox teams, and "we girls" and cousin Fred tended the cows.[9]

Like the female diarists, some of the letter writers discussed their families. Virginia Reed talked about her mother and siblings but paid more attention to her step-father, even though she sent both of her letters to a cousin on her mother's side. In her first letter Virginia mentioned "Paw's" hunting expeditions and his Fourth of July observance in which "severel of the gentemen in Springfeld gove paw a botel of licker and said it shouden be opend tell the 4 day of July and paw was to look to the east and drink it and thay was to look to the West an drink it at 12 oclock paw treted the compeany and we all had some lemennade." In a second letter Virginia reported that "Paw" went to California alone, then returned to rescue his family. Before he reached them, Virginia, her mother, and other Donner party members made an unsuccessful attempt through the mountains. The first relief team finally arrived, and Virginia, her mother, and five-year-old James went with it. But Patty and Thomas "giv out & so the men had to take them

---

[9]Clarke, "Journal Kept," 17–18; Millington, "Journal," 235–236, 256–261, 266–269.

back" to the cabins. Patty said, ". . . well ma if you never see me again do the best you can." On her way out Virginia met "Paw" who continued on to the cabins to save Patty and Thomas. Virginia described her siblings' rescue, but since she was not present, "Paw" must have provided the details. Mary Murphy, who was in the same relief party as Virginia, and four siblings reached California alive, but their "poor mother and brothers . . . are dead thair bodies to feed the hungry bears and wolves for there was no chance of burying them the snow was so deep." Left an orphan, Mary voiced a prevalent nine-teenth-century belief in life after death. "[I] am tiard of this troublesome world and i want to go to my mother i know that she is in a better world."[10]

In letters to grandparents Margaret and Catharine Scott did not share family trail experiences, but they noted their mother's illness and Catharine described her death. West of Fort Laramie their mother

> was taken verry violently with diareah about 2 oclock in the morning she did not awake anny one as she thought she would soon get over it but she continued to get worse until we became alarmed about her, we called in two physicians which done all that they could do but it did not seem to do her anny good and she [*died about*] 5 oclock in the eavning. . .

Almost thirteen, Catharine longed for her mother. "I now know what I never knew before that is to be bereft of a Moth-ers advice." Later on the trail, little brother Willie "was taken sick with Direah" and "his deasease terminated to dropsy of the brain he could not speak for several days before he died but would take a cup and hold it out for water was the only sign he would make, after nine days sickness he died leaving us in a wild desert place to mourn over him."[11]

Many of these young writers mentioned death in their accounts. Death was common in the nineteenth century whether at home or on the trail, and youngsters were not

---

[10]Murphy, "Virginia," Letter 1:1–2 and Letter 2: 4–5; Murphy, Letter TN, 2.
[11]Sisters, "Letters," 141, 146, 157–158.

shielded from it. Parents taught their children from the Bible that heaven was a place where the deceased lived with God. But religious teachings did not quell feelings of fear, loneliness, and loss when a family member, especially a parent, died on the trail. Children have always depended upon adults for survival; as a result, one of their basic fears is abandonment, loss, or separation from their caretaker.[12] Seeing bodies of loved ones buried on the barren prairie for wolves to unearth could be an unnerving experience to children. While older siblings provided support to younger ones, they, too, mourned and suffered when a loved one died. Historian Elliott West noted that although fewer than one in twenty travelers died going west, most young emigrants encountered death in some way.[13] According to the 453 contemporary and reminiscent accounts which I studied, the vast majority of young pioneers confronted death—through immediate or extended family, members in their company, or others on the trail. One-fourth of the contemporary accounts noted family members dying, and three-fourths mentioned the death of others. Over half (55%) of the 430 reminiscences included "I remember" death experiences, and many "we remember" memories discussed this topic as well.

Of the twenty-three diary, journal, and letter writers, why did some mention family members before or after but not during the journey? Perhaps they thought their diaries might be read. More likely, though, family was common to a child's daily life, and young pioneers preferred to describe new scenes and experiences. Girls usually tended younger siblings as they traveled, yet no diarist mentioned this. A few writers talked about associating with but not caring for smaller siblings. Clearly, other aspects of the journey interested them more than daily routine, especially if parents were nearby to provide security. According to child development experts, beginning at the age of ten young people seek independence from parents and

---

[12]See Rieck, "Geography of Death," 13–21, and Yamamoto, *Their World*, 1–10.
[13]West, *Growing Up*, 37–40; West, "Youngest Pioneers," 96.

deeper relationships with peers.[14] All of the writers which I studied were ten years old or older.

Why were fathers included in more female writings? In nineteenth-century patriarchal society the father was in charge, and mother and children were taught to obey. A father's work may have seemed more important to girls, or perhaps male activities appeared exciting. Men took responsibility for their family's safety, and they moved in and out of the wagon train while women and children remained within relatively confined areas. Also, girls probably saw their fathers more on the trek than at home. A few writers anticipated meeting their fathers near the end of the trail and, when they did, made entries about them. In her research Lillian Schlissel detected a dark thread in women's diaries from "painful subservience to the authority of husbands and fathers," but this did not appear in the girls' writings. They wrote more about their fathers than mothers and expressed positive feelings toward them.[15]

FAMILY RELATIONSHIPS IN REMINISCENCES

What did child pioneers remember about family relationships when they recorded their trail experience as adults? Families played a major role in oral and written memories. Only 4% of the 430 reminiscences I studied did not mention parents, and 16% did not discuss siblings; however, many of these accounts were oral interviews in which questions about family were not asked. Also, some reminiscences only described one or two incidents, and these did not include family. Fourteen per cent of these young pioneers crossed the plains with one parent (10% with mothers and 4% with fathers) while 8% traveled with no parent, and more than 75% journeyed with two parents or step-parents. One-third of the adolescents, ages

---

[14]See Table 1, page 69, for a list of the twenty-three writers. See also Blodgett, *Centuries*, 58, and Irwin and Simmons, *Lifespan*, 292, 298.

[15]Schlissel, *Women's Diaries*, 95.

thirteen through fifteen, made the trek with one or no parent; most of these were Mormons.

Single-parent Crossings

Of the children who migrated on the California and Oregon trails with one parent, four accompanied mothers and eight went with fathers. Why did they travel with only one parent? A father waited at a destination, a parent died so the other moved west with extended family or friends, or a father took his sons for a temporary stint like the gold rush. Some young pioneers like Elisha Brooks struggled along the way, while others like George Stokes had a relatively easy trip. Distance to one's destination and year of travel influenced these experiences. Elisha Brooks's father left for the California gold fields, then two years later asked his family to join him. In the spring of 1852, Elisha's mother packed up their few belongings and with her five sons between the ages of four and eleven, a thirteen-year-old daughter, and a hired teamster, she began a 2,800 mile trek from Michigan to California. When the teamster deserted them at Council Bluffs, the mother asked her children "if we wanted to go on, and if we thought we could drive the team, and if we were afraid of the Indians." The family chose to press forward, but "in the loneliness of that night, we saw her . . . kneeling beside a log" praying for guidance. This was a busy travel year, and the family joined various wagon trains, but they fell behind due to "our many delays . . . so that the pastures were almost all fed bare and our cattle were getting gaunt and weak. Once in a while, a belated train would overtake us." The Brooks family reached the Humboldt sink in Nevada with no food. Their father rescued them and "reinforced our team with his mule, replenished our exhausted stores, and we could smile again." In contrast, George Stokes's father sold his business in Missouri and went to the gold fields of Colorado in 1861. Eighteen months later, he sent for his wife and fifteen-year-old son. During the 650-mile journey,

George and his mother enjoyed fine weather and camped at ranches and stage stations along the Platte.[16]

Several youngsters on the California and Oregon trails made the trek with their fathers. In 1850, Upton Swingley's father caught the "gold fever," and leaving his family in Illinois, he took fifteen-year-old Upton and twelve other men with him. They joined a wagon train, traveled to California, worked in the gold mines for two years, then returned home by way of Panama. Elizabeth Shepard (Holtgrieve) went west with her widowed father, her sister, and a paternal uncle and aunt. At the Boise River Elizabeth's father met a young woman whose train was camping nearby. "Father suggested to Miss Nelson that they should take advantage of the minister's being with them and get married." The ceremony was performed, and Miss Nelson "brought her things over to our wagon."[17] Another father married a sister of his deceased wife after she accompanied the family to Oregon. Living on the frontier required the combined efforts of father, mother, and children, and widowers in new settlements needed women to raise their motherless offspring.

Pioneers on the Mormon Trail emigrated for religious reasons and, as a result, were bound by a common purpose and a single vision. If a parent died before or during the journey, the surviving parent and children continued to Zion with L.D.S. traveling communities assisting them. Widows and children easily joined Mormon companies because of the nature of the church's migration. From its inception President Brigham Young issued the "will of the Lord" concerning the trek west, and this encompassed caring for the poor, widows, and orphans. Of the 264 Mormon reminiscences I analyzed, thirty-seven writers described going to Utah with their mothers, and in twenty-five cases their mothers were widows. A few children traveled with widowed step-mothers. Four

[16]Brooks, *Pioneer Mother*, 10, 15–16, 24, 30–31; Stokes, *Deadwood Gold*, 8–12.

[17]Swingley, "Gold Rush Fever," 459, 461; Helm, *Conversations*, 155, 157.

youngsters lost fathers in or near Nauvoo, the fast-growing Mormon gathering place in Illinois, as a result of sickness or other experiences in and around this Mississippi River community. Some fathers died before leaving Europe or on the way to the Missouri River. In 1847, William Mitton's father sailed to America to earn money to bring his family, but he died two years later. William's "mother was anxious to get to Utah," so the family found jobs and provided the means to send the two oldest boys. They, in turn, helped the others reach Boston. Finally six years later, the Mittons emigrated to Utah. William recalled, "It surely was a hard journey." He and his brother slept in a small tent and one morning discovered a snake under their bed. "I soon wore my shoes out and had to walk bare footed most of the way." William "began to think we never would get over those ridges." But many times his mother reminded him, "We're going to Zion and we will surely get there."[18]

Some young Mormons pulled handcarts to Utah with their widowed mothers. Between 1856 and 1860, the church organized ten handcart companies to economically transport European converts across the plains. Four or five people pulled two-wheeled wooden carts weighing sixty pounds with hundred-pound loads. A few freight wagons accompanied the several hundred walkers and hauled the heavier baggage and supplies. At night approximately twenty people slept in one large tent. Jacob Bowers emigrated from England with his family, then his father died on the way to Iowa, and his mother and six children walked across the plains in 1856 with the first handcart company. "We traveled about 12 to 18 miles a day, through heat, dust, rock, rain and mud and waded river and streams" to reach the Salt Lake Valley. Samuel and Richard Rowley walked with their mother and five other siblings in the Willie company, which left that same year too late

---

[18]Allen and Leonard, *Story of L.D.S.*, 223, 237; Doctrine and Covenants 136: 3–9; Mitton, "Sketch," 1–4.

in the season. Samuel remembered, "We were delayed at times on account of our handcarts becoming rickety, having been made of green timber." At the last crossing of the Platte Samuel's "clothes were frozen so that I could scarcely move. I stood by the fire with a blanket around me while Mother dried my clothes by the fire." Richard recalled reaching the last crossing of the Sweetwater "entirely out of food and the fact that the snow was two feet deep did not lighten the burden on our minds." Early October snowstorms trapped the emigrants in Wyoming, and approximately one-sixth of the Willie company died. Thomas Rowley's "right hand froze while pushing on the back of the handcart. My brother, John, overcome by exhaustion, was laid by the roadside to await the sick wagon. When he was picked up, he was frozen in two places on the side of his body nearest the ground."[19]

Twelve Mormon children went to Utah with mothers who were not widows. One father sailed with Samuel Brannan around Cape Horn to San Francisco while the family crossed on land; another joined the Mormon Battalion in the war against Mexico. A third refused to go west because a thief stole some of his supplies, and he blamed church members. A few fathers traveled to Utah ahead of their families, while others emigrated later. Josephine Hartley (Zundle) joined the church in England with her mother and siblings, but her father was not baptized "and the family never saw him again." The Hartleys crossed to Utah in the Martin handcart company, which left two weeks after the Willie company. To push faster through Wyoming they lightened their loads, which included bedding, and then the snow began to fall. Approximately one-fourth of the group died in Wyoming blizzards. When their food was gone, Josephine's mother scraped flour sacks with a knife "to make some cakes and mush to help sustain life." In

---

[19]Bowers, "History," 1; Rowley, "Biographical Sketch," 1–2; Rowley, "Richard Rowley," 1. See Hafen, *Handcarts to Zion*, and Carter, "Mormon Handcart," for facts about Mormon handcart companies.

MORMONS CROSSING THE PLAINS.

"Handcart Pioneers," from *Ballou's Pictorial*, Sept. 20, 1856.
Courtesy of L.D.S. Church Historical Library.

THE PIONEERS.

"The Pioneers," from T.B.H. Stenhouse, *The Rocky Mountain Saints.*

the evenings Josephine attempted to dry her wet skirt by the fire; her brother's "feet were frozen, and he lost one leg below the knee."[20]

Nine Mormon children crossed the plains with fathers, and in all cases except one the mother had died. Isabella Siddoway's (Armstrong) family left England and lived in the eastern United States for several years during their mother's illness. After the woman died, ten-year-old Isabella and her younger brothers helped their father pull a handcart to Zion. "Our shoes were so badly worn that, at night, after a long day's walk over the rough ground I would have to bathe the pebbles from my little brother's torn and bleeding feet as well as my own." When Andrew Shumway's father was selected to go with the first pioneer company to the Salt Lake Valley, the youth "burst into tears. My mother having just died, it seemed more than I could endure to be left alone," so the boy was permitted to accompany his father. The train roster, however, listed the fourteen year old as an adult. Thomas Davis's father joined the L.D.S. church in Wales, but his mother, a devout Baptist, did not. She learned that Mormon converts went to Utah and many died along the way, so she and a seven-year-old son remained while other family members, including a four-year-old son, left Wales without her.[21] Of 264 Mormon reminiscences only four stated that one parent consciously chose to never accompany the family to Zion.

Migration without Parents

Some children crossed the plains with no parents. On the California and Oregon trails 4% of the youngsters I studied made the trek alone, while 10% of the Mormons did. Why did these young people go? Mrs. M. A. Gentry was eleven when she followed her sister and brother-in-law to Califor-

---

[20]Carter, *Pioneer Heritage*, 9: 457–458. For details about the Willie and Martin Handcart companies, see Hafen, *Handcarts to Zion*, 91–141.

[21]Armstrong, "Sketch of Life," 169–170; Godfrey, *Charles Shumway*, 108; Bagley, *Pioneer Camp*, 130; Davis, "Autobiography," 7–8, 11–12.

nia as a young "forty-niner." Hearing that General Sutter's daughter collected gold nuggets, "I begged and pleaded until my sister consented." For several years Mrs. Gentry had lived with her sister 250 miles from home and helped with household chores. Their mother learned about the trip when a letter arrived from the trail. At first she was shocked, "but realizing that I was in safe hands, she calmly faced the inevitable." After Daniel Giles's father died, his mother married a poor man, and at "eight years old I found it necessary to seek a living for myself." Giles worked at odd jobs until age fifteen when he went with his sister's family to Oregon. Some years after Daniel Drumheller's father died and left his mother "with a big brood of children," Daniel's mother consented to let the fourteen year old help a friend transport cattle to California. Fourteen-year-old William Gay became a bullwhacker with freight contractors going to Fort Laramie during the Civil War. "Hands were scarce at that time. . . so they were often obliged to employ young boys." James Farmer's mother died when he was a small child, and his paternal uncle and aunt who took care of him had a son who "was a species of snob." Whenever the boys fought, James "got a severe thrashing." So he ran away and joined an army unit to Utah in 1858.[22] Albert Dickson's mother remarried after his father's death, and the boy was bound out to a family "by mutual agreement and according to a current practice . . . until he should come of age." When the family went to the Montana gold fields, the thirteen year old did too.[23] It was not unusual for children of this period to leave home if their families were large and had little means of support or if one or both parents died.

Of twenty-seven Mormon children who crossed the plains

---

[22]Ross, "Child's Experiences," 300; Giles, "Indian Wars," 248–249; Drumheller, *Uncle Dan*, 1, 4; Gay, "An Extract," 1; Giese, *My Life*, 15–17. For additional information about children leaving home, see Kett, *Rites of Passage*, 17–36; and Gillis, *Youth and History*, 7–8, 17, 43, 44, 47.

[23]Dickson, *Covered Wagon*, 20, 23. This published account of Albert Dickson was a narrative written by his son from Albert's private journals, original memoranda, notes, and papers. According to the preface, Albert Dickson was alive when his son wrote it, but the author did not say how much input the pioneer provided.

without parents, thirteen left from Nauvoo, Illinois. Between 1839 and 1846, the Mormons transformed Nauvoo from a sleepy village to a thriving city with a population of over 11,000. During this time, American, Canadian, and British converts flocked to the church headquarters on the Mississippi River. But Nauvoo and nearby towns contained residents other than Mormons, and the two groups clashed about religious tenets and social, economic, and political ideas. As a result, Joseph Smith the Mormon Prophet was killed, and the stage was set for the church to move west.[24]

Children who left Nauvoo without parents between 1846 and 1850 were influenced by what happened in this city. Louisa Norris's (Decker) father was killed in a battle against an anti-Mormon mob, then her mother and newborn infant died in Iowa. The twelve-year-old girl accompanied a church family to Utah by driving teams and assisting with chores. After the mother gave birth on the trail, "the babe became a great comfort" to Louisa because "it was something to love . . . The family never knew how the orphan girl longed for the kind words they so freely gave their own and that I had been so recently deprived of." Edwin Pettit's parents died within two weeks of each other from hardships and the unhealthy climate in Nauvoo. The thirteen-year-old boy secretly left his guardian and went to Utah with a sister and husband. After Harrison Sperry's parents died in Iowa and Nebraska, the fifteen year old and his siblings "hitched up our teams and loaded in our outfit and goods and started for the west" in a Mormon company. "Before Father died he called all of us around his bedside and requested us to follow on after the heads of the Church who were moving west." Aurelia Spencer's (Rogers) mother died thirty miles west of Nauvoo, and her father took the family to Nebraska, built a log cabin, and left on a mission to edit a church newspaper in England. He

---

[24]For information about Nauvoo, Illinois, see Flanders, *Nauvoo*; Allen and Leonard, *Story of L.D.S.*; Mc Gavin, *Nauvoo the Beautiful*; Roberts, *Rise and Fall*; Hallwass and Lanius, *Cultures in Conflict*; and Miller and Miller, *Nauvoo*.

planned to take his family to Zion, but Brigham Young asked him to remain in Britain another year. So the Spencer children went to Utah in Brigham Young's 1848 company.[25]

Compelled to leave Nauvoo before selling homes and property or making sufficient preparations, Mormon pioneers in the 1840s made due with what they had. Often that was not enough, and people died from lack of provisions, over-exposure, and disease, especially during the winter of 1846–47 at Winter Quarters, Nebraska. Such was the case with the families of Harrison Sperry, Aurelia Spencer, and Louisa Norris. In addition, five hundred men heeded Brigham Young's call and enlisted in the Mormon Battalion to fight in the war against Mexico. Their women and children cared for themselves or relied on other church members. John Young explained, "Owing to the poverty of our people, and to the lack of men [due to the Mormon Battalion], conditions were such that in making up the Pioneer Company many families were divided." While Young's father and little brother went to the Salt Lake Valley with the first pioneer contingent, ten-year-old John and another brother traveled in a different train. Their mother who was in poor health followed a few years later. Young remembered the journey without his parents:

> . . . during that pilgrimage I was like a waif upon the ocean. The camp fire was my home, and I was everybody's chore boy. While this arrangement taught me self-reliance, it chilled my heart, and turned me against those finer, more tender endearments of life. . . and from this experience I have learned to pity the child that grows up without a mother's care and caress."[26]

John Young needed his mother on that trip.

So did almost seven-year-old Hannah Hill (Romney) who wrote, "I haven't many pleasant remembrances of my child-

---

[25]Decker, "Reminiscences," 42, 49–50; Pettit, *Biography*, 6–7; Sperry, "Short History," 2–3; Rogers, *Life Sketches*, 35, 47, 66, 76.

[26]Young, *Memoirs*, 56, 60–61. For information about Winter Quarters and the Mormon Battalion, see Allen and Leonard, *Story of L.D.S.*, 225–238; Church Educational System, *Church History*; and Ludlow, *Encyclopedia*. For an older but more extensive history, see Roberts, *Comprehensive History*.

hood days, for while in Winter Quarters my mother took sick and died owing to exposure and hardships." The father left her "brother Samuel with his father and mother, my sister Rebecca with one sister, and I with another, and he started with the pioneers to find a home in the west." Two years later he sent for Hannah, and "I was very excited and thought we were going on a pleasure trip, but found it was a very long, hard one." The child "started out with strangers; they cut off all my hair. I traveled bare-footed and bare-headed; sometimes we would travel two or three days without water." Finally, Hannah's "father met us in Emigration Canyon with vegetables and melons which we enjoyed very much."[27]

In an analysis of young California pioneers, psychologist Emmy Werner observed that younger children felt secure on the trail if they were encircled within the bounds of the extended family. "Only the loss of a parent, especially the mother, could unravel this basic sense of security."[28] Even though Mormons migrated as church families and cared for the basic needs of widows and orphans, children like Louisa Norris, John Young, and Hannah Hill longed for nurturing parents. Yet adolescents like Patrick Murphy, Daniel Drumheller, and James Farmer seemed quite content traveling on their own. Age, experience, and degree of independence made a difference in feeling secure on the trail.

European children who emigrated with no parents traveled greater distances alone. After leaving home, they went to Liverpool, climbed aboard a ship, crossed the ocean, and made their way across the United States to the jumping-off place where they joined wagon or handcart companies to the West. Some youngsters went alone in wagon trains; others accompanied siblings, relatives, or friends. Twelve Mormon writers remembered leaving foreign countries by themselves. Two arrived in America with families, but their parents died before making the trek to Utah. Ellen Perks'

[27]Carter, *Pioneer Heritage*, 5: 263.   [28]Werner, *Pioneer Children*, 4.

(Johnstun) father left for America before he was drafted in the Crimean War. He found work in Illinois and sent for his family, but Ellen's mother "was very sick on the trip and gave birth to a son the day we landed." The mother and new-born infant died in New York. "This left my little sister, Clara, three years old and myself alone. . . . Father sent money to President Taylor and he sent us with a man going to St. Louis, but he did not care for us," so the railroad conductor looked after the girls. After Clara died in Illinois, "it was decided that I should go West to live with my Grandmother Perks." Almost twelve years old, Ellen Perks crossed the plains alone in a handcart company.

After Christopher Alston's father died, his mother sent her two oldest children, Christopher (10) and John (8), to America with a friend. The in-laws opposed them going to where the "awful Mormons" lived. Near the Missouri River, "John strayed away and was lost for several days." He was found "early one morning, nearly naked and almost starved, by a farmer in the neighborhood; from which exposure he suffered a shock from which he never fully recovered." Although the boys traveled with friends, John Alston needed his mother's loving arms and watchful care.[29]

Living in an English coal mining town with limited income, George Beard's parents could only send a married son to Utah, then that son earned money to help other family members go, which he did one or two at a time. George and two sisters sailed with their mother who died on the voyage, so the children completed the journey in a church train. Their father arrived several years later. George explained that "many families under similar circumstances left their homes and migrated to Zion" in the same way. Sometimes European converts were advised by missionaries or church leaders to do this. According to Louisa Mills (Palmer), the president of the European Mission counseled members to send their families a few at a

---

[29]Clayton, "Biographies," Box 2: 2–3; Alston, "Biographical Sketch," 1; Alston, "Thomas Alston," 14.

time if they lacked means to travel together. Two of her siblings made the journey, then ten-year-old Louisa went the next year. She recalled being homesick at Florence, Nebraska, but mentioned nothing about it while crossing the plains. Perhaps she attached herself to the Morris family, for she said they walked ahead of the train together. Ten-year-old John Hayes was determined to go to Zion, so he found his own way. "Brother Morris made it pleasant for me crossing the plains, being very kind to me all the way, and took the place of a good kind father." Even the teamsters looked after John by letting him ride and taking him fishing.[30] These three children must have felt fairly secure traveling with church members, or perhaps in their recollections they forgot—or chose not to share—the feelings of youngsters so far from home alone.

Only three Scandinavians talked about going alone to the land with a strange language. After his mother died on the ocean and his father and sister in New York, ten-year-old Hans Larsen and his brother went to Utah with church members. Non-Mormon relatives in Denmark contacted the Danish consul and unsuccessfully attempted to have the boys sent home. Fourteen-year-old Augusta Dorius (Stevens) emigrated from Denmark with a family who paid her way. ". . . I wonder sometimes how I received courage to leave my family and go to a strange country and then too, when I did not know how far we should have to travel to get to Zion and I could not talk the language." Even though Augusta had faith in her religion, "I had my sobs and cries and pangs of sorrow. What comfort it would have been to me if I could . . . speak or understand the English language." Georgina Norr (Miller) remembered that a church member approached her widowed mother in Denmark and offered to take one child to Zion. Since she was the oldest, thirteen-year-old Georgina was chosen, and after a lonely and discouraging journey she arrived

---

[30]Davies, "George Beard," 11–12; Carter, *Pioneer Heritage*, 13: 455–457; Carter, *Pioneer Heritage*, 13: 438. See Taylor, *Expectations*, 127–129, for facts about families emigrating in stages.

in Salt Lake City. Although other pioneers were met by friends, "no one came for me." She lived with church members until her mother arrived two years later.[31] Augusta Dorius and Georgina Noor seemed more despondent during the journey than did English children. Perhaps the language barrier contributed to their frustrations of being alone.

These reminiscences indicate that the majority of children who crossed the plains without parents traveled with at least one sibling, and this may have tempered their feelings of loneliness. Fewer children on the California and Oregon trails went by themselves, probably because their trains did not have a strong support system for youngsters without parents. These lone travelers ranged in age from eleven to fifteen. Mormons often assisted each other; as a result, younger children could make the trek by themselves. One was only six years old; the others were between nine and fifteen.

Travels with Two Parents

While children occasionally crossed the plains alone or with one parent, more than three-fourths traveled with two parents or step-parents. Since most of the reminiscences mentioned families, what did they remember about these relationships? Childhood memories can easily be distorted after fifty to eighty years, and sometimes it is difficult to distinguish between primary and secondary memories, or if they happened at all. One way to catch the vision of the trail through the eyes of young pioneers is by considering the "I remember" or "I did" experiences separately from the "we remember" incidents. The "we remember" happenings may have been acquired around an Oregon Pioneer Trail Association's campfire, discussed by parents and older siblings who made the trek, or obtained from primary and secondary sources which resulted in shared and collective memory, adult views, and nostalgia. While some "I remember" incidents were

---

[31]Larsen, "Autobiographical," 2, 4–6; Stevens, "Autobiography," 2, 4; Carter, *Pioneer Heritage*, II: 202.

probably rehearsed over the years, they appear to portray a more accurate rendering of the child's perspective, especially if they reflect the child's age and awareness of life at the time of the original experience.

During the twentieth century, psychologists and child development experts formulated theories of learning, thinking, and stages of development in children, particularly in Caucasian subjects. Piaget, Erikson, Vygotsky, Bruner, and others are currently studied to gain insights into children. Yet their ideas evolved from centuries of philosophical thinking about childhood. For example, in the seventeenth and eighteenth centuries, John Locke and Jean-Jacques Rousseau altered the Puritan thought of their day. Today, as new ideas appear, theories of the past are questioned. Still, certain characteristics of human growth and development are common to youngsters regardless of historical time and cultural expectations.[32] I have used these to analyze the memories of 430 pioneers who crossed the plains as children. Even though age levels and maturational abilities overlap, I have divided the reminiscences into three groups for convenience: young children one through six years old, middle-year children seven through twelve, and adolescents thirteen through fifteen.

"I Remember"—Ages One Through Six

Young children see life through a narrow lens because of limited language, training, and experience. This lens widens as they learn and develop. Perception, memory, knowledge, and understanding grow with the child. Small children can think and reason, but their thinking is directed to the real world and to real-life situations. They respond to life through their senses with curiosity, a sense of awe and wonder, and spontaneity.[33] Their experiences revolve around the family and espe-

---

[32]See Santrock, *Children*, 6–11, 34–52; Wood, *How Children Think*, 34–36; Berger, *Developing Person*, 31–53; Berk, *Child Development*, 1–32; Owens, *World of Child*; and Aries, *Centuries*.

[33]Wood, *How Children Think*, 32–34, 59, 72, 77; Donaldson, *Children's Minds*, 90, 127; Yamamoto, *Their World*, 106, 148–149; Irwin and Simons, *Lifespan*, 150.

cially the parents. Although these youngsters actively explore their world, they do not usually seek close attachments with people outside the home. Five and six year olds develop some independence and ability to play cooperatively with other children. They become involved in pretend play and adult imitation either by themselves or with other youngsters. But they consider friends as convenient playmates and not necessary appendages to their lives.[34]

Of 58 young pioneers between one and six who crossed the plains with two parents, all mentioned their families in their reminiscences. Though twelve did not describe personal recollections, thirty-four pioneers recalled specific "I remember" incidents with their families.[35] Personal memories of youngest children resemble snapshots or fragmentary images. Such images may return years later, unexpectedly and involuntarily, often from a prompt complete with feelings, sounds, and smells—but with no indication of what occurred before or after that moment. These memories are unlike those of an adult, for a child sees, reasons, and reacts differently. Of twenty-five accounts from youngest pioneers, ages one through four, seventeen described "I remember" snapshots. These most often involved parental care, sensory impressions, and fear. Angus Wright, almost three, recalled parental care when "walking once with mother and crossing a small stream while holding to her hand." Frances Clelland (Peabody) admitted that many incidents she experienced at four years old were "preserved only by what my mother told me, but minor things you wouldn't expect a child would remember are still fresh in my mind—the creaking and jolting of the wagon, the straining of the oxen over rough places, . . . the clanking of the big heavy chains." Yet these sensory impressions are ones young children would

---

[34]Berger, *Developing Person*, 219, 223. Mildred Parten studied the social play of young children and identified five types: solitary, onlooker, parallel, associative, and cooperative.

[35]In Palmer, "Voices," III, I noted 64 reminiscences by youngest pioneers, but in this book I eliminated accounts that said "tiny tot" or "small child" instead of a specific age as well as accounts that did not say they traveled with two parents.

remember since they learn about life through their senses. Two-year-old Laura Caldwell encountered fear when she was "left out of our covered wagon. I was frightened. Mother told me to go to Father. He reached down from the wagon, told me to hold my arms up, and lifted me into the wagon."[36] Little children tend to fear what threatens their immediate security, especially separation from parents.

One small emigrant described disobedience, and another mentioned death. Jane Bybee (Stowell) recalled being contrary when she was not quite three years old. Developmentally, she was in the phase which today we label "the terrible two's." Recovering from cholera, Jane "was very cross and peevish and wanted a pair of small scissors my mother had brought along." At first her mother refused because "she was afraid I would lose them," but Mother gave in and handed her the scissors. Jane "threw them across the wagon. They hit the wagon cover and slid down and out onto the ground. We could not stop so that was the last of Mother's precious scissors." Her mother probably reminded her of this incident, but Jane did not embellish it with adult details. Instead, she said, " I can still see those scissors sliding down the wagon cover."[37] Eliza Burdett (Horsepool) recalled her little sister's death and burial, although she did not understand it. "I can hear my mother crying and saying, 'Those poor little bones.' I realized as I grew older that she meant that they would be crushed by the weight of the dirt and rocks as the grave was filled in." Eliza's three-year-old mind registered her mother's tears and sad comment.[38]

Young children have a short attention span and are distractible with so much to see and do in their world; consequently, they are not likely to rehearse experiences in order to

[36]Wright, "Autobiography," 5; Peabody, "Across the Plains," 72; Helm, *Conversations*, 265–266.
[37]Carter, *Pioneer Heritage*, 11: 184. Carter said she published Stowell's account verbatim.
[38]Genealogical Society, *Utah Pioneer*, 13: 112–113. See Irwin and Simons, *Lifespan*, 476–477, and Dickinson and Leming, *Understanding Dying*, 100–103, for information about young children and their concept of death.

remember them. But five and six year olds begin to understand causal relationships and to process information at a less
shallow level. Five- and six-year-old emigrants recalled snapshot memories. They included more "I remember" events and
details like seven- and eight-year-old children, that is if they
did not receive assistance with recall. Major themes involved
fear, pleasure, responsibilities, and curiosity—with fear being
the most common, for they lived in an environment they did
not understand. Six-year-old Ann Wilden (Johnson) was
tending her little sister in the wagon when her brother asked
her to drive the sheep. As she climbed out of the wagon, the
oxen kicked her under the moving vehicle. "A wheel struck
my back and squeezed up my dinner, and my prized lead pencil was lost in the food . . . Though I was not badly hurt, I
mourned the loss of my pencil." Her parents, who had been
visiting a nearby company, came running when they heard the
commotion. Ann and her family probably discussed this
frightening event over the years, but fretting over a prized pencil was a child's memory. Six-year-old Peter McBride from
Scotland recalled the Martin handcart company's suffering in
the premature Wyoming winter. "I shivered so much I knew
I would die." When the wind knocked the tent down, the others crawled out. "I began to feel warm and the tent closed down
around me, the snow fell on it, I went to sleep and slept warm
all night." The next morning Peter heard someone ask how
many in their tent were dead, and his sister answered, "Well
there are five children . . . My little brother Peter must be frozen
to death." By now, death had become common to this handcart company. "They jerked the tent loose, sent it scurrying
over the snow, my hair was frozen to the tent. I picked myself
up and came out quite to their surprise."[39] With this recollection's detailed image, it may have been seasoned by family
retellings.

Five- and six-year-old pioneers also recalled experiences

---

[39]King, "Long Journey," 9; Carter, *Pioneer Heritage*, 13: 362.

involving pleasure. After being confined in the wagon, Mary Boatman's father let "Sarah and me out to run along beside him" while he drove the ox team. "Often we would try to catch the end of the long whip." Mary was five and her sister was three. Some youngsters listened to stories, picked flowers, and played tag. Six-year-old William Colvig learned to read, but his rec- ollection differed somewhat in two accounts. In one reflection he said, "During the six months or more we were on the plains Mother had me recite to her, so that by the end of the trip I was reading in the [McGuffey's] Second Reader." In a second account his mother sat at the foot of the wagon bed, "with a babe in her arms--and I remember that she taught me to read during that summer, using an old 'Elementary Spelling Book' as a text book." Since Colvig mentioned that his mother's trav- eling library contained *Webster's Elementary Spelling Book* and McGuffey's *First* and *Second Readers*, perhaps he learned to read from all of them.[40] Still, this example shows that memories are constructed, not reproduced, and they fade or are re-developed and re-cropped over time. Colvig may have verbalized this scene over the years and, thus, revised his snapshot memory.

Some five and six year olds remembered responsibility and curiosity themes. The nineteenth-century work ethic appeared on the trail with young pioneers who most often mentioned gathering buffalo chips and sagebrush for mothers to cook sup- per. A few children picked wild berries. Girls cared for smaller siblings in wagons while their mothers moved about outside. One boy rode a spare cow or ox every day, and a few young- sters routinely walked beside full wagons. These young pio- neers were also curious about their new surroundings. Buffalo and graceful antelope tantalized their sense of wonder, so did a few individual train members and Native Americans.

In research studies of early childhood memories, Waldvo- gel and Dudycha and Dudycha noted fear and joy or pleasure

---

[40]Boatman, "Crossing the Plains," 6; Helm, *Voices*, 162; Colvig, "Annual Address," 339–340.

as the most common themes their subjects remembered.[41] All of the youngest pioneer "I remember" memories with or without family totalled 148. Of these, 41% involved a general category of sensory, trivia, responsibility, and curiosity themes. Negative recollections of trauma/fear, sadness, pain, and disobedience constituted 37%, and positive experiences of pleasure and parental care/security comprised 22%. The largest single themes of youngest pioneers were fear (26%), pleasure (16%), sensory (15%), and trivia (12%), which corraborates with the studies.

"I Remember"—Ages Seven Through Twelve

In comparison to their younger counterparts, children between seven and twelve look at life through a wider lens. They are taller with increased motor skills and powers of concentration, attention, and memory. Although they are keen observers through their senses, their perceptions, knowledge, and understanding have expanded through experience and training. They are still limited to concrete images and have difficulty extracting abstract meanings. As middle-year children grow, they develop a time perspective of past and future, and near the age of ten they grasp the chronological arrangement of the historical past. They begin to step beyond the family and build relationships with peers, but their families are still most important to them. Their communication skills increase, and they grow in moral reasoning and understanding of societal values and emotions, such as guilt and pride. They enjoy cooperative interaction, games, and reciprocal friendships. Their sense of humor expands, sometimes at the expense of others, and they display an ability to share.[42]

---

[41]Waldvogel, "Childhood Memories," in Neisser, *Memory Observed*, 76; Dudycha and Dudycha, "Childhood Memories," 268.

[42]Yamamoto, *Their World*, 32, 81; Irwin and Simons, *Lifespan*, 147, 206, 208, 245–246; Bryant, *Perception*, 178; Wood, *How Children Think*, 150; Gardner, *Frames of Mind*, 248–249; Norton, *Through the Eyes*, 13. For information on sensory, short-term, and long-term memory, see Irwin and Simons, *Lifespan*, 205–208.

Of 171 accounts of middle-year children who crossed the plains with two parents, their "I remember" experiences contained more description and detail than youngest children's recollections.[43] Their long-term memory was improving through knowledge, experience, and the ability to rehearse and make associations for retention. Rather than sensory, trivia, or curiosity themes, their family experiences involved these themes listed according to frequency of occurrence: illness/death; responsibilities; animals, fear, and values/religion; and pleasure/play. Minor topics were lack of thinking/disobedience and accidents/pain.

Middle-year pioneers most often mentioned the theme of illness/death, a concept youngest children do not understand but nine to twelve year olds fear. These youngsters noted disease, accidents, cholera—the main cause of death on the trail—and graves along the way. One girl traveling in 1850, a heavy cholera year, recalled that her father quit counting graves when he reached 1,000. Sarah Palmer's (Sharp) mother was ill most of the way across the plains. One day her father said, "You must get out and walk or you will die in the wagon." He challenged the woman to walk from one new telegraph pole to another. "She took his arm and, oh my, I will never forget how slow. When they reached the pole he let her rest and then got her in the wagon." Each day Sarah's mother walked one pole farther. Lydia Thrower (Holdaway) from England recalled her father dying of pneumonia. "They rolled him in a blanket and buried him and how terrible it seemed to me for him to be left on that lonely plain and of wondering if the wolves would get him." Lucy Henderson's (Deady) little sister died from an overdose of laudanum after Lucy and a friend found the medicine and sampled it while the young child watched. After the older girls left, the child "got the bottle and drank it all."[44]

---

[43]In Palmer, "Voices," 115, I noted 198 reminiscences and memories of middle–year children, but in this book I left out accounts that did not state they traveled with two parents or did not provide a specific age.

[44]Sharp, "Autobiography," 8–9; Holdaway, "Life Story," 1; Henderson, "Young Adventure," 89–90.

At times the themes of illness/death and responsibility merged. Nirom Hawley's mother, who was ill with mountain fever, saw a snowbank in the distance and begged for snow in her drinking water. Nine-year-old Nirom rode his horse to the place which was farther away than it appeared, and the snow was "so hard that I could hardly get it in my pail." The boy accomplished the task even though it took "most of the afternoon." Elizabeth Jacobson (Pulsipher) from Norway cared for her siblings after her mother fell out of the wagon and was badly injured. Many nights the twelve-year-old girl held a quilt over her mother to protect her from the rain. "My little sister was very sick also, her condition was so that I held her on my lap." After the child died, Elizabeth "had to bathe her and put a little dress on her and sew a cloth around her body to be buried in as there was no coffin. As small as I was no one came to help me and Mother was not able to do any- thing." This young girl prematurely followed in the footsteps of women of her time who acted as healers, nurses, and mor- ticians.[45] Illness and death forced some youngsters to assume challenging responsibilities.

But most young emigrants recalled tasks suitable to their age. They had already learned the nineteenth-century work attitude back home; now they pitched in with jobs on the trail. Seven- through nine-year-old boys and girls collected buf- falo chips and picked wild berries and plums with their moth- ers and siblings. The first time Mary Ann Parker's (Wilgus) father asked the children to gather buffalo chips for fuel, "we told him we would not pick up the dirty stuff, but we did and soon didn't mind at all." Girls also tended smaller siblings in wagons and assisted with simple chores, while boys helped with loose cattle. As they grew bigger and stronger, middle-year children drove teams or loose cattle and took additional responsibility with animals, camp duties, and family members.

---

[45]Clark, "Nirom Hawley," 54; Pulsipher, "Life History," 3. See Schlissel, *Women's Diaries*, 15, for women as healers and morticians.

Usually boys helped fathers and girls assisted their mothers. Eleven-year-old Oliver Beagle went with his father to "get a buffalo." While he and another boy held the horses, the men chased after a big bull, but it "got away from them. I saw he was coming in our direction, . . . and as he galloped by I shot at him. I happened to hit him in a vital spot," and Oliver's father and Peter Burnett butchered the animal and carried the "rump, loin, and tongue back to the wagon train."[46]

Sometimes middle-year emigrants switched roles and responsibilities, with girls helping fathers and boys assisting their mothers. At times these tasks strained their capabilities. Ten-year-old Diana Eldredge (Smoot) became proficient at driving a team when her brother was ill. As they neared the Salt Lake Valley, her father asked if she could lead the oxen down the mountain. Diana mounted her pony, and "Father instructed me to hold the reins close to the bit to prevent the pony from falling if he stumbled on the rough, bushy trail." Before Diana reached the bottom, "the tears were streaming down my face, but father kept cheering and encouraging as he followed beside his team." Nine-year-old George Himes helped his mother carry his smaller siblings on the last stretch of the Oregon Trail. They abandoned a wagon, and their father fell behind because of the "wretched condition" of the horses. George put his little brother on his back and "did what I could to lighten my mother's burden by carrying the baby." He took the little ones across a river on a "footlog," then assisted his mother who became dizzy and fell into the water. "Luckily I was in reaching distance of overhanging bushes, which were instinctively grabbed with my left hand, still clutching her left hand with my right," and George helped his mother to safety.[47]

Trail responsibilities provided middle-year Mormons from Europe an education as well. Jane Hooper's (Blood) father sent

[46]"Mary Ann Parker," III; Helm, *Voices*, 311.
[47]Smoot, "Autobiography," 3–4; Himes, "Annual Address," 148.

her "to tell the men driving the loose herd that he needed some cattle for replacements. In the bustle of changing cattle" and crossing a river, she was accidentally left. "I was frightened when I saw that all the wagons were gone," but a man in the company found her and helped the nine-year-old girl rejoin her family. Jane became more independent on that trip, for "I had never done any work, not even dressed myself" in England. Bertha Jensen (Eccles) came from Denmark and, since her father knew nothing about oxen, he purchased one without teeth. "Father bought a quantity of damaged flour from an army post and mother baked this into bread." Each time the train stopped, Bertha fed the animal a piece of bread, and the toothless ox took them to Utah.[48] European families were more naive about the ramifications of covered wagon travel than were most American travelers.

Mormon children who traveled by handcart had unique and often difficult responsibilities. Mary Powell's (Sabin) brother pulled a cart "all the way from Iowa City to Utah" in the first handcart company of 1856, while twelve-year-old Mary and her father "took turns pulling the other one. When I was not pulling father's handcart I was helping to pull someone else's .... Sometimes when father or mother took sick I worried, as I did not want them to die by the way side." Twelve-year-old John Oborn from England walked with the Willie company late in the 1856 season. "Father would usually pull and mother and I would push." Food ran out, and "we resorted to eating anything that could be chewed; even bark and leaves of trees. We youngsters ate the rawhide from our boots." John Stucki from Switzerland remembered his experience with the Stoddard company in 1860. "When I, a nine-year-old boy, would be so tired that I would wish I could sit down," John's father asked "if I could not push a little more on the Handcart." After the people were placed on half-rations, a buffalo was shot and the meat divided. Stucki's father put their small share in the back of the cart, but

---

[48]Hill, *Jane Wilkie*, 14; Genealogical Society, *Utah Pioneer*, 9: 26.

"I was so very hungry all the time and the meat smelled so good ... and having a little pocketknife, I could not resist, but had to cut off a piece or two each half day." When his father brought out what was left of the meat, "instead of giving me the severe scolding and whipping he did not say a word but started to wipe the tears from his eyes."[49] Most youngsters in handcart companies recalled being hungry and tired, and many shouldered greater burdens at younger ages than did those who traveled with well-equipped wagons. The long distances they walked with less than adequate food for their growing bodies probably intensified hunger pangs.

Besides topics of illness/death, responsibilities, and animals, fear contributed to recollections of middle-year children, and it often combined with other themes. Jane Hooper became afraid after she obeyed her father and was accidently left behind. Diana Eldredge's apprehension reflected in her tearful face when she lead the oxen down a mountain near the Salt Lake Valley. Young people feared family members dying or getting lost. Sometimes they were afraid to share frightening personal trail experiences with parents, and many probably never did. Rebecca Moore (Tanner) confessed to two incidents. At the Elkhorn River, the seven-year-old girl

> wandered off alone and was walking along the bank where dirt had been washed out. Suddenly the dirt gave way, and one of my feet went into the water. I saved myself by throwing my body against the bank, for there was nothing to catch hold of. Had I fallen in they would never had known what became of me. After that, I didn't wander away, but I didn't tell the folks about it until I was grown.

Another day Rebecca stopped at a spring where she found some little shells.

> I picked up one, perhaps an inch long, and a head came out of the shell and cut my finger just like a sharp knife would have cut it. It bled quite freely, and I was badly frightened. I kept that to myself also, for I was afraid of getting a scolding.

These two unembellished recollections came from a child's

---

[49]Sabin, "Mary Powell," 9; Carter, *Heart Throbs*, 6: 365–366; Stucki, *Family History*, 43–44.

viewpoint. Not sharing frightening experiences for fear of being reproved by adults for doing something wrong is typical of youngsters this age. Rebecca's comment about "had I fallen in they would never had known what became of me" reflected the adult looking back. Rebecca the terrified child may have worried about another scolding.[50]

One aspect of nineteenth-century family life whether on the trail or off was belief in God, and the next important theme in many middle-year emigrant accounts was values/religion. Religion played a greater role in that era than it generally does today. S. W. Campbell, who went west at the age of nine, said, "It is important to mention here that in those days people worshipped God and had prayers on retiring at night." Historian Merrill Mattes observed that the majority of emigrants were churchgoers who kept the attitude of the Sabbath even if they traveled on Sunday or worked when they camped. Most pioneers relied on their faith in God to get them to their destination. Many children were taught to pray and to read and learn the scriptures. Eugene Foster's father was a great teller of Bible stories. "All my life I have been more indebted to his stories for my knowledge of the Bible than to my own reading." When the journey was tough and pioneers pulled through, they gave credit to God. Some, like Newton Finley, attributed a successful journey to "no travel on Sunday unless it was actually necessary" and "God was with us."[51]

Middle-year Mormon children also included values/religion in their reminiscences. They discussed right and wrong and religious feelings more frequently than did other pioneers, probably because they intended to convey spiritual values to their posterity. Anna Clark's (Hale) mother lost her sewing needle on the trail, and "the next day I showed up with a needle and told Mother I had found it." Several times her mother

---

[50]Lesson Committee, *Enduring Legacy*, II: 365–366. For insights into the child's perspective, see Young, *Life Among the Giants*.

[51]Campbell, "Oregon Trail," 3; Mattes, *Great Platte*, 74–75; Sexton, *Foster Family*, 187; Finley, "Memories," 4.

asked where she got it, and finally the seven year old confessed she had visited another camp and saw a lady sewing. Next to the woman was a cushion with pins and needles, so Anna stole one. "Mother made me take the needle back and apologize to the lady," which "was one of the hardest things I ever had to do." John Oborn remembered pulling handcarts into a circle for nightly religious services and instructions with the Willie company. He never forgot "the testimony and the wonderful spirit of sincerity and loyalty of all members of our company" even though many died. But arriving in the Salt Lake Valley produced mixed feelings among the religious wayfarers. Seven-year-old John Squires from England remembered having their belongings dumped on the ground and the borrowed wagon taken away. His mother burst into tears and said, "And this is Zion for which we have sacrificed so much and travelled so far to reach!" Unlike John Squires, Lucy White (Flake) remembered reaching Utah and seeing her mother cry. Seven-year-old Lucy could not understand the tears until her mother said, "When people are as happy as I am, they can not keep from crying."[52]

The last theme middle-year pioneers remembered with their families was pleasure/play. One wonders where this topic would fit in actual diaries of youngsters this age. Margaret West's (Irvin) family sang as their wagon rolled slowly toward Oregon, for "singing helped us pass the time and was good to raise our spirits." Margaret's father "had a high, strong voice and was always singing when he felt well enough." He liked the song "We'll Camp Upon the Mountain," and "I can still hear his high, strong voice leading while we children joined in and sometimes, if my mother was not too tired, she would hum or sing softly along with us as she held baby Sarah in her arms." Mothers and older siblings sometimes helped younger ones make dolls and other playthings, and celebrations such as wed-

---

[52]Hale, *Memoirs*, 17; Carter, *Heart Throbs*, 6: 365; Squires, "Notes of Interest," 2x; Flake, "Last Frontier," 5.

dings brightened trail experiences. One night at a camp wedding Nancy Osborne's (Jacobs) father threw an armful of sagebrush on the fire so everyone could see the ceremony.[53]

"I Remember"—Ages Thirteen Through Fifteen

Compared to middle-year children who see life through an expanding lens, adolescents from thirteen through fifteen have greater capacity to understand the world around them. They have grown in experience and expertise, in relevant and prior knowledge, and in levels of competence. They begin to think in terms of possibility and moral reasoning rather than concrete reality. Their concentration span increases, their motor skills improve, and they can do more physically. As they advance through their teens, their bodies change biologically, although most adolescents in the nineteenth century probably did not mature physically and sexually as early as teens do today. Puberty occurred near the age of fifteen, and physical growth was more gradual instead of by spurts. During adolescence, peer socialization is more pronounced, and young people are moody and idealistic. Ralph Waldo Emerson noted this idealism in the mid-nineteenth century when he said, "In youth, we clothe ourselves with rainbows, and go as brave as the zodiac." But today's concept of adolescence as a unique stage of life with gradual independence and responsibility was not common to mid-nineteenth-century thought. As young children they were expected to work, and by the teen years they were assigned adult tasks. They assumed adult roles early in life and sometimes left home quite young.[54]

Of 88 adolescents who crossed the plains with two parents, almost all of them mentioned their families, and many wrote "I remember" recollections. Some of their experiences were like those of middle-year youngsters, especially twelve year

---

[53] Adams, "Covered Wagon," 17–18; *Told by the Pioneers*, 1: 80.
[54] Wood, *How Children Think*, 150, 155; Berger, *Developing Person*, 14, 321–322, 344, 369–370; Kett, *Rites of Passage*, 44, 135–143, 169; Gillis, *Youth and History*, 6–7, 64; Emerson, *Conduct of Life*, 37.

olds like Elizabeth Jacobson whose accounts could easily fit in this section. Themes were similar to those of middle-year children, although they noted accidents and pain more frequently. Again, illness/death and responsibilities were most often discussed, while pleasure/play was last. Conversely, in contemporary adolescent accounts responsibilities came first, and pleasure/play appeared next. Themes in reminiscences in order of frequency were: illness/death; responsibilities; fear, accidents and pain; values/religion and animals; pleasure/play and lack of thinking. Teens shouldered responsibility, but if their parents were healthy, young people assisted with tasks without adult worries. Those forced to assume adult roles prematurely found the journey almost more than they could handle. Still, they persisted and survived, with faith and idealism propelling them forward.

Adolescents who made the trek with both parents relied on them to provide security, carry their load, and take charge. When Mary Jane Long's shoes wore out as she helped her father search for water, he tore her apron in strips to cover her feet. They encountered danger along the way, but Mary Jane did not worry because she was with her father. "I was young and did not consider the danger we were in, but I understood the change in father's face." Emma Shepard (Hill) and her sister lost their comfortable bed inside the wagon because their father and brother became ill. "My sister and I were now obliged to sleep under the wagon. We were wrapped in quilts, and were as comfortable as our mother could make us; but we had a feeling of loneliness, and many nights were unable to sleep" because of fear. "Our only consolation was that we were doing what we could to help our mother," and their parents were nearby.[55]

With parents in charge, adolescents drove teams, herded and tended animals, milked cows, stood guard, cared for and carried small children, cooked meals, and assisted with the sick

---

[55]Long, *Crossing the Plains*, 4–5; Hill, *Dangerous Crossing*, 27–28.

and dying. When Priscilla Parish's father contracted mountain fever, "Mother couldn't drive the oxen, so I drove them
and she drove the cows until father got well." Henry Crane's
father appointed him to take their cow across the plains and
milk her daily, "a task that I succeeded in doing" on that thou-
sand-mile trek. Margaret McNeil (Ballard) from Scotland
assisted her sick mother by cooking meals, milking the cow,
and watching her young brother. "I walked every step of the
way across the plains and drove my cow, and a large part of
the way carried brother James on my back." Mary Jane Long
helped her mother tend the sick and wash and dress the dead
for burial. Through adult eyes she said, "What a blessing youth
is, for one can take a good cry, go to bed and sleep sound and
be up bright and early the next morning, ready to help
again."[56] These young people assisted with adult tasks but were
not required to carry the full load.

In contrast, some adolescents like Henry Garrison recalled
intense hardships because they were given too much responsibility. Not yet fifteen years old, Henry took charge after his
father became bedfast with inflammatory rheumatism and was
forced to stay in the wagon. After seven-year-old Enoch broke
his leg, Henry's father, who could not move a joint from his
neck down, asked his oldest son, "What shall we do?" Henry
saw the condition of the leg and felt that it should be ampu-
tated, "for mortification would be shure to set in." But the doctor scolded Henry and "said I was nothing but a boy." For five
days Enoch rode in the wagon with Henry never leaving his
sight. Finally, the doctor decided to amputate. But Enoch did
not improve, and he told his mother and brother, "I am going
to Heaven . . . to where there is no more broken limbs, neither is there any more suffering." Henry Garrison was over-
whelmed by his father's disability, his little brother's sickness
and death, and the heavy burdens placed upon him. Thirteen-

---

[56]Carter, *Heart Throbs*, 9: 444; Carter, *Pioneer Heritage*, 19: 409; Ballard, "Margaret McNeil," 12,
13, 15; Long, *Crossing the Plains*, 9.

year-old Heber McBride and his older sister took their parents' place when their mother and father became ill. Traveling in the Martin handcart company, these Mormons had no wagon in which their sick could ride. While their parents lagged behind, Heber and his sister pulled the cart and cared for their younger siblings. "We used to pray that we might die to get out of our misery," for it was cold and everyone was starving. "We would find Mother laying by the side of the road first then we would get her on the cart and haul her along." Then they let their father ride. One morning Heber discovered his father "under a wagon with snow all over him and he was stiff and dead."[57] If a relief party had not come, these young Mormon pioneers would not have survived. Their tasks were beyond their capabilities to fulfill. Although these two experiences were more dramatic than most, some adolescent emigrants did bear burdens larger than their size and ability.

"We Remember"

While many "I remember" episodes captured childhood feelings and perceptions of the experience, the "we remember" sections of young pioneer accounts added information unknown to children, described events in depth, and involved shared or collective memory. Sometimes it was difficult to distinguish between "I remember" and "we remember" in older children's accounts unless they wrote in first person, since they tended to recall events in more detail than younger ones did. Youngest children's "we remember" reminiscences were most often related by family members who added to their snapshot memories. Three-year-old Troy Shelley would not have known that his father was financially well-to-do and that he reached Oregon with two hundred dollars in his pocket unless someone told him. Angus Wright admitted he did not remember when their wagon train neared Salt Lake City and Mormon

---

[57]Garrison, "Reminiscences," 15–18; Berrett, "Heber McBride," 10–12.

families stopped to clean up before arriving. Angus's mother put a new velvet suit on him, and the boy exclaimed, "My! Brigham [Young] won't know me, will he mother?" Angus's mother probably shared this story with him as he grew older and appreciated the humor of it.[58]

Middle-year children who included "we" events about their families sometimes used prompts to help them remember. How much of John Rogers James's account came from his own recollections is hard to say because his father kept a trail diary, and John referred to it. Allene Taylor's (Dunham) mother made a list of what they ate for their Fourth of July dinner, but "most of it is still fresh in my mind"—perhaps because she kept the list. A tintype of Margaret West's (Irvin) father dressed in his crossing-the-plains outfit helped her recall his clothing and hair style. Their family Bible and Methodist hymnbook with the "warped covers and the water stains on their leaves" reminded Margaret of their Platte River crossing.[59] Most likely these items instilled shared memory within her family.

Since some reminiscences described certain events in depth, pioneers who made the trek as children probably relied on shared or collective memory. After Mary Dart's (Judd) brother died, he was buried without her knowledge and she remembered her distress. Later, she reflected through adult eyes, "It was perhaps wise to not permit my young mind to be impressed with the rude coffined way in which they were obligged to put his remains." Mary went to bed while her father and sister tended the sick and dying, then early the next morning another tragedy struck when the sister died. Family members who witnessed what Mary did not expanded her childhood memory. Jean Frederick Loba's father found a black and white animal "gliding rapidly like a cat through the tall prairie grass." He killed it and noticed "the air was blue with a very

---

[58]Helm, *Voices*, 235; Wright, "Autobiography," 5.
[59]*Told by the Pioneers*, 2: 69; Dunham, *Across the Plains*, 10; Adams, "Covered Wagon," 10, 14.

unpleasant odor," but he did not connect the smell with the animal. The captain of the train convinced the Swiss emigrant to throw the creature away and burn his clothing. This was the father's first introduction to the "American pole cat."[60] Jean Loba probably learned the details from his father's constant retellings, for he was only seven when it occurred and he related it from his father's perspective.

The "we" reminiscences of adolescents were similar to those of younger emigrants. They included shared and collective memory, adult viewpoint, and information from other sources. John McBride's father and Martha Gay's (Masterson) brother kept diaries during the trek, and these writings probably triggered memories of the trail as John and Martha recorded their own experiences. H. N. Hansen from Denmark mixed his adult perspective with memories from his parents. At one time his father became weak and could not keep up with the train. One night when he did not arrive in camp, the family became alarmed. The father finally appeared and said that "he had become so tired and having being left behind, that he very near had given up in despair not thinking himself able to reach us." By following the campfires, he located his family. After relating his father's story, H. N. Hansen added his own adult observation, "I believe he would have been left and perished in the wilderness rather than having asked for the privilege of riding."[61] Other "we remember" recollections combined family and personal memories in a similar way.

CONCLUSION

While some of the twenty-three diary, journal, and letter writers discussed family members, almost all of the reminiscences included them and expressed deep feelings about parents and siblings. Diarists who made day-to-day entries

---

[60]Judd, "Sketch," 13; Loba, "Reminiscences," 8.
[61]McBride, "Overland, 1846," 28, 36; Barton, *One Woman's West*, 40; Hansen, "An Account," 765.

inserted family members here and there. By the time older pioneers narrated their childhood memories, they saw the bigger picture, albeit through adult eyes, and included the most important participants, the family. Young diarists had a new world to think and write about, and family was common to their lives. But contemporary accounts provided insights through young people's eyes.

When eleven-year-old Harriet Scott (Palmer) wrote her letters shortly after reaching Oregon, she briefly mentioned the deaths of old Flower, their cow, and their mare Sukey who "got got drowned in snake river." Yet she said nothing about her mother and brother Willie who died on the trail. In an adult reminiscence Harriet reflected upon these sad happenings. Her mother, who was not physically strong before she left Illinois, feared the perilous journey, and Harriet added, "I think as a child I partook of her feelings in this great sacrifice." If young Harriet had kept a diary, she might have voiced this childhood concern—if it truly was a concern. Instead, we learn about this qualm years later. The adult Harriet described the death and burial of family members in nostalgic terms: ". . . the passing of that dear, beloved mother was a crushing blow to all our hopes. We had to journey on and leave her, in a lonely grave. . . . The rolling hills were ablaze with beautiful wild roses—it was the 20th of June, and we heaped and covered mother's grave with the lovely roses."[62] Harriet Scott's reminiscence contained more pages, additional subjects, and adult thoughts; but her letters revealed eleven-year-old feelings and topics she chose to discuss at that moment. This was a notable difference between young pioneer diaries and letters and reminiscences written years later.

What were other common threads and differences in contemporary and reminiscent accounts that involved family relationships? From the age of five and above, pioneers noted trail responsibilities as first or second in importance to dis-

---

[62]Scott Sisters, "Letters," 159, 160; Palmer, *Crossing Over*, 1, 3.

cuss. Doing chores with siblings and caring for smaller ones were common memories, yet contemporary accounts basically ignored these. Many reminiscences recalled gathering buffalo chips, but only a few contemporary writers mentioned this task. Both types of documents discussed animals and often linked them to family members or responsibilities. While adolescent reminiscences rarely included the theme of pleasure/play, it was the second most important topic in the teenage diaries I analyzed. New adventures on the trail allured young people, and they were eager to discover them with family members. These young diarists did not carry adult burdens; parents and others supervised their trail experience. Even when tragedy struck, as in the case of Virginia Reed and Mary Murphy, they were not required to be the adult. Yet Henry Garrison and Heber McBride recalled taking adult roles. Only youngest pioneer reminiscences noted sensory, trivia, and curiosity themes, but to diary and letter writers these topics were a significant part of their daily experience. In both types of documents young emigrants discussed the illness or death of family members, both included values/religion—except youngest pioneer recollections—and both expressed fears. Though the death of family members affected one-fourth of the contemporary writers and they mourned deeply, this was one part of their trail experience and the effects of the loss were still to come. The young diarists who wrote regularly focused on happenings of a particular day and did not let one subject consume their writings. Even though contemporary records are the preferred documents for ascertaining a young emigrant's perspective of family relationships, one can gain insight into family relationships by sifting through the adult nostalgia, philosophizing, and extraneous information in childhood reminiscences and comparing "I remember" sections to actual writings of young people, for these reminiscences usually included parents and siblings.

CHAPTER IV

"My Train and I":
Diaries, Letters, Journals, Reminiscences

> *Fletcher Royals man Laurence Johnstone has become dis-*
> *satisfied. Several times lately he has been reproved and*
> *scolded in such a way that his sensitive feelings were*
> *wounded, and before they knew any thing about it, he had*
> *his clothes all packed up ready to leave. He had made*
> *arrangements to go with Mr Burns, a company travel-*
> *ing near us, but Mr Royal persuaded him not to leave our*
> *company, and so he has taken up quietly with us. He is a*
> *Swede talks quite broken, but is an good young man.*[1]

Nearly fifteen when she wrote the above entry, Rachel Taylor learned that relationships had their ups and downs on the
trail, even in a preacher's wagon train. A three- to six-month
trip half-way across the country could bind or separate individuals in a company, for human nature was the same at home
or abroad. Flora Bender wrote in her diary, "But they say on
the plains is the place to lose one's temper and 'fall out' with
the best of friends."[2] Since emigrants did not go west alone,
a successful journey required cooperation not only among family members but also with other traveling companions—
extended family, small parties, and large trains. These were
sources of support to children crossing the plains, and young
people built relationships within them. Some of these companies formed in home towns; others met at the jumping-off
places. Still others joined along the trail, and just as easily as

---

[1]Taylor, "Overland Trip," 168–169. [2]Bender, Typescript, 1.

they formed, they separated and created new traveling groups. Large companies often broke into smaller ones because big trains generated tension and took longer to reach a destination. By the 1850s, more people were traveling the overland highway; and families could easily move from one company to another or stick to smaller parties for increased privacy, mobility, and interpersonal relations. During the late 1850s and 1860s, groups formed more loosely for protection against such dangers as threats from Native Americans. Trains provided safety and camaraderie on the trail, but families also traveled as self-sufficient entities. As a result, there was no way to enforce meaningful discipline, and with men's individualistic attitudes divisions occurred. If leaders proved incompetent, fell out of favor, or lacked support, they usually relinquished their position or were replaced. Many emigrants, however, tried to select leaders who were experienced on the trail. Some of the earlier trains hired guides, but most were just that--guides. Andrew Sublette quit his job after taking a company to Independence, Missouri, and "despairing of ever preserving order and discipline." According to Merrill Mattes, Oregon trains with family ties held together better than those going to California for gold.[3]

MORMON TRAINS

In contrast to Oregon and California companies, Mormon trains were larger and systematically organized into hundreds, fifties, and tens with a captain over each and a disciplinary policy set by church leaders. This type of organization was altered slightly over the years and not always strictly observed. But emigrants believed they were led by God through His designated leaders, and they generally obeyed counsel and followed train rules. If they did not, offenses might be punishable by material and church penalties.[4] In his 1862 diary, James

---

[3]Mattes, *Great Platte*, 32–36.

McKnight described the organization of the train in which he and Lucy Canfield traveled.

> <u>Monday, July 28, 1862</u>. In the evening of this day a meeting was held on the camp-ground near Florence, Nebraska Territory, at which Joseph W. Young presided, and Apostle, Amasa M. Lyman was also present. After a few appropriate remarks by Elder Young, Isaac A. Canfield was unanimously chosen captain of the company, William C. Neal, Sergeant of the Guard, James McKnight, Chaplain and Clerk, and Christopher Dickson, Captain of the first Ten.
>
> <u>Tuesday, July 29</u>. We assembled for further organization at Florence. Joseph C. Stickney was chosen as captain of the second Ten and Milan Russell as captain of the third Ten.

Train leaders were often "sustained" in traditional Mormon fashion with members voting to accept the man designated by church authorities, in this case Isaac Canfield, and then following his instructions on the trail. Other candidates might be nominated by emigration agents, church leaders, or the people themselves. Sometimes the person directing the voyage from England continued as captain across the plains. Most leaders of later trains had made the overland journey at least once and were familiar with the route.

After commencing on the trail, James McKnight wrote, "The camp was aroused by the blowing of horns at 5:30 a.m. At the breakfast we had singing and prayer as usual." Mormon companies usually began and ended the day with singing, prayer, and instructions. In another entry McKnight said,

> After breakfast we convened in a grove near the camp and held a meeting, in which Captain Canfield gave us some directions regarding the observance of the Sabbath, interdit[c]hing, hunting, fishing, etc., He advised all, except the guards to stay in or near the camp when the company rested on the Sabbath, whenever it was consistent to do so. The Chaplain requested a prompt attendance at camp devotions in the mornings and evenings.

Later that day he added,

---

[4]According to Bashore, "Pioneer Companies," some Mormon trains contained four hundred to six hundred people. See also Taylor, "Mormon Crossing," 327–328, and *Deseret News Church Almanac*, 166–176. Kimball, *Historic Resource*, 18–19, discusses discipline in Mormon trains.

We spread a large awning and held meeting at 6 p.m., at which remarks were made by Captain Canfield, Elder J. J. M. Butler and Chaplain James McKnight. Profane swearing and cruelty to animals were deprecated, and obedience and resignation to the will and providence of God, and the counsels of his servants, were urged.

At another camp meeting "after singing and prayer, the Captain and Chaplain spoke against killing snakes on the road, and exhorted the brethren to diligently cherish the spirit of peace."[5]

Mormon pioneers crossed the plains in three types of companies: church funded, independent, and private. Church-funded groups included Perpetual Emigrating Fund (PEF), Ten Pound, handcart, and down-and-back trains. These emigrants received assistance for part or all of their travel from the church. Occasionally individual members helped finance those without the means. Families traveling in independent trains paid their own way but were usually organized and dispatched by church agents. Private companies included freighting, non-Mormon, and Mormon groups.[6] According to 271 L.D.S. accounts, most children and adolescents who emigrated with one or no parents traveled in church and independent trains and built relationships within them.

Mormons had several challenges that travelers on other trails did not. First, the people were generally poorer than those who went to Oregon or California. During the 1850s and 1860s, missionary work spread through northern Europe, particularly in England and Scandinavia, and new members were instructed to gather to Zion. Many converts did not have the financial means to do so. Between 1849 and 1857, more than fifteen thousand British Saints crossed to Utah, often with assistance from the church's PEF which supervised funds,

---

[5]Journal History, 16 Oct. 1862, 1–2, 5.
[6]Bashore and Haslam identified many of the pioneer companies in "Mormon Pioneer Companies." Bashore estimated numbers traveling in these companies in "Pioneer Companies." See also *Deseret News Church Almanac*, 167–176; Ludlow, *Encyclopedia*, 673–675; Arrington and Bitton, *Mormon Experience*, 129–136; Arrington, *Great Basin*, 98–101.

Mormon Encampment in Wyoming, Nebraska, 1866, by Charles R. Savage. *Courtesy of L.D.S. Church Archives, Salt Lake City, Utah.*

loaned money, and directed migration. Church members who paid their own way received help as well. PEF agents chartered ships or sections of ships at cheaper rates for European Saints to sail to America. Agents arranged travel to the jumping-off place and helped organize the trek to Utah at reduced costs. Those who borrowed from the PEF were expected to pay it back after they settled in the West. When funds grew low, Brigham Young instigated handcart travel, but this cheap mode of getting to Zion had several drawbacks: pioneers could not take many belongings with them, emigrants suffered when they became weak or ill and could not ride, and they often lacked proper food and clothing for the long trek on foot. During the 1860s, Brigham Young used down-and-back church trains to get the Saints across the plains as cheaply as possible. Wagons with Utah oxen and flour headed east from Salt

Lake City to Florence, Nebraska, in the spring of the year; then they acquired passengers and eastern goods and transported them back to Utah in the fall. The same wagons and teams completed the six-month round trip, which saved purchasing outfits in Nebraska. The young diarist Thomas Griggs was a member of one of the church's first down-and-back trains.[7]

A second problem confronting Mormons was the lack of skills and experience among Europeans to deal with oxen, tools, weapons, wagon repairs, and outdoor living. Most British converts came from industrialized regions, but even those from rural areas lacked skills for trail travel. Scandinavians with farm backgrounds could handle teams, but others had limited or no experience. James Lindsay from Scotland remembered waiting for the down-and-back trains to arrive. "It was a strange sight to us when they did come. We had never seen oxen and men driving them with their long whips and shouting, 'Whoa, Ha, and Gee.'" The journey was "very trying" because of heat, dust, and wind. "We did our cooking in skillets over smokey fires and slept in tents with ten to fifteen men, women, and children. Flour and bacon was about all the food we had." Hyrum Weech from England thought "it was amusing to see the way the teams were herded along. Very few of the company had ever driven cattle before." Early on the trail "some of the steers ran around and broke several wagon tongues and then the people had to cut a green tree and put in a new tongue, and they did not get into camp until way in the night." While many Americans knew what to take and how to use it, European Mormons required assistance from outfitting centers or PEF agents. These pioneers reached the Missouri River after weeks of travel by ship, steamboat, and train without getting exercise.[8] They were not conditioned to walk the many miles,

---

[7]See Bergera, *B. H. Roberts*, 4; Allen and Leonard, *Story of L.D.S.*, 279–287; Kimball, *Historic Resource*, 10; Hartley, "Florence Fitout," 345–347; Hartley, "Down–and Back," 23–34.

[8]Lindsay, "History," 2; Weech, "Autobiography," 2–3; Taylor, *Expectations*, 225.

especially when large numbers of women, children, and older folks crossed the plains and food was sometimes rationed near the end. Conditions of the trail, such as early snowfalls and river crossings, perplexed inexperienced travelers as well.

A third problem Mormons faced was the language barrier among European converts. Christian Christensen from Denmark wondered, "How they managed such a babble of tongues is more than ordinary mortals can tell. Danes, Swedes, Norwegians, German and English, and none of them had ever seen an ox team in their lives before. It must have been a stupendous undertaking."[9] The church's assimilation process helped combat this obstacle. According to William Mulder, "Mormonism produced a break with the convert's past, separating him from mother church, fatherland, and native tongue." Preparations for this break began before members left for America. Classes in English, religion, and writing were often held on Sundays before church, and later on board ship members were organized into well-ordered communities where English instruction continued.[10] Many European converts journeyed with members who spoke their native tongue, and sometimes returning missionaries interpreted what was spoken in English. This assistance relieved some anxiety--but not for all foreign emigrants. Mary Ann Williams (Jenkins) from Wales was almost left behind when her railroad car started moving before she was ready. "I often wondered what would have happened had I been left behind because I couldn't speak a word of English." During the entire six- to nine-month journey, European converts were being assimilated into the Mormon religion and culture. Charles Nibley from Scotland remembered that at Florence, Nebraska, "I first began to get the least insight into Mormonism and Mormon methods. Meetings were held regularly, hymns sung everywhere and

---

[9]Christensen, "Leaves," 2.
[10]See Mulder, "Scandinavian," 147–149, and Mulder, "Mormons from Scandinavia," 235, 236, 239.

oft and the religious enthusiasm and spirit of the people were entirely different from what we had left behind in the east." When weary pioneers reached Zion, the Saints gave them a hearty welcome and sometimes a feast, then helped them merge into their new society.[11]

TRAIN MEMBER RELATIONSHIPS IN DIARIES, LETTERS, JOURNALS

Whether Mormon or non-Mormon, American or European, pioneers who traveled together provided safety and security and met the social needs of young and old. Sometimes relatives and neighbors from the same hometown accompanied each other on the trail. A wagon train became a temporary community with births, deaths, religious worship, individual and group chores, neighborly visits, artisan and medical assistance, and social life.[12] Young people had plenty of friends and associates with whom to play, visit, and explore their new world. They traveled and slept in crowded wagons and tents and walked on congested trails, but many families were accustomed to small quarters, several children to a bed, and little privacy.

What did young people say about relationships with extended family and other members of their trains? Most of the twenty-three diary, letter, and journal writers which I studied were adolescents. G. Stanley Hall, the founder of American developmental psychology, noted that adolescents have strong social instincts and a desire for excitement and groups beyond the nuclear family. Born in 1844, Hall was a contemporary of these young pioneers, and he may have gleaned some ideas about adolescence from his own time period.[13] The diary

---

[11]Martin and Carpenter, *Samaritans*, 140; Olson, "Proselytism," 196–198; Nibley, *Reminiscences*, 17.
[12]Burgess, "Migrant Women," 67.
[13]Kett, *Rites of Passage*, 217, 220; Irwin and Simons, *Lifespan*, 246, 288; Berger, *Developing Person*, 331–332; Berk, *Child Development*, 8; Johnson and Malone, *Dictionary*, 129–130.

and letter writers, some of whom were Hall's age, described relationships within their trains. With a dearth of male diaries, it is difficult to read the thoughts of young male pioneers. But of these twenty-three accounts, age of companions did not seem especially important, although most associated with individuals near their age or older. Few mentioned younger children. Major themes discussed in order frequency were: responsibilities, pleasure/play, animals, discord, illness/death, and values/religion. Minor topics were accidents/pain, fear, and literacy. Writing about responsibilities and pleasant experiences far outnumbered other topics.

All of the young writers at least mentioned train members, and the majority wrote extensively about them, more than about their families. People in their companies helped each other with guard and camp duties, transportation tasks, animal care, food and water procurement, river crossings, road and bridge building, burials, and sundry other chores; they also socialized and quarreled. In traveling communities families could not be as self-contained and private as they were on farms back home, but these young writers seemed to fancy their new associations. Even so, at times they needed their space to read, write letters or diary entries, and investigate their surroundings alone. Their nineteenth-century culture followed them with female interpersonal relationships and gender division of labor—although work boundaries sometimes blurred. Flora Bender watched four men perform female duties and could not "help laughing to see them cooking and washing dishes."[14] In a few of the female diaries the personalities of certain train members evolved as the girls made entries along the trail. The only letter writer who included train members to any extent was Virginia Reed in her letter from California after many of the Donner party died. How were train relationships portrayed in these diaries, letters, and journals?

---

[14]Bender, Typescript, 3.

Male and Female Writings

According to John Mack Faragher, men's diaries contained action and generalizations, whereas women talked about people and interpersonal closeness. Such differences conformed to their social and cultural lives of the time.[15] Of twenty-three diary, letter, and journal writers, the few boys and almost all of the girls followed this pattern. William Pace did not discuss personal relationships in his Mormon Battalion company; instead, he stated general facts about the group except when he wrote about the last part of the trek as an adult. Then he volunteered information about his companions. Near Wood River, Nebraska, a mule gave out and the starving men "agreed to make a supper out of the old Jack." So "Abraham Huntsucker Elisha Averett & others with a gun and knives a marching to the field of Battle" made quick work of the animal and prepared it for eating. A few men "stood off and would not partake while others piched into it like as many raveous wolves Devouring their prey."[16]

Patrick Murphy wrote impersonally about the fellows in his stock train. They were co-workers and remained nameless in his diary. One man was thrown off his mule and injured. Others lost their way while hunting during the coldest night of the season. Their "negro cook" became ill, rode in Murphy's wagon, "and was very well churned before we got through" a canyon and river. Once Murphy inferred adolescent apprehension when he took his turn as night guard. The other guard had fallen asleep, "and I could not find him, as the night was very dark; I rolled up in my blanket and reclined under a sage bush until morning." Near the Nevada desert, Murphy could not sleep "as I kept thinking of crossing the desert. I was driving a team, so I took the place of one of the guards." He may have heard gruesome stories about that stretch of trail—pos-

---

[15]Faragher, *Women and Men*, 129–133. See also Schlissel, *Women's Diaries*, 14.
[16]Pace, "Diary," 33–34.

sibly from men in his own company—and his youthful anx-
ieties kept him awake.[17]

While William Pace and Patrick Murphy traveled with
small, all-men contingents, Thomas Griggs and Andrew Jenson went to Utah in large down-and-back trains. In his diary
Griggs mentioned a friendship with Brothers Paxman and
Paye and noted church leaders who visited camp, but he never
talked about his peers in a company of over four hundred emigrants. Yet Zebulon Jacobs, three years his senior and a teamster in another down-and-back train that year, shared a
youthful tidbit: "As we woke up in the morning all hands began
laughing at each other, as our faces were besmeared with tar
and wagon grease. Some of the boys from the other camp had
paid us a visit and left their compliments upon our faces." Did
Thomas Griggs participate in escapades such as these? When
he stated that the "travel worn teamsters and emigrants" held
a grand ball with "all enjoying themselves well," one wonders
if Griggs danced with some fine young ladies.[18]

Just as none of the male diarists detailed personal relationships with train members, neither did Andrew Jenson in his
journal. In one entry an anonymous young man lagged behind
the others leisurely eating wild berries. That evening the night
guard searched for him, and at prayer meeting the captain gave
strict orders for all emigrants to keep up with the train. Even
though Jenson's entries were impersonal, he noted general relationships among old and young, European and American
Mormons. Young foreigners adjusted to life on the plains more
easily than older overlanders or adults with large families. Lack
of fuel and water, meals seasoned with rain and wind, and other
challenges taxed their energies. "But we soon learned to look
upon these things as the unavoidable difficulties of crossing
the plains with teams, and we bore them without murmur or
faultfinding." To alleviate the language barrier in their com-

---

[17]Murphy, "Across the Plains Diary," 2, 5, 7, 11, 13.
[18]Journal History, 23 Sept. 1861, 7–8; Griggs, "Crossing the Plains," 39.

pany, a Norwegian missionary interpreted the captain's remarks. Before reaching Utah, fifteen-year-old Andrew had "learned sufficient of the English language to feel quite independent of such translations, though as yet I could speak but very little."[19] These comments, however, were made with Jenson's adult hindsight and not from adolescent insight.

Although most of the young female diarists adhered to Faragher's observation of women discussing interpersonal relationships, most of Sallie Hester's entries about fellow travelers were impersonal. Her missionary train to California started out with 134 men and many women and children, yet she provided no mental picture of individuals. Traveling in such a large company, did Sallie make friends with other girls? Her adolescent feelings about friendships did appear in two entries, however. In Wyoming, she climbed Devil's Gate with her brother, younger sister, and the preacher's son and noted that "this mountain" was "somewhat perilous for youngsters not over fourteen," which was approximately her age. Then Sallie added,

> We made our way to the very edge of the cliff and looked down. We could hear the water dashing, splashing and roaring as if angry at the small space through which it was forced to pass. We were gone so long that the train was stopped and men sent out in search of us. We made all sorts of promises to remain in sight in the future.

Then a month later "some of our company left us, all young men. They were jolly, merry fellows and gave life to our lonely evenings. We all miss them very much. Some had violins, others guitars, and some had fine voices, and they always had a good audience. They were anxious to hurry on without the Sunday stops."[20]

In contrast to Sallie Hester's few notations about train members, other female diarists discussed friends and extended family. Eliza McAuley included them throughout her diary. The

---

[19] Jenson, "Journals," 73–74, 75, 82.
[20] Purdy, "Isaac Owen," 49; Hester, "Diary," 238–240.

young Meeker family joined her company, and Eliza wrote that "Margaret and Mrs Meeker are washing today, and I am to get dinner for the boys, and take care of little Dick," the Meeker's baby. In another entry, everyone "gathered in Ezra's tent this evening and had a merry time." Later, Ezra Meeker was "very sick with the mountain fever, but is better now." Eliza also talked about "the boys" who accompanied them. "While out with the cattle, the boys caught a little antelope and brought it to camp. We have named it Jenny," and it remained with them for over a month until it was accidently killed. Eliza's sister Margaret made "some cakes, but the boys steal them as fast as she can bake them." The boys "discovered a pass by which the mountain can be avoided," so their small company stopped for a couple of weeks to build a road. They found "thickets of wild currants," which the boys chopped down and "we" made jelly, currant wine, vinegar, and pie.[21] In her diary Rachel Taylor talked about Mary Royal, the minister's twenty-year-old daughter. The friends rode horseback and "had a very pleasant time. We tried to reach the timber but could not." Another day "Mary and I undertook to climb one of the highest and steepest mountains that we could see," and the teams and wagons "looked very diminutive and 'beneath our notice.' The hillside is covered with evergreens intermingled with flowers of different kinds. A beautiful place, and we would love to stay longer but the advancing train reminds us that we must be hurrying forward." One Sunday in July, Mary was "quite unwell to day, but better towards evening and able to walk around."[22]

Ada Millington had quite a bit to say about train members, but some of the details may not have been in her original diary. Thirteen-year-old Ada associated with her eleven-year-old cousin Fred and occasionally her aunt, uncle, and younger cousins. Near South Pass she and Fred walked ahead of the

[21]McAuley, Diary, 20, 27, 31, 50, 51, 53–54.
[22]Taylor, "Overland Trip," 161, 167, 170–171.

wagons "till we got rather tired and still the wagons did not come in sight, so we stopped and built a little rock chimney. Went on apiece and built another, and still farther and built a third." Then Ada's father met them, and they climbed in the wagon and rode. The writer also related anecdotes about other members of her company. The hired men were washing clothes in the creek, and Jake Shontz "discovered what he thought was a beaver. On punching it with a pole it proved to be one of his flannel shirts." When her dog Watch got lost, Ada's half-brother rode to the Sweetwater Station to inquire about him and "learned that a dog answering to the description of ours had been there but was gone again." Two weeks later, Mr. Ream, a fellow in their train, was tending the horses and felt something jump on him. He turned around and saw the dog. "Watch was so glad he nearly eat him up." Mr. Ream "brought him to camp, and . . . there was great commotion in that tent. Watch would go first from one to another," and train members were just as excited to see him.[23]

Discord

Besides describing friendships and positive relations, frustration and contention crept into some of the writings. Unhappy California and Oregon trail pioneers left one group and joined another, for emigrants were not only "joiners" but also "separatists." Competition, strength, and steadiness of character were characteristics of nineteenth-century masculine culture. Men quarreled over which trail to take, whose wagon should go first, how fast the company should travel, whether or not they should make Sunday stops, and a number of other reasons. Much of the dissension occurred during the last half of the journey when food supplies decreased and people grew weary. Arguments erupted as a result of tension, anxiety, and pride, then progressed to fights, train divisions, and occasionally death. According to John Mack Faragher,

---

[23]Millington, "Journal," 218, 228, 231, 234.

fist fights were common on the trail, and many adult diarists noted them, with women writers shaking their fingers in disapproval. From my observations, adolescent writers sat by and watched male disputes, then recorded what happened, sometimes with personal opinions. Young females occasionally wrote about their own spats with friends where they ignored each other, then became chummy again. At Ash Hollow in Nebraska, Patrick Murphy reported a confrontation without elaborating: "Two of our boys had a fight here but no one was injured." Three weeks later "at the last camp, there were several of us going to leave the train because we were dissatisfied with their traveling."[24] The other male diarists said nothing about quarreling and divisions, but with so few male diaries it is difficult to make generalizations.

The girl writers, on the other hand, described such scenes in some detail. At times Rachel Taylor seemed exasperated with her Uncle Sylvester because his overloaded wagon kept getting stuck in the mud. Finally, to everyone's satisfaction, her uncle purchased another wagon and divided his load. When a hired man and Reverend Royal's nephew talked about leaving the company, Rachel Taylor supposed "there will not be many tears shed even if such should be the case." A few days later, Blake "picked up his 'duds'" and "bid us all a kind farewell." But that did not end their troubles. Two of Reverend Royal's nephews threatened to go, and Phil, one of the hired hands "who every day gives some evidence of his weak mind, thinks he will leave if they do. We know no cause for this resolution." They "made a treaty of peace," but another quarrel festered because "Will sold his Uncle a yoke of cattle and now refuses to give them up. He used abusive language to his Uncle and aunt and finally went to Burts" wagon. Soon Phil caused trouble again and was "profane and bad tempered. We have treated him just as well as we know how, but he has

---

[24]Schlissel, *Women's Diaries*, 25, 89; Faragher, *Women and Men*, 101–102; Murphy, "Across the Plains Diary," 3, 4.

his seasons of anger without any cause." Most of their problems resulted from the younger men becoming hot-tempered and dissatisfied. Near the end of the journey with provisions dwindling, some of the company wanted to travel on the Sabbath, but "Father Royal says he will not put a yoke on one of his oxen on Sunday."[25]

Like Rachel Taylor, Edith Lockhart complained about contention in her train, although she did not elaborate. When "Mr Stanley and Scott had a little dispute," Edith did not explain what it was. Three days after her group left the main body, "Capt Davis invited us to rejoin the train, as they had a split up yesterday----The Burlington Boys and Gates having got into a scrape with the German settlers causing quite a disturbance. The rest of the train withdrew from them." Two weeks later "Mr Stanley and Dobie had a little quarrel this evening." Then Mr. Winn and Mr. Dobie were told to leave the train at Fort Laramie. Edith's company continued to split up, get back together, and combine with others. Internal conflict seemed to be the norm for these travelers. Near the Humboldt River "Mr Stanley and Dobie had a quarrel today----no one seriously hurt." But the next day "as we passed the first wagons of the Hall train, Mr Stanley was shot through the right breast, by Wm Dobie----he lived about an hour and a half." Even then, Edith Lockhart did not explain what promoted the killing. A week later "Bill Dobie was brought in at Midnight," and they "talked of having a trial but done nothing with him." Edith's account makes readers scratch their heads and wish for additional details about her train's discord.[26]

Mary Warner also noted disharmony within her train. "Ben got mad and left our company (to the great joy of all) and hired Mr. Hageboom to take him as far as Salt Lake." In eastern Nevada, tensions mounted and "one of the boys refused to do something which he was asked to do, which caused some trou-

[25]Taylor, "Overland Trip," 154, 160, 166, 171, 173, 175.
[26]Humphrey, "Original Diary," 4, 5, 6, 8, 13, 14.

ble." Mr. Lord was asked to help settle the conflict, and he "rather upheld the boy, which made the matter worse. Pa (who was taking charge of the train) refused to do so any longer, and Uncle Chester would not." So Mr. Lord agreed to lead. The company stopped at noon, and "as Mrs. Lord ordered dinner cooked it was done." Relationships continued to disintegrate until the train separated, and the trek became a race to see which of the two divisions would reach Austin, Nevada, first. Mary reported, "As soon as they saw us coming, they hitched up, and started just before we got there." They stopped to eat, so "we passed them and camped a mile this side of them and started before they did." When both parties rested, "we did not pay much attention to them, <u>especially</u> Mrs. Lord." Finally, Mary Warner's division traveled all night and arrived in Austin first.[27]

The Feminine Culture

Flora Bender and Mary Warner discussed both positive and negative relationships in their diaries while imitating nineteenth-century ideals of womanhood. Religious beliefs of their time emphasized women as the "heart" who should sympathize, love, nurture, show tenderness and compassion, and not strive for status or achievement. Women's lives revolved around the family and also other females during such times as birthing, nursing the sick, and preparing the dead. Being the "heart" suggested that they needed interpersonal associations with each other since men did not understand their feelings. Only a woman could know the heart of a woman, and females relied on each other for emotional expression and introspection.[28] Like their adult counterparts, "girls often came to see each other as sisters in deeply spiritual and emotional ways, tied together by almost sacred bonds of friendship and mutual religiosity." Such attitudes initiated them into a "woman-defined culture."

---

[27]Warner, "Diary," 15, 22–25.

[28]Cott, *Bonds*, 164, 168, 173, 185–186. See also Faragher, *Women and Men*, 122, 126.

One practical application of this culture was "calling" or visiting, a custom which had been popular since at least the eighteenth century. Pioneer women and girls visited each other as they rode, walked ahead of the wagons, went on short excursions, and met at each other's campsite.[29]

During adolescence friendships are quite complicated, and friends want common interests, compatible personalities, and interdependence. Throughout her diary Flora Bender shared nineteenth-century female culture, adolescent friendships and moodiness, and train relationships. Near the beginning of the trek "Mr. Marvin's train passed us and Mary came up to see Nellie . . . I do hope we will catch up with them and travel with them for Mary is such a nice girl." The two groups formed a company of twelve wagons, and Flora wrote, "I am so glad we are come together." On Sunday she "went over to Teachont's tent. Nothing would do but I must sing. So I went and got Nell and Mary Marvin and we had some melodious singing." Flora Bender revealed adolescent emotions as she discussed train members. "Nellie went up to Marvin's but I was too mad & cross to go with her. Mary came back with her, she is just as friendly as ever." Flora did not explain why she was upset. She also said, "There is one girl here of my age, but I don't like her much. How I wish I had some of my Bell Creek friends here tonight." Flora's attitude about a woman in her company surfaced when she wrote, "Mrs. Hopson is dreadful mum, didn't have anything to say. Mary Marvin is the only one that I care much about."

Problems arose when several wagons went ahead in search of grass and the others disapproved. Flora Bender inserted her own—and Shakespeare's—opinion about the situation. "I hope it will be all over in a few days, for we had such a nice company, and it is too bad to be broken up in this kind of a style. But it was not our fault . . . and what's the use of mak-

---

[29]Boylan, "Growing Up," 172; Watson, "Cult of Domesticity," 26. See also Jeffrey, *Frontier Women*, 41.

ing such an ado about nothing." The train divided, and rumors flew that Mr. Marvin was "secesh," an enemy to the republic, and had run away from the Civil War.[30] At Fort Laramie a soldier asked Flora Bender if someone in their train was secesh, and "I, like a dunce, told him I had heard Marvin was but could not vouch for the truth of the story." Feeling guilty about tattling, she confessed to her diary, "He asked me and I couldn't lie." Mr. Marvin was arrested for hiding a deserter, and Flora wrote, "Poor Mary Marvin I care more for than all the rest. Mary said she would write to us at Virginia City." Marvin was later released, and his family continued westward. By then Flora's group had joined another train in which the people seemed "cold and distant, only one lady has called on us, a Mrs. Clayton." Women who did not go "calling" were considered snobbish. Flora added with nineteenth-century propriety, "I shall never speak to those girls till they speak to me. I only know one - Becky McCutchin - got acquainted with her coming down a big hill. She spoke first though - I'll assure you." Flora Bender's company continued with a join-and-separate attitude for the rest of the journey, but whenever Marvin's train camped nearby, Flora renewed her friendship with Mary.[31]

Although Mary Warner was the same age as Flora Bender, her writings did not display adolescent moodiness, but they did contain female culture and relationships. Her closest friend was her father's sister Celia, who appeared to be unmarried and possibly quite young. Together they rode horseback or in a carriage, drove a team, sketched the landscape, walked ahead of the wagons, and discovered their surroundings. In the Black Hills of Wyoming, Mary Warner and Aunt Celia "went down a very steep hill into a ravine where the bluffs above our heads nearly touched. We followed the ravine until we came to the

---

[30]Bender, Typescript, 3, 4. Mattes, *Platte River*, 558, provided the definition for "secesh," or secessionist.
[31]Bender, Typescript, 6, 9; Watson, "Cult of Domesticity," 26.

road when we climbed the hill with the rest. By this time we were nearly tired out and when the teams overtook us we rode in the wagons and I went to sleep and had something to eat and felt better." Another day "Mrs. Hayward, Fannie, Aunt Celia and I visited Split Rock . . . We went upon the highest point and did not reach camp until dark." In Nevada, "Aunt Celia, Aunt Lizzie, Libbie and I went on ahead" to Mammoth City, a town with twelve houses, where "about a hundred chickens followed us. We went a little further and fifteen or twenty pigs followed us till we were out of sight of the town."[32] The adolescent must have built a close bond with Aunt Celia; she also associated with other ladies in her train. Mary did not include her mother in her activities, but her mother was probably busy with three other children and trail responsibilities until their father met them in Salt Lake City. Perhaps the fifteen year old purposely sought friendships outside her immediate family since this was characteristic of her age.

Train Member Relationships in Reminiscences

Children who crossed the plains and later wrote reminiscences described "I remember" relationships with extended family and other train members, but age of travel and maturation played a role in what and how much they recalled. Older pioneer children elaborated on experiences, and youngsters who journeyed without parents provided additional information about people in their trains. Unlike the boys' diaries, male memoirs frequently included relationships with train members. But none of the reminiscences revealed personalities from a young person's perspective quite like the female diaries did.

"I Remember"—Ages One Through Six

Youngest emigrants had few memories about individuals

---

[32]Warner, "Diary," Introduction, 9, 13, 26. Schlissel in *Women's Diaries*, 135, said that Aunt Celia was a married lady, but the introduction to Warner's diary does not confirm this. Perhaps Schlissel mistook Uncle Chester's new wife Libbie for Celia.

outside the immediate family. Only one-third mentioned "I remember" encounters with people in their trains, and these involved themes of trauma/fear (52%), pleasure (26%), care/security (11%), and pain (11%). This agrees with twentieth-century research studies in which fear and pleasure are the most common early memories from childhood. No three-year-old pioneer related incidents with train members, and only two four-year-old emigrants did. Child development experts remind us that the family is most important to little children, not external relationships. Clearly, five- and six-year-old emigrants provided the snapshots, but they sometimes seasoned them with shared or collective memory.

Youngsters most often remembered trauma/fear themes with train members. They were afraid of river crossings, thunderstorms with animal stampedes, and gun accidents. As six-year-old Catherine Anderson (Ross) watched her father carry her mother across the Platte, "I let out a scream, because the river looked so wicked to me. The teamster, Brother Albert Shales, quieted me some, but no sooner had he pacified me until Father slipped and fell with Mother, but soon recovered himself." With adult embellishment Benjamin Bonney remembered a terrible storm, but one wonders how much he actually saw through six-year-old eyes. "The thunder seemed almost incessant, and the lightning was so brilliant you could read by its flashes." Oxen bellowed, children cried, men shouted, and thunder rolled "like a constant salvo of artillery; with everything as light as day from the lightning flashes and the next second as black as the depth of the pit."[33]

A few youngsters recalled fear from gun accidents. Five-year-old David Bulloch was playing in his wagon with two siblings and a loaded gun. The gun "accidentally went off. The bullet passed through a feather bed we had, through the hind end of our wagon and just grazed Brother Stoddard's head." Brother Stoddard "was standing near his own wagon" but

---

[33]Butcher, *Hakan Anderson*, 416; Lockley, *Across the Plains*, 3.

immediately came to assess the situation. "He found the wagon full of smoke and feathers and David frightened nearly to death." Sarah Zaring (Howard), age five, recalled a man returning from a hunting trip and exclaiming that one of their party "had accidentally killed himself by letting his revolver fall from his belt." The victim's son, age five or six, "clapped his hands and excitedly said: 'Oh, goodie, goodie, goodie! I'll get dad's old jack-knife!'" Sarah "never forgot how that boy looked. I can see him yet." Youngest children are literal and live in the immediate present; as a result, their reactions to situations like death may seem strange and even distorted.[34] At the time neither Sarah nor the little boy understood the full impact of what had occurred.

The second theme youngest emigrants recalled with train members was pleasure. Manomas Gibson (Andrus) described a woman who "rode in a carriage, not like the wagons the rest of us had, and sang all day long, 'On the Road to California.' This old lady churned and made butter as she rode along. I can't recall her name, but she seemed happy." The driver of Mary Creighton's wagon had an "endless supply of old English and Scotch ballads which he trolled out by the hour to his own comfort and my delight." Young children ate their evening meal by the campfire, then listened to stories or watched fiddles appear for people to sing and dance. Mary Ann Chapple (Warner) heard tales around the campfire, but they did not always bring pleasure. "So terrorizing were some of these stories, that I could hardly move. After the evening prayer, when silence claimed the camp and everybody was asleep, I often lay awake, afraid to even close my eyes."[35]

Two children related care/security incidents in which they depended upon adults. Christian Christensen from Denmark recalled the kind acts of an old German gentleman in his com-

---

[34]Carter, *Pioneer Heritage*, 18: 216; Howard, "Crossing the Plains," 2; Irwin and Simons, *Lifespan*, 476–478; Young, *Life Among the Giants*, 71.

[35]Genealogical Society, *Utah Pioneer*, 3: 199; Creighton, "To My Grandchildren," 4; Federal Writers Project, "Mary Ann," 3.

pany. After Christian's father died on the trail from a gun accident, the old German walked ahead of the train with the little boy. They became companions without understanding each other's language, and the old man "provided me a lunch each day and I shall never forget the many times he would say, 'Du haf en gut fadder.'" Six-year-old Francis Donner (Wilder) mentioned a Mr. Stanton from their train who went on to California, then returned to assist the Donner party out of the mountains. He brought a few provisions, and "Patty Reed came round with her apron full of buiscuits, & gave one a peice to the children." In his attempt to rescue his friends, Mr. Stanton lost his own life.[36]

Two other children had snapshot memories that involved emotional or physical pain with train members. Peter McBride of the Martin handcart company was starving, and "they gave me a bone of an oxen that died. I cut off the skin, put the bone in the fire to roast. When it was done, some big boys came and ran away with it."[37] Ann Wilden (Johnson) was walking barefoot when her train left the road to camp. "The great prairie was covered with thick high grass, and hidden underneath the grass was cactus." The cactus thorns poked into the child's bare feet, so she sat down to pull them out, and they stuck in her hands.

> The wagon soon got so far ahead of me that I was sure I was lost. The people behind did not know of the cactus and thought I was lingering because I had gotten into a stubborn spell. In a short time, which seemed like hours to me, my brother came for me on horseback. After my thorny condition was discovered and doctored, I was petted and comforted.[38]

This basic memory came through a child's eyes—the painful thorns, the dilemma of having them attack both feet and hands,

---

[36]Christensen, "Leaves," 4–5. Christensen's quote means, "You have a good father." Wilder, "Letters," April 17, 1879.

[37]Carter, *Pioneer Heritage* 13: 362. One should remember that the accounts published in the DUP volumes *Treasures*, *Heart Throbs*, *Enduring Legacy*, and *Chronicles* may have been paraphrased or edited from the originals.

[38]King, "Long Journey," 9; see Young, *Life Among the Giants*, 77, for insights into young children's perceptions.

the reaction by train members, the fear of being lost, and the feeling that it took hours to be rescued when time to a small child is the immediate present.

"I Remember"—Ages Seven Through Twelve

While only a third of the youngest pioneers recalled "I remember" memories of people in their companies, over half of the children, ages seven through twelve, who emigrated with one or two parents did. This logically follows the developmental pattern for their age. These young pioneers expanded their horizons outside the family. Major themes in order of frequency were: pleasure/play, fear and animals, responsibilities and illness/death, and values/religion. Sometimes several of these themes wove through one experience.

Middle-year emigrants most frequently described pleasure/play relationships with train members, for pioneer children found time to play. Young people this age have a sense of awe and wonder about life, and play is a means for learning and problem-solving. Middle-year youngsters begin to enter two worlds, the adult's and their peers', and pioneers related stories about both. With fondness they remembered adults who shared their wagons, drove their teams, and displayed interesting personalities. Jesse Applegate slept in a tent with an old man the family had adopted years earlier and named "Uncle Mack." Snuggled next to Uncle Mack probably helped seven-year-old Jesse feel safe. Eleven-year-old Margaret West (Irvin) was intrigued by their French driver who caught bullfrogs and cooked the legs. "We children liked them, or thought we did, at least we enjoyed the fun of it, but mother did not like frog legs and would not sample them. I can just remember the face she made."[39]

Some adults were interesting enough that ten- through twelve-year-old emigrants inserted them in their memoirs. Lucy Henderson (Deady) wrote that a Mr. Smith reluctantly threw

---

[39]Applegate, *Recollections*, 14; Adams, "Covered Wagon," 12.

away his rolling pin when the company was forced to discard extra weight. "I shall never forget how that big man stood there with tears streaming down his face" because the rolling pin belonged to his mother and he could not part with it. Catherine Camp (Greer) recalled a funny couple from England who

> had a little two wheeled cart and one little bull to pull it. They called him "Bullie," and whenever we would start out in the morning he would start to "boo" like a bull, and when they came to a creek he would wade all around in the water with them. They had a tent and everything they wanted, and all done up in that cart, and one day, we had a stampede and this little fellow run right after them and going "Boo-oo, boo-oo," but he did not get scared, but just followed them all around and over the sod and that old couple couldn't do a thing with him. . . . I never saw anything as good to mis-behave sometimes, as "Bullie."[40]

Middle-year pioneers especially enjoyed pleasant times with peers. Children this age sometimes segregate themselves according to gender, with girls cooperating and expressing feelings and boys playing physical, competitive games. Typical for their age group, some young emigrants imitated adult behavior and division of labor through their play. Mrs. John Gowdy and her playmates cooked dough and slices of bacon on a small fire, and with "a tin cup of coffee" they "spread it all out on the dusty grass or leaves" and had "a fine spread."[41] Other children enjoyed active times with peers. Ten-year-old Sarah Palmer (Sharp) associated with about a dozen boys and girls her age. "When the cattle came in, we would start to walk ahead of the train," then after dinner they walked again. Youngsters climbed Independence Rock and other famous landmarks with their peers. When almost ten-year-old Joseph Fish came in sight of Chimney Rock, he and his friends walked toward it. They "traveled some little distance when we gave it up and we did not get even with it until the next day."[42] Young trav-

---

[40]Helm, *Conversations*, 88; Greer, "Anecdotes," 10–11.

[41]Faragher, *Women and Men*, 89, mentioned children playing at being little men and women. Gowdy, *Crossing the Plains*, 2. For children's play, see West, "Youngest Pioneers," 90–96, and West, *Growing Up*, 101–117.

[42]Sharp, "Autobiography," 8; Krenkel, *Life and Times*, 27.

elers noted the deceptive appearance of distances in the West, just as adult overlanders did in their writings.

A few middle-year pioneers mentioned humorous play-times—sometimes at the expense of others—or harmful pranks with friends or extended family. Jesse Applegate and his friends amused themselves with the swollen stomach of a slaughtered ox. They ran and butted their heads against it, then bounced back. A boy named Andy bolted toward it with all his might while the others shouted, "Give her goss, Andy!" But the child's head stuck in the stomach, and he had to be pulled out by his legs. To his expense, "Give her goss, Andy" became a joke among the boys. Middle childhood youngsters steadily improve in physical coordination, and they desire vigorous activities, like stomach punching and tag. Boys this age tend to tease and become physically aggressive. One day Jesse Applegate was gathering buffalo chips, and a boy tried to take one of his. "But I caught him in the act and threw another into his face with such violence as to . . . make the blood come. I think I was urged to this by the elder boys, for I remember they laughed, when I could see nothing to laugh about." Barnett Simpson had never tasted liquor and his year-older nephew John "thought it would be funny if he could get me drunk." The boys took turns tipping the jug, but John only pretended to drink. When the jug was empty, Barnett "fell in a stupor." The adults "worked over me all night. I foamed at the mouth and had convulsions and they thought I was going to die." But he recovered, and he vowed never to touch whiskey again. This prank nearly cost Simpson his life, and what began as pleasure/play turned into near disaster.[43] These two tales appeared in California and Oregon trail accounts. Few Mormons discussed childhood pranks; their reminiscences tended to be serious with stories that promoted values, faith, and trying times. Still, children are children, and

---

[43]Applegate, *Recollections*, 19, 25; Helm, *Voices*, 29–30.

young Mormons certainly had moments when they tormented each other on the trail.

Second to pleasure/play, middle-year emigrants recalled themes of fear and animals with train members. Like youngest pioneers, they noted dangerous river crossings, buffalo and oxen stampedes, and accidents where individuals were injured or killed. They also feared drowning. Eight-year-old Annie Taylor (Dee) waded into a stream which "got deeper and deeper until it was above my waist, and it was very cold" and frightening. Without saying a word a man in her company "picked me up and put me on his shoulder and took me across the stream and set me down." Mary Perry (Frost) and her brother "lingered behind the wagons to gather gum from the pine trees," then they tried to catch up. With a river separating them from their train, they attempted to cross, but the weight of her clothing and the force of the current threw Mary down. Fortunately, a cousin came after the stragglers and "rescued me not five minutes too soon." Ten-year-old Orson Stearns went swimming in a stream with his brother and cousin. Since Orson and his sibling could not swim, they ventured into water up to their knees. Soon they found a waist-deep pool but, unknown to them, it contained a dangerous hole. Orson "went under, and when I tried to emerge found no bottom." He yelled for help, "but the water ran down my throat, strangling me, and under I went again." Finally, he grabbed some grass at the edge of the pool and slowly pulled himself out. Safe on the bank again, Orson discovered that his brother had almost drowned, too, for their cousin thought the boys were competing to see who could stay under the water longer and, therefore, did nothing to save them.[44]

Another fear of middle-year children was getting lost, and in some instances train members came to their rescue. Howard Egan's mother allowed him to walk when their wagon was at

---

[44]Dee, *Memories*, 14; *Told By the Pioneers*, 1: 104–105; Williams, "Diary of a Trip," 205–206.

the back of the train. But the eight-year-old dawdled as boys his age would do, and he "gradually fell back till I could hardly see the wagon." Frightened, the boy "ran at my fastest speed, but soon was out of wind and went very slow again to gain my breath, and took another run, but I was getting father behind all the time." Howard Egan's mother sent George Redding after him, and the man

> took hold of my hand and tried to make me run the whole distance to the train, but finding I was about all in he swung me on his back and tried to rattle my teeth out by running at a dog trot, stamping his feet as hard as he could to give me a good jolting, and something to remember him by, which this proves I do, for I never got very far from the wagon again.

Twelve-year-old John Labrum and his brother were getting tent pegs near the Elkhorn River when their company left. Neither their widowed mother nor fellow travelers realized they were gone. "We lost our way and went around and around and up and down and could not find our way. We were very much frightened." Finally, they "saw the last wagon go over the hill. We sure ran fast so we could catch it before we lost sight of it."[45] Many middle-year pioneers found themselves almost getting lost because of lack of thinking on their part or because they were completing tasks assigned to them.

The next two themes middle-year emigrants recalled with train members were responsibilities and illness/death. Some of their chores were like those of little children—gathering buffalo chips and picking wild fruit—but as youngsters grew, so did their tasks. Boys drove teams for others in their company and rode horses or walked while herding loose animals, sometimes to help pay their way across the plains. On long drives without water or in the high mountains, they pitched in with more strenuous jobs to get wagons and people through. Girls cared for small children while their mothers did chores, and sometimes drove teams or pushed handcarts. In most of

---

[45]Egan, *Pioneering*, 142; Lesson Committee, *Enduring Legacy*, 2: 335.

the accounts, though, middle-year children mentioned collecting buffalo chips and helping with loose cattle.

During times of illness or death, adults were often helpful to youngsters. Catherine Camp (Greer) remembered a woman some thought was crazy. "But I believe she was so sorrowful because she had lost her husband, and she used to take an old tin cup and go ahead of the wagons and gather some kind of herbs." Catherine became ill with cholera, and the woman "told mother to give me a spoonful of medicine she had made and all the water I wanted and I would get well, and sure enough, it did cure me." Nine-year-old Louisa Sweetland was impressed when her uncle volunteered to make a coffin for a child who died if others would donate wood, nails, and lining materials. "Each one gladly gave the best they had, and the dear little one was laid to rest with the help of the kind people." But even with the assistance of adults, death frightened middle-year children. J. C. Moreland was "wakened one night by loud screams of one in pain, and the next morning about sunrise a hole was dug beside the road." The man was wrapped in a blanket and buried "out on those arid plains." To Moreland's young mind "death was terrible in any form, but out there under such conditions it was simply horrible." Metta Mortenson (Rasmussen) from Denmark traveled in the Willie handcart company and "always severely censured myself for taking from the pocket of one of the dead women a crust that I knew she was saving." That guilt remained in her memory for years.[46] Middle-year children are conscious of moral values, and they feel guilty when they think their actions cause psychological or physical harm to others.

Death on the trail affected a traveling community when two parents succumbed. Catherine Sager (Pringle), age nine, and her two younger sisters Elizabeth, age six, and Matilda, age four, remembered the kindness of train members who rallied

---

[46]Greer, "Anecdotes," 9; Sweetland, "Across the Plains," 191; Moreland, "Annual Address," 27; Carter, *Pioneer Heritage*, 2: 250.

together for the seven orphaned children. In 1844, Henry and
Naomi Sager and their six children left Missouri in a train led
by Captain William Shaw. Near present-day Seneca, Kansas,
Naomi Sager gave birth to Henrietta, her seventh child. It was
a hard delivery, and the mother never fully recovered. Later,
their wagon overturned and seriously injured Mrs. Sager.
According to Catherine, "A tent was set up and Mother carried into it, where for a long time she lay insensible." Then
other calamities occurred. Catherine jumped from the moving wagon, caught her dress, and fell, and the wheels rolled
over her leg and broke it. A few days later, Henry Sager took
sick and did not recover. Before he died, he said to Catherine, "Poor child! What will become of you?" He begged Captain Shaw to look after his family, for "his wife was ill, the
children small, and one likely to be a cripple."

Mrs. Sager "hired a young man to drive, as mother was afraid
to trust the doctor" who knew little about driving oxen, "but
the kind-hearted German would not leave her, and declared
his intention to see her safe in the Willamette." Naomi Sager
failed rapidly, even though the other women cared for her and
the baby. "We travelled a rough road the day she died,"
Catherine said. Her mother's "last words were, 'Oh, Henry!
If you only knew how we have suffered.'" Within twenty-six
days seven Sager children—John, Frank, Catherine, Elizabeth,
Matilda, Hannah, and Henrietta—became orphans.

Before she died, Mrs. Sager asked Dr. Dagon and Captain
Shaw to care for her family, which they did. The doctor's funny
German accent made Elizabeth Sager (Helm) giggle. "He may
have talked broken English, but if there was ever a man with a
heart of gold, it was this same German doctor," for he "took
care of us children and was both father and mother to us." Baby
Henrietta "was passed from one mother to another," and,
according to Matilda Sager (Delaney), "Mrs. Eads took the tiny
baby and the big-hearted travelers shared their last piece of bread
with us." When the wagon train reached the Whitman Mis-

sion, Captain Shaw arranged for the Sager children to stay, and Dr. and Mrs. Whitman began raising them as their own. Three years later, "the emigration of 47 brought the measles among the Indians and great numbers of them died." A man named Jo Lewis spread rumors that Dr. Whitman was poisoning them; as a result, Cayuse Indians killed the Whitmans and most of the people at the mission. Only four Sager girls survived.[47]

The fourth theme middle-year youngsters recalled with train members was values/religion. Like the Sager company, many adults taught young pioneers to live the Golden Rule by their example; they applied the Biblical teachings they preached. But other adults challenged their values or religious beliefs. A young man in George Riddle's company shared trail expenses with an older man and his family. The older man, identified as "B," tormented and abused the boy, and train members "advised him to give B a threshing." Finally, on the desert after "B" hit him with a whip stock, the young man "proceeded to wipe the desert sand with him." Joseph F. Smith's widowed mother asked a Mormon agent for help in crossing the plains, but he refused and advised her not to go. She informed him, "I will beat you to the valley and ask for no help either," and he replied, "You will prove a burden to your company." Unfortunately, the Smiths were assigned to the company in which the Mormon agent was captain, and he made their trip unpleasant. In spite of this and several mishaps and setbacks, the Smith family reached the Salt Lake Valley a day ahead of him. Twelve-year-old Mary Powell (Sabin) from Wales felt sorry for a woman in her handcart company. The husband was lazy, and "for the sake of the wife and child, I had often helped pull his cart." Near the end of the journey, they went down a slope and "I simply let his cart go." The lazy man "sprang forward and caught it in the nick of time."[48] Mid-

[47]Pringle, *Across the Plains*, 5–8, 19; Pringle, "Letter," 354–356; Pringle, "Account," 3–6; Delaney, *Survivor's Recollections*, 8; Helm, *Conversations*, 47; Thompson, *Shallow Grave*, 10–11.

[48]Riddle, *Early Days*, 19; Smith, "True Pioneer Stories," 165, 171; Sabin, "Mary Powell Sabin," 13.

dle-year children tend to judge acts according to harm done, rules violated, or fairness; to them the world is black or white. These young pioneers could see the unfairness of some adult behaviors.

"I Remember"—Ages Thirteen Through Fifteen

Whereas only a third of youngest pioneers and over half of middle-year children recalled "I remember" train relationships, 83% of adolescents from thirteen through fifteen who emigrated with one or two parents and 100% of those who went without parents did. Themes they mentioned in order of frequency were: responsibilities, illness/death, animals, pleasure, fear and discord, and values/religion. Both contemporary accounts and reminiscences noted responsibilities as the topic which adolescents most often discussed about train members. Diarists next emphasized pleasure/play, then illness/death and values/religion appeared last. Yet illness/death was second in significance in reminiscences; however, these pioneers may have traveled during times of greater sickness. Values/religion surfaced more in Mormon accounts, and discord entered more often in non-Mormon documents.

The most important topic adolescent emigrants noted with train members was responsibilities. Teens were assigned heavier tasks than middle-year children, for as "Aunt Phoebe" Newton noted, "I was a woman grown. I was upwards of 15 years old when we headed our oxen westward." Their jobs varied depending on year of travel, trail conditions, traveling companions, and individual train circumstances. In her analysis of young people on the California Trail, Emmy Werner noted that adults relied heavily on the contributions of adolescents. Her observation agrees with what I found on the California, Oregon, and Mormon trails.[49] However, almost all of the experiences came from male reminiscences; only a small number of girls described train member duties, unlike the female

---

[49]Helm, *Conversations*, 225; Werner, *Pioneer Children*, 4.

diarists. By this age, though, young women usually helped their mothers with family and camp responsibilities and young men stepped into the adult male world. They drove teams, herded loose stock, milked cows, moved animals away from camp-sites to feed, hunted wild game, butchered animals and made jerky, stood guard at night, buried the dead, and acted as chore boys. Many of their responsibilites related to animals, and learning new jobs took time and practice. Thirteen-year-old Thales Haskell had never driven an ox team, and he broke an axletree by running a wheel onto a bank. "I heard a great many making remarks about me being a very careless boy to let such an accident happen," and he continued to receive "daily lec-tures about careless driving." Sometimes male adolescents were given tasks to complete with peers or alone, and several acknowledged being afraid. In fact, most of the fears in male or female reminiscences related to responsibilities. George Tribble, age fourteen, and four other boys took their cattle down the river in Oregon. At one spot "if an animal made the least misstep it would fall one hundred and fifty feet on a bar of the river. Hundreds had made that misstep. Consequently there was a pile of dead animals" with hungry wolves devour-ing them. "We had to stand guard all night to keep the wolves from attacking us." Fifteen-year-old John Smith went by him-self to search for a lost woman. "I had not gone far when I came up with a dead carcass, which was covered with wolves, fighting and howling. I walked past as fast and as quickly as possible. I travelled six miles before I came up with any wag-ons. During this distance I passed about twenty such fright-ful scenes." He finally found the lost woman "safe with her mother."[50]

Adolescents emigrating with one or two parents mentioned illness or death of train members from cholera, mountain fever, measles, scurvy, starvation, over-exertion, over-exposure, and

---

[50]Lesson Committee, *Enduring Legacy*, 2: 324; Tribble, "Autobiographical," 4; Smith, "Autobi-ography," 4–5.

accidents. But instead of elaborating as they did about their families, they usually made a brief statement. A few noted the kindness of others during traumatic times with family. After Ann Jarvis's (Stickney) mother died, "the sisters were very kind to us, they washed her and put some clean clothes upon her and sewed her up tight in a white bed blanket" before she was buried. Thirteen-year-old Margaret McNeil (Ballard) carried her sick little brother on her back as the train moved on and her parents remained behind to search for lost oxen. "That night a kind lady helped me take my brother off my back," and "the people in the camp were very good to us and gave us a little fried bacon and some bread for breakfast." Ann traveled for a week without her parents. "Each morning one of the men would write a note and put it in the slit of a willow stuck into the ground, to tell how we were getting along."[51]

While adolescent diaries described specific pleasure/play experiences with train members, most of the reminiscences spoke in generalities. Young people gathered around the campfire to play games, dance, and sing popular and religious songs. European Mormons learned American dances and told stories of the home and friends they left behind. Landmarks attracted young people, boys relished the wild country and chores like buffalo hunting, and girls took walks and picked flowers with their peers. One thirteen-year-old female remembered when the Scandinavian boys in her train carried the girls across streams on their backs. She was beginning to appreciate her associations with the opposite sex. Caroline Cook (Dunlap), another thirteen year old, was thrilled when Catherine's family joined their company. The new friends "gathered curios," played make-believe, and fixed each other's hair. Catherine plaited "two sixteen strand braids; then, spreading them out over my shoulders, would tell me how beautiful I looked. I was not so skilled with hair and could only do Catherine's into two tawny pigtails, but I decorated them with flow-

---

[51]Carter, *Pioneer Heritage*, 9: 439; Ballard, "Margaret McNeil," 6–7.

ers." Feeling secure without taxing responsibilities, adolescents were permitted to clothe themselves "with rainbows and go as brave as the zodiac."[52]

A few adolescents described incidents that tickled their funny bones. Rebecca Nutting (Woodson) remembered that Mrs. Baker refused to cross the river in a small boat; instead, she wanted to use the ferry for her precious possessions.

> She was an extreordinary neat woman While the rest was content to get things fixed comfortabl when we camped at night Her tent had to be fixed just so It was like steping into a parlor to go in her tent consequently they were always late getting started mornings . . . . Thier wagon must be arranged just so It was a picnic for the boys to unload thier wagon and put the things in the boat Some would call her attention one way while the others picked up a load and ran with it to the boat.

Then they "caught her and her little step daughter and put them in the boat." Mrs. Baker "went screaming she knew she should be drown." Dilius Ward arrived at a hot springs before his company "and not waiting for a cup, stretched myself out, boylike, on my stomach, for the purpose of getting a good drink of cold water." To his surprise, the water was boiling hot. "I was disappointed, but had my wits about me sufficiently to keep my mouth shut until several others who had rushed up about the same time with their cups, had made a like discovery."[53] Young people found moments to make light of situations on the trail.

Like the young diarists, adolescents emigrating with one or two parents noted discord among train members. Pauline Wonderly recalled two young men in her train who shared a wagon and three oxen and after an argument "concluded to travel singly." So "the provisions were divided, the wagon cut in two parts and one man bought the other's share in the third ox. After that one headed the train and the other brought up the rear, as far apart as they could get." While diaries most

---

[52]Dunlap, "Ancotty," 11–12; Emerson, *Conduct of Life*, 37.
[53]Woodson, "Sketch," 13; Ward, *Across the Plains*, 43.

often described contention among adult male emigrants as Pauline Wonderly did, reminiscences related more personal incidents with the adolescent fighting peers or the family clashing with train members. Fourteen-year-old Henry Garrison was harassed by a bully named David Inglish. This tormentor "threw a buffalos head and it struck me in the back and knocked me sprawling on the ground." After several confrontations, Garrison retaliated. His father expected him to be punished, but the captain of the train stood up for the youth. "He knew that I was always busy looking after our stock . . . that I had to take a mans place" since his father was disabled. David Inglish continued heckling. He pulled out a butcher knife and said, "Here you die," but Garrison reciprocated with, "If you ever attempt from this time on to raise a row with me, I will kill you." Just then the captain intervened and stopped them. Garrison concluded, "Mother afterwards told me that Capt said I was not to blame, and she guessed that Daves Father had whipped him nearly to death." Finally, the bully left Henry Garrison alone. One night Heber McBride's family reached camp late with their handcart. It had been raining, "and mother was very sick we thought she was going to die and we had gathered a few sunflower stalks and wet Buffalo chips and had just got a little fire started when all hands were ordered to attend prayers." Only their father attended, "and because we did not go to prayers Daniel Taylor came and kicked our fire all out and spilled the water that we was trying to get warm to make a little tea for Mother."[54]

"I Remember" with No Parents

Youngsters who crossed the plains without parents had their own "I remember" experiences with train members, but almost all of these were Mormon reminiscences. As a result, it is difficult to assess if youngsters on the California and Oregon trails responded to experiences of being alone in the same way. Still,

---

[54]Wonderly, *Reminiscences*, 9; Garrison, "Reminiscences," 21, 35–37; Berrett, "Heber McBride," 11.

we can see how some lone travelers handled the circumstances in which they were placed. Middle-year children had their own unique and often unsupervised times, and they talked about responsibilities, pleasure, kind and not-so-kind individuals, and their own lack of thinking. Ellen Perks' (Johnstun) father sent the almost twelve year old to Utah alone in the Bunker hand-cart company. One day she and two girls "took a handcart and filled it with little children, too small to walk," assuming this would help train members. When the girls grew tired of pulling on the sandy road, they moved off the trail to rest and missed their train. "We traveled until dusk, then seeing the campfires down near the river, found they had had supper and that a few men were ready to start out to hunt for us. We were very tired and received a lecture never to be forgotten."[55]

Nine-year-old Brigham Roberts and his older teenage sister went to Utah in a church train to meet their mother and sib-lings. From his many adventures, Brigham probably received less supervision than did many young pioneers, perhaps because he went without parents. At a shallow river crossing his com-pany received strict orders to walk across. But Brigham watched a teenage girl being smuggled into a freight wagon, and he decided if she could ride, he could too. So he "tumbled into the wagon among the bags of light brown sugar, side bacon, and hams." All went well until they reached the middle of the river bed and the captain told the driver to leave the wagon and assist another caught in quicksand. Uncomfortable with his predica-ment, Brigham decided to leave, but the young lady began to cry and begged him to stay. All night the wagon vibrated back and forth in the sand. The next morning the teams returned for the freight, but not until the stowaways had feasted on sugar, bacon, and hams.[56] B. H. Roberts, who became prominent in the L.D.S. church and a prolific writer, most likely detailed and embellished these autobiographical writings.

As with adolescents with parents, young people who went

---

[55]Clayton, "Biographies," Box 2, folder 75: 4.   [56]Bergera, *B. H. Roberts*, 28–29.

alone recalled responsibilities with train members first, then illness/death. Fear appeared as important as illness/death to lone travelers but was at the bottom of the list for the others. Often teens without parents handled adult responsibilities, carried heavy burdens, and worked with disagreeable people. Fourteen-year-old William Gay hired on as a bullwhacker, and "the wagon boss, and his brother the assistant were cross, surley, selfish, and overbearing men, us boys received but little assistance and no sympathy from them." They herded both day and night, and Gay called his job to Fort Laramie "the toughest time of my life." Fourteen-year-old Louisa Gittens (Clegg) and her sister from England hired on with a private company going to Utah. The family for whom Louisa worked had a husband, wife, four children, a teamster, and two loaded wagons. "The teamster, their oldest boy and myself rode when we could, but very little did I ride as they would say they had too much of a load." Louisa's main chore was to procure water, but she did other tasks as well. "If it had not been for the hired man I should have fared very poorly before the journey was through. He sometimes would help me get the wood and water, but he had a hard time of it too." The sixteen-year-old son did nothing but boss the hired help. Occasionally "on a bright moonlight night" Louisa Gittens and other young folks made molasses candy, which lightened the drudgery of the trail. Fifteen-year-old John Henderson traveled alone in an L.D.S. church train. After a cattle stampede, he and two men searched for the animals and finally located three head. "If I had been left to myself, I would have returned with the three we had found here because there were no signs of any more." After more riding and searching, the men sent John back with the three animals. "I had always been taught to listen to those older than I," so John obeyed but "began to feel my loneliness more keenly than ever." He had trouble getting the animals to camp, and his horse was about to give out when two fellows from the train found him. Back at camp John discovered that his co-workers had returned several hours earlier.[57]

Sometimes adolescents without parents noted depressing or frightening times with train members. Thirteen-year-old Georgina Norr (Miller) left Denmark with a church member. "Traveling across the plains was hard enough, but toward the end of the journey food became very scarce." Her shoes wore out, and her stockings burned when she dried them by the fire. "I asked someone in the company for a pair, but they could not spare any, so I got some rags and tied them around my feet." When she reached Salt Lake City, "the man who had brought me from Denmark had forsaken me." Fifteen-year-old Eliza Duncombe (Fletcher) from England traveled with a family in which the parents, their oldest son, and baby died of mountain fever. One day Eliza fell asleep by the road. "When I awoke it was nearly night and I didn't know which way to go, but I suppose I was inspired to look for the oxen tracks and followed them until I saw a man going for water." She "hurried to catch him and found the camp had eaten supper and had not missed me."[58] Although Mormon church trains were like big families, individuals still could be ignored.

Some adolescents without parents described pleasant memories with train members. Fourteen-year-old Augusta Dorius (Stevens) from Denmark traveled with the Ravens family who gave her "most unusual treatment and care .... Especially did I appreciate the kindness of sister Ravens as she cared for me as her own child." Sometimes Augusta walked ahead of the wagons and socialized with other girls. Coming from Denmark "I thought the emigrant wagons most remarkable vehicles as I had never seen any thing of the kind." In contrast, she remembered feeling "so tired I should often have been glad to have gone to bed without my supper but I always had to help with

[57]Gay, "An Extract," 1; Clegg, "Life of Louisa," 12–15; Henderson, "Life," 17–18.
[58]Carter, *Pioneer Heritage*, 11: 202–203; Carter, *Pioneer Heritage*, 2: 333.

the dishes and help with the camp duties including the preparing of beds." When thirteen-year-old George Beard from England and his friend Joe Barber discovered they were covered with lice, they looked for a spot where they could strip and "delouse" themselves. "We went over a knoll and found a depression, but a bunch of girls from camp beat us to it. None of them had a rag of clothing on; there were fat girls, thin girls, and just girls." The females ordered the boys to leave, but "Joe and I lingered around there and made haste very slowly." These young adolescents followed their developmental pattern of being curious about the opposite sex. Beard probably enjoyed retelling this story for years; in fact, readers today can hear him chuckling to himself. He also recalled the teamsters from Utah being "a happy, jolly, healthy-looking lot of men who used to entertain the immigrants at the campfires every night, dancing and singing and telling stories." The teamsters even helped boys without parents. When a scorpion stung Beard on the thumb, one fellow opened the wound, sucked the blood, and covered it with his own chewing tobacco.[59]

"We Remember"

Many "we remember" recollections included shared or collective memory and information borrowed from others. This was most obvious in reminiscences of youngest pioneers who could not have remembered or understood what older children and adults did. David Bulloch from Scotland must have obtained the details about the division of his private train to Utah from others, since he was only five when it happened.

> In traveling in this large company we were hindered considerably. Some of the men had never driven oxen before, others had only little experience and their troubles would hinder the whole train. Therefore, after a few days of travel with the train, our Company from St. Louis broke with the main company and traveled on ahead of them to Salt Lake. We were called The Independent Scotch Company.[60]

---

[59]Stevens, "Autobiography," 2, 4–5; Davies, "George Beard," 17–18.
[60]Carter, *Pioneer Heritage*, 18: 216.

Of approximately two hundred and fifty companies that trekked to Utah, probably less than ten per cent separated as Bulloch's did. When large trains broke away or spread out from each other, it was often due to scarcity of feed for their stock. Pioneers could not scatter far when they followed the Platte; but when they reached the mountains, they had less chance of threats from Native Americans and more water sources and, therefore, could branch out.[61]

Most of the "we remember" train relationships contained generic information that a group would assume all accounts should include. The most common were the gathering of buffalo chips, campfire activities, stampedes, and facts about the train and its leader. Five-year-old Mary Culmer (Simmons) recalled "moonlight nights when the camp was all settled and made safe; the people would gather around the campfire and after some singing and prayer, there would be dancing. Some would be mending clothes for the next day, others would be mending harness by the light of the fire." Six-year-old Robert Sweeten noted that "children would play around the wagons and camp fires; after supper the older folks would get out the fiddles and have dances around the fires, some of them dancing in bare feet, as they had no shoes. Every week we would have religious services."[62] Did Mary Culmer and Robert Sweeten remember these activities on their own or after discussions with other pioneers?

Since many Mormon reminiscences intended to preserve the history of the trek for posterity, the church, or organizations like Daughters of Utah Pioneers, they often added facts acquired elsewhere. Sarah Palmer (Sharp) traveled in the same down-and-back company as diarist Thomas Griggs, but she added information he did not record. For example, teamsters in down-and-back companies "were called as missionaries to drive. They

---

[61]Bashore, telephone interview, identified ten to fifteen instances in 250 companies where Mormon trains divided.

[62]Carter, *Pioneer Heritage*, 12: 32; "Robert Sweeten," 9.

received no pay, only their food . . . . The train was made up of 46 wagons with passengers, two belonged to the Captain and 6 carried supplies, and the night herders slept in them in the day." Sarah claimed her company contained forty-six wagons, but recent estimates place the number at sixty-three. Griggs noticed other companies near his but did not explain that "they traveled three trains, about 1/2 day apart, so if any serious accident with Indians occurred, they could help each other." Since Sarah Palmer was ten when she went to Utah, she probably gathered additional facts as she grew older.[63]

CONCLUSION

From this analysis of contemporary and reminiscent documents about train member relationships, it appears that child development factors influenced what young people said. Three-year-old pioneers recalled no personal associations with train members, and only two four year olds did. This is consistent with their developmental pattern. Five and six year olds began to remember train member experiences. Children this age move toward relationships outside the family, but the family is still their focal point; consequently, most of their memories with train members related in some way to parents or siblings. Middle-year youngsters most frequently described pleasure/play incidents, and this fits developmentally with their need to play and to relate to adults and peers. Often these youngsters segregated themselves according to gender; at times they associated with mixed company and older people. Adult train members helped to provide a secure environment, even if it meant giving them swats or carrying them on their backs to discipline them for lack of thinking. The new world of the trail and sometimes the tasks assigned them drew them away from the wagons. Few middle-year youngsters remembered being treated badly by adults.

[63]Sharp, "Autobiography," 6–7; Deseret News Church Almanac, 174.

Adolescent diarists wrote more about train members than they did about their families; obviously, expanding their relationships was important to this age group. Nineteenth-century culture followed these young people on the trail with gender division of labor and female interpersonal relations. Gender differences became pronounced as adolescents discussed train members and females revealed social needs and nineteenth-century conventions. Diaries and reminiscences emphasized responsibilities as their main topic of discussion about train members, and a bigger picture emerges when both are analyzed together. Teens were treated as adults when extra hands were needed, and sometimes these new jobs frustrated them. Young people without parents emphasized train responsibilities as well, although theirs were often more difficult than their peers.

All ages of children noted fear when discussing train member relationships. Five and six year olds recalled this as their most significant topic, and middle-year youngsters recalled it as second in importance. Adolescents, too, discussed their fears and often connected them to responsibilities. As they described difficult tasks without adult participation, it became obvious why they were frightened. Even diary and letter writers noted fear. Fifteen-year-old Flora Bender "crossed the Loup Fork on the ferry part of the way and had to ford the rest. I was frightened because I was afraid our mules would get to prancing around." When her brother Charlie was ill, "he was all cramped up and imagined every one was going to kill him . . . All the campers, hearing him scream, rushed right into our tent and I was frightened nearly to death. They soon got him quieted, however, and he sleeps now." Although John Mack Faragher and Lillian Schlissel suggested that adults "schooled their feelings" and did not discuss their fears freely, youngsters, whether male or female, tended to express theirs in their writings and recollections.[64]

Discord among train members appeared in both contem-

---

[64]Bender, Typescript, 1, 11; Faragher, *Women and Men*, 90–91; Schlissel, *Women's Diaries*, 30, 111.

porary and reminiscent adolescent accounts. According to Faragher and Schlissel, adult diaries also noticed fighting on the trail, and "nearly every diary recorded at least one incident." Women worried when men quarreled because they might become separated from female friends. Flora Bender expressed the same concern about her friend Mary Marvin when their train divided. She also reported that "Mrs. Hopson actually cried when she saw we were going to leave."[65] From the young female diaries we can observe how California or Oregon trail companies joined and separated, with wagons traveling as self-sufficient entities. Even in religious groups like Rachel Taylor's preacher train or Heber McBride's Mormon handcart company, there were troubles among train members.

When youngsters talked about train member relationships, contemporary and reminiscent accounts filled in the holes from what the other left out, and their experiences complemented each other. Most of the contemporary writers seemed optimistic and pleased with friendships among train members, and they carried a "what will be will be" attitude when their trains divided. Most reminscences did not let time cast a rosy glow on their retellings of experiences with train members; they, too, told their stories with a reality check.

---

[65]Faragher, *Women and Men*, 101; Schlissel, *Women's Diaries*, 25, 30, 89; Bender, Typescript, 5, 8.

CHAPTER V

Friend or Foe:

Young Pioneers' Interactions with Others on the Trail

We passed several Indian wigwams today. I went up to one – there were Indians and half breeds and their tents were neat and clean. . . . We passed a train of oxteams – about 200 wagons. They were on their way to Omaha from Salt Lake, after the Mormon emigration.[1]

In her diary fifteen-year-old Flora Bender noticed others besides her family and wagon train on the Platte River road. By 1863 travelers were moving east and west on the great highway between the Missouri River and the Pacific Coast. The wagons Flora mentioned belonged to Mormon down-and-back companies which traveled down the Platte River road from Utah to Nebraska and brought back emigrants. Pioneers from the East and Midwest, Mormons from Europe, soldiers, freighters, stage drivers, mail carriers, settlers along the trail, people with relief wagons, family and friends at their destination, and Native Americans all played a role in children's interactions and relationships on the journey west. During the 1860s when Flora Bender emigrated, way stations and white settlements had increased and the telegraph improved communication. Roadside messages were not as vital to communication as they had been earlier because pioneers could leave notes at stations and post offices or send telegraph messages across the country.[2]

---

[1]Bender, Typescript, 5.   [2]See Mattes, *Platte River*, 5.

Seeing other wagon trains nearby gave young people a feeling of security and a sense of community. Flora Bender commented on five other companies camping close to hers, and Patrick Murphy made diary entries about being "in sight of five trains" and "in sight of eight trains," or he noted "a great many trains" within view. Thomas Griggs passed mail coaches, down-and-back trains like his, and telegraph workers raising poles. Harriet Hitchcock saw the road full of emigrants, and

> we are now camped near the river fifteen families on one acre of ground. There is a man just taking the census. I think he will need to understand the first rule in Arithmatic in order to count all of the children for they are so thick they can hardly tell to which wagon they belong. It is quite amusing to look around among the different families, some are churning others are baking bread and preparing supper, while others are scolding their children and probably would use the rod of correction if they had any, but as we are getting out of the region of bushes and trees it is hard to find a rod and they are obliged to use threats instead.[3]

Harriet probably wrote this as she witnessed the scene, for she said, "There *is* a man *just* taking the census" [italics mine]. Today's reader can climb into Harriet's mind and observe what she was seeing at the moment because the adolescent created a photograph of words: many families camping on one spot of ground, a man counting travelers, chores being done, and children irritating their parents. In other words, Harriet was depicting life on the trail in 1864. This chapter discusses individuals and groups whom young pioneers met along the trail, such as other trains and relief parties, Missourians, Mormons, and Native Americans.

During the years of overland travel, pioneers from various trains assisted and socialized with each other as a large traveling community. They located animals that wandered or were stolen, and strangers built bridges and roads together. Sometimes they helped despondent travelers tend the sick and

---

[3]Bender, Typescript, 13; Murphy, "Across the Plains Diary," 2, 3; Griggs, "Crossing the Plains," 42, 52, 59; Hitchcock, "Thoughts," 238.

injured, bury the dead, and find their camps if they were lost. Emigrants from nearby trains visited, spent the night, attended Sunday religious services, and took people in when they needed help or were abandoned. In a single diary entry Eliza McAuley described two different encounters with trains on the trail. Two brothers who had been hunting were waiting for their train and one of the men's guns went off, "the ball passing through his lungs. He was still alive, but sinking rapidly when we left. We gave them all the fresh water we had, which was all we could do for them, as their train had come up." Later that day, the McAuley company stopped where many emigrants were camped, "and a merrier set I never saw. Just after dark we were treated to a variety of barnyard music in various parts of the camp. Roosters crowed, hens cackled, ducks quacked, owls hooted, pigs squealed, donkeys brayed, dogs howled, cats squalled, and all these sounds made by human voices."[4]

Another type of assistance mentioned by young writers and memorists was relief from trains, stations, or family and friends near the end of the trail. Mormons especially mentioned this topic when they included other people in their reminiscences. A few diarists also talked about those who brought assistance. Lucy Canfield reached Echo Canyon in Utah and "met some of the boys from the City with Flour." Two days later they "camped at Mr Merrels they gave us some butter. Went down there in the evening[.]" Eliza McAuley started into the Nevada desert and "met a man hauling water from the Truckee for the relief station who gave us some drinking water." Members of the Donner party and the Willie and Martin handcart companies particularly remembered the succor they received. Virginia Reed (Murphy) recalled her father "hurrying over the mountains." He "met us in our hour of need with his hands full of bread" and fourteen men. After the four relief parties rescued the survivors, "the generous hearted cap-

---

[4]McAuley, Diary, 67–68.

tain" at Sutter's Fort gave them assistance. John Oborn with the Willie company remembered seeing rescue wagons appear. "Those of you who have never had this experience cannot realize its intensity. . . . We were cared for by a dear brother who was very kind to us. He seemed like an angel from heaven. We left our handcarts and rode in his wagon and slowly, but safely, he brought us to Zion."[5]

Young Pioneers' Perceptions of Others

How these young pioneers perceived others on the trail depended partly upon their family values and society's views. Overlanders sometimes stereotyped Missourians, Mormons, and Native Americans. When emigrants referred to "Missourians," they did not necessarily mean people from Missouri; in fact, of 712 documents the largest number of young non-Mormon pioneers hailed from Missouri.[6] Rather, "Missourians" or "Pikers" were rowdy emigrants of lower social status and poorer backgrounds from regions in and around Missouri—particularly from Pike County—who swore, drank, and mistreated their animals and women. Their females were sloppily attired and bedraggled from physical labor normally delegated to men.[7] Many citizens from Missouri did not fit that description.

Two childhood "I remember" reminiscences illustrated pioneer feelings about "Missourians." Remembrance Campbell recalled sitting around the campfire telling stories with travelers from various states when a question arose about the meaning of a particular word.

They decided to leave it to be settled by some one in the adjoining camp.

---

[5]Margetts, "My Journal," Oct. 12, 14; McAuley, Diary, 75; Murphy, *Across the Plains*, 31, 33; Carter, *Heart Throbs*, 6: 366.
[6]See Table I in Appendix A.
[7]Myres, *Ho for California*, 41; Myres, *Westering Women*, 133–134; Schlissel, *Women's Diaries*, 105–106. See the Remington illustration of "Two Pike County Arrivals" in Bidwell, "Life in California," 174.

They went over to the camp, but they had all gone to bed. One man poked his head out from a tent and asked what was wanted. He was asked if there were any grammarians in that camp. He replied, "No, we are all Missourians," and pulled his head in again.

Six-year-old Eugene Foster giggled for years about the time his family's pack animals climbed the mountains by Donner Lake after a rain when the rocks were slippery.

> There was a party from Pike County Missouri, along about the same time. Old Jule was packed with the tent which, being wet, was very heavy. She was grunting aloud when she slipped and fell, giving out a great grunt. A woman from Missouri standing near exclaimed: "There! That critter is dead. I heard the breath go out of her body."[8]

In contrast to the infrequent mention of "Missourians" in young pioneers' accounts, writers talked about Mormons, especially if they paused at Salt Lake City. Mormons in Utah had become vocal against Midwesterners after their struggle for survival in Missouri and Illinois during the 1830s and 1840s. Emigrants passing through their city were offended when they attended church services and heard fiery sermons delivered against the "Gentiles." Such an attitude intensified prejudice. But the main cause for discrimination was polygamy. Mormons were white, Christian, and generally well-educated but, according to non-Mormon emigrants, they lived in sin. Mormons, on the other hand, believed plural marriage was a commandment from God and must be obeyed. Even so, no more than twenty to twenty-five per cent of church members practiced polygamy, which most often involved two wives. Large families like Brigham Young's were the exception. Sensational anti-Mormon novels, scathing newspaper and periodical accounts, and Mormon haters passing through or wintering in Salt Lake City kept controversies and rumors alive. Most novels were authored by New England women who had never been to Utah and, as Julie Roy Jeffrey observed, what they wrote revealed more about middle-class America than about

---

[8]Campbell, *Brief History*, 16; Sexton, *Foster Family*, 185.

those they attacked. In a study of British women emigrants, Rebecca Bartholomew found it difficult to find realistic treatment of Mormon pioneers in the writings of the period.[9] Since Mormons lived in tightly knit communities and were leery of outsiders after their Midwest experience, emigrants stopping at Mormon settlements received superficial contact with them. Some overlanders even chose not to go to Salt Lake City at all.

Most young California and Oregon trail diarists did not talk about interactions with Mormons until they approached the settlements. Mary Warner was one exception. Near South Pass she "met a Mormon train consisting of fifty wagons" and "Uncle Chester sold one of our provision wagons to them." Within sixty miles of Salt Lake City, Flora Bender

> nooned at a village called Coal Ville. Put the stock out to pasture at 10 cts per head for two hours. We also see nice looking wheat and vegetables growing. It reminds us of the past, after travelling over such a barren country. For dinner we had onions, lettuce and radishes – quite a treat to us. . . . The Mormons have settled in every spot large enough for a garden.

In Echo Canyon Flora saw "a great deal of travel on this road – Mormons hauling wood from the mountains." Then in Salt Lake City, "no sooner were we camped till the Mormons were flocking around, with vegetables to sell or trade." Ada Millington and several reminiscence writers also described being hounded by women and children. In her original diary Ada said, "We had hardly stopped before girl [came] around & wanted to get our washing to do then we were just perfectly haunted by people with vegetable to sell of all kinds."[10] Mary Warner

> went up town – we were very much pleased with the City. The streams are very wide, and on each side of every street is a stream of water – nearly all of the walks are fine and shaded by large trees. We went up

[9]Ludlow, *Encyclopedia*, 1094–1095; Jeffrey, *Frontier Women*, 149; Bartholomew, *Audacious Women*, 16.

[10]Warner, "Diary," 13–14; Bender, Typescript, 11; Clarke, "Journal Kept," 23.

Great Salt Lake City in 1853, looking south. As rendered by Frederick Piercy in
James Linforth, ed., *Route from Liverpool to Great Salt Lake Valley.*

to Brigham Young's yard but we could not get in. His yard is surrounded
by a high stone wall and guards are stationed at the entrances and they
would not let us pass in as it was Sunday. We went to the Temple and
but we could not get in to see either of them.

Mary should have said tabernacle because the Salt Lake
Temple was not completed until three decades later. Edith
Lockhart "nooned near a Mormon settlement and went to
church----had a very poor sermon." Flora Bender did not like
the preaching in the Salt Lake Bowery either.[11]

Reminiscences also gave opinions of Mormons. William
Gay remembered seeing Welsh, Dane, Russian, and English
converts enroute to Utah in 1863. They "were the queerest

---

[11]Warner, "Diary," 17–18; Humphrey, "Original Diary," 11; Bender, Typescript, 11.

dressed, and most peculiar looking people I had ever seen." Mrs. M. A. Gentry had heard "tales of the hostility of the Mormons toward all Missourians," probably because she came from that state. "The year before, the Mormons had been driven out of Independence, Missouri, and were alleged to have sworn eternal vengeance against all citizens of the State. So many threats of retaliation had I heard that my fear of Mormons amounted to a possible terror." When her train chose not go through Salt Lake City, the girl was relieved.[12] Although Mrs. Gentry recalled her childhood terror, her memory failed when she said the Mormons were ousted from Missouri the year before her 1849 emigration. It had been over ten years since they left the state.

In a "we remember" reminiscence, Pauline Wonderly said, "We had dreaded the Mormons as much as the Indians and did not expect fair treatment from them. The tales told of the Mormons in those days were worse than those of the Indians." Allene Taylor (Dunham) wrote that "many of the Mormons were to be dreaded more than the Indians and the Mormons led the Indians on many times." In Salt Lake City, she "saw Brigham Young and a good many of his wives and children. At this time he had a young bride and was then courting another." An old lady "asked mother if she could give her a teaspoon to take her medicine in. I remember her, she seemed so old and forsaken. Mother gave her the teaspoon." The Mormon "women and children looked so wretched."[13] Allene's memory could have been colored by her mother's prejudices; even so, poverty and hunger were prevalent throughout early Utah settlements.

While young diarists mentioned other people on the trail, 62% of California and Oregon trail emigrants and 42% of Mormons included them in their reminiscences. But only 19% and 11% discussed them in "I remember" writings. If others on the

[12]Gay, "Extract," 2; Ross, "Child's Experiences," 303.
[13]Wonderly, *Reminiscences*, 4; Dunham, *Across the Plains*, 11–12.

road influenced them personally, then youngsters recalled them to memory. On the other hand, Native Americans became a common topic for discussion. The writers referred to the native inhabitants as "Indians," "savages," "red men," or "redskins." The term "Indian" seemed to be a generic reference, for most young pioneers did not specify the tribe. All the diarists and one letter writer mentioned Native Americans. This differed from John Unruh's observation that letter writers gave these people more emphasis than diarists. Twelve letters written by five youngsters, however, cannot be a large enough sample to prove or disprove Unruh's statement. Of 430 reminiscences, 80% who traveled the Oregon and California trails mentioned Native Americans, whereas 51% of the Mormons did. Yet only 36% non-Mormon and 18% Mormon accounts contained "I remember" incidents. In other words, the majority of experiences with Native Americans were not seen through children's eyes. Most likely they had been discussed and improved by fellow travelers over the years and, thus, became shared or collective memory. John Unruh noted that embellished hostile accounts appeared more in later writings than in trail diaries.[14] Of the 430 reminiscences, any embellished incident usually occurred in published or lengthy, descriptive pieces. The most detailed accounts were published by non-Mormon pioneers.

Even though half of the Mormon accounts mentioned Native Americans, most did not elaborate for several possible reasons. First, their reminiscences were written for posterity and not for publication, and instilling faith was a primary objective. Second, many Mormon memoirs became life stories. The trail experience was one brief moment in a person's existence. Next, Utah pioneers sometimes described experiences with Native Americans during the early settlement days. These were often more dramatic than those on the trail. This was true for some of the Pacific Coast pioneers as well. Also, many WPA interviewees gave terse answers to ques-

---

[14]Unruh, *Plains Across*, 175.

tions about Native Americans. By the time the interview was conducted, the pioneer was elderly and either did not remember the details or found no cause to embellish. Finally, the Mormon Trail ended before the most dangerous part of the journey in Idaho and Nevada, while Pacific Coast travelers passed through the region where most attacks occurred.

Nine diarists and letter writers experienced no problems with Native Americans. Virginia Reed and Sallie Hester went west in the 1840s when Native American and white relations were relatively peaceful. Eliza McAuley and the Scott sisters crossed during the heavy emigration year of 1852. Thomas Griggs, Lucy Canfield, and Andrew Jenson went to Utah in the 1860s when troubles had escalated, but they traveled in large Mormon trains which protected them. Also, most L.D.S. emigrants followed Brigham Young's advice to treat Native Americans with patience and kindness and feed rather than fight them.[15] Lucy Canfield's train "saw some Indians on horse back gave them some flour & meet," and "did not build fire." Edith Lockhart and Flora Bender went west during the troubled 1860s but did not mention problems. Six writers noted minor difficulties, such as stealing and begging. Of nineteen contemporary accounts of the journey, no young pioneer experienced major conflicts with Native Americans. Some, like Harriet Hitchcock, witnessed the results of attacks on others. Only 3% of the reminiscences described murderous assaults on their own trains. Some described minor problems, and a small number mentioned atrocities committed to others. As John Unruh observed, almost all emigrants completed their trans-Mississippi journey without being physically harmed by Indians.[16]

Nevertheless, many young pioneers developed preconceived notions even before embarking on their journey. If they

---

[15]See Madsen, *Shoshoni*, 29. Also, several Mormon pioneer reminiscences mentioned Brigham Young's counsel to them. For example, see Eliza Horsepool's account in Genealogical Society, *Utah Pioneer*, 13: 112.

[16]Margetts, "My Journal," Aug. 23; Unruh, *Plains Across*, 200.

did not read the popular captivity novels of the day, they heard exaggerated newspaper reports. Or, family members planted visual pictures in their minds of "fiendish Indians" and thus expanded the frontier myth.[17] Jesse Applegate remembered talking about the journey long before his family left.

> Oregon was, in my mind, a country a long way off, and I understood that to get there we would have to travel through a country swarming with wild Indians who would try to kill us with tomahawks and scalp us. Some girl cousins, older than I, would take a coffee cup after drinking the coffee, and turn the mouth down, and . . . look into it for pictures of future scenes.

Seven-year-old Jesse visualized "covered wagons and Indians scalping women and children." Virginia Reed (Murphy) listened to her grandmother's tales of an aunt who was taken captive in early Virginia and Kentucky, then lived with her captors for five years before escaping. Harriet Zumwalt (Smith) recalled her grandfather's tales of Indians in the War of 1812. George Waggoner's father "told so many hair-raising stories of the atrocious conduct of the red men on the borders of Kentucky, when he was a boy, that my only ideal of an Indian was that of a monster seeking for little boys with a tomahawk and scalping knife in his hand."[18] Most contemporary and reminiscent accounts did not discuss preconceived notions, but what young pioneers wrote revealed they had been warned. Impressions from home, gossip at the jumping-off place, tales around the campfire, and parents' anxiety filled children's minds with tomahawks and scalps. As they moved along the trail, children learned harrowing accounts from other travelers, roadside warnings, and guidebooks which told them to treat Indians with suspicion and distrust. But most young pioneers learned that rumor was worse than reality.

According to John Unruh and Glenda Riley, many adult

---

[17]See Jeffrey, *Frontier Women*, 20; Myres, *Westering Women*, 48–50; West, *Growing Up*, 35–37; and Williams, "My First Indian," 14.

[18]Applegate, *Recollections*, 9–10; Murphy, *Across the Plains*, 3; Smith, "My Trip Across," 2; Waggoner, *Stories*, 8.

diarists detailed first encounters with Native Americans, but the few young diarists who mentioned these meetings did not elaborate. Mary Warner wrote, "There were two Indians come to camp begging – they were the first we had seen and we were afraid of them." Sallie Hester saw "a small Indian village. There is a mission at this place, about thirty pupils, converts to the Christian faith."[19] In contrast, Ada Millington and Andrew Jenson, who revised their teenage diaries, provided detailed descriptions of the first Native Americans they met. How much they added to their adolescent impressions cannot be ascertained without studying the original entries. In her journal Ada said,

> I thought the Indians were very ugly. They were of a dull copper color, or of wet clay and had rather long black straight hair. They were very friendly and would want to shake hands with us, and say "how, how." . . . They always rode as fast as the horse would go, and though they were a great curiosity to us children, we were considerably afraid of them too. They belong to the Sioux Tribe.[20]

Near Fort McPherson, Nebraska, Andrew Jenson wrote about the first Native Americans he saw.

> About one hundred Indians were encamped here and some of their tents were large and confortable. These were the first Indians we had seen on our journey, and after we had subdued our fear and timidity they became the object of our greatest attention and curiosity, and as they were a friendly band, a number of them soon appeared in our camp. Some of the young warriors entertained us by showing us their skill as marksmen with their arrows. Most of them were scantily clad, and some of the young boys were entirely naked, a feature which was rather shocking to us people from the north who had never seen anything like it before. Some of them who made themselves more free with us than the rest partook of our food and seemed to be particularly fond of our bread and pan-cakes.

Several days later Jenson learned that "the Indians in this locality were said to be very hostile, and those of us who walked were instructed to keep near the wagons." After burying two

---

[19]Unruh, *Plains Across*, 386; Riley, *Women*, 124; Warner, "Diary," 5; Hester, "Diary," 236.
[20]Millington, "Journal," 213.

train members on the plains, he wrote, "Yes, there they rest, where the wild Indians sing their war songs, and where the buffalo and other wild animals roam at large."[21] Andrew Jenson was the only diarist to provide a Scandinavian viewpoint. From the books they read, Europeans pictured the American West as an untamed wilderness, a mythical land with utopian features. Perhaps Jenson heard stories of the land where "Indians sing their war songs" and "buffalo and other wild animals roam at large," or he may have added the descriptive language when he revised his diary. Thomas Griggs was the only young diarist from England; however, he lived several years in the United States before emigrating to Utah. His first mention of Native Americans was, "The sight of some Indians on the river banks enabled us to pass away the time pretty well." Later, several Pawnees came into camp "begging vituals, and the way they took it rather astonished us 'green uns' taking it from us by the plate full."[22]

Sometimes reminiscences described first encounters with Native Americans. Many of these stories appeared in published works, and some authors like Jesse Applegate and Dilius Ward rambled with details of what they remembered or thought they recalled. The Applegate train camped near a Caw Indian town where huts and cabins lined the river.

> It was said those Indians grew corn, beans, and pumpkins. I admired several of the Indian men I saw here. They were more than six feet tall, straight, and moved with a proud step; wore blankets drawn around their shoulders, and leggins. Their hair was shorn to the scalp, except something like a rooster's comb on top of the head, colored red.

Jesse Applegate remembered gazing up into a face and not being afraid. Looking up at an adult would fit the memory of a seven year old, but other details belonged to an older person. Thanks to his father's terrifying stories, George Waggoner dived into some brush when he saw his first Native Ameri-

[21]Jenson, "Journals," 77–80.
[22]Nash, "European Image," 7; Griggs, "Crossing the Plains," 21, 33.

cans. "They were a couple of young Pawnees, with red blankets around their shoulders and vermillion paint on their faces." Approximately five hundred men in war paint approached John Goulter's train and asked for tobacco. They were looking for U. S. soldiers and went on their way after receiving the tribute. Since Goulter traveled in 1864 when relations were tense, Native Americans could have been chasing soldiers, and a nervous adolescent from England may have thought he saw five hundred warriors whether he did or not. Ruth Blair (Evans) from England encountered her first Native American in Salt Lake City. "I went over to pick up an ear of corn that I saw on the ground but the Indian beat me to it. I was terribly frightened of him, but he didn't say or do anything."[23]

In addition to describing first experiences, youngsters shared opinions about the tribes along the trail. Most diary and letter writers provided superficial views because of brief exposure to the other culture. Sallie Hester described the Pawnees as "a dangerous and hostile tribe. We are obliged to watch them closely and double our guards at night. They never make their appearance during the day, but skulk around at night, steal cattle and do all the mischief they can." Little did Sallie realize that the Pawnees had once been a self-sufficient people who did not rely on stealing and begging to survive. Their Sioux enemies had killed or ousted them from their villages, then overlanders destroyed wood, wild pasture, and game. As a result, begging Pawnees developed a bad reputation among the pioneers.[24]

In her trail letter, Virginia Reed remarked that the Sioux were the prettiest dressed of the tribes she had seen. Eliza McAuley thought the Sioux were "better looking," and Flora Bender described them as friendly. Physically, the Sioux were large people with physiques that suited their rugged environ-

---

[23]Applegate, *Recollections*, 12; Ward, *Across the Plains*, 15–16; Waggoner, *Stories*, 8; Genealogical Society, *Utah Pioneer*, 11: 120 and 9: 93.
[24]Hester, "Diary," 237; Hyde, *Pawnee Indians*, 223–225, 236.

ment. They carried themselves with dignity, and their culturally imposed behaviors, such as sitting quietly and absorbing
knowledge, presented a composed appearance.[25] According
to Glenda Riley and Sandra Myres, adult diarists considered
the Sioux "real" Indians because they were handsome, clean,
intelligent, athletic, and friendly. Perhaps they most closely
resembled the "noble savage" image portrayed in novels of the
time.[26] In addition, their qualities approached nineteenth-century Anglo-Saxon standards.

At the Platte Bridge in Wyoming, Flora Bender noted a store-
keeper with "a great ugly squaw for a wife," and the Snake Indians at Fort Bridger were a hostile, dirty-looking, savage race.
Sallie Hester described Indians on the Sweetwater as "mostly
naked, disgusting and dirty looking." To Patrick Murphy the
Paiutes were a dirty, miserable tribe. Rachel Taylor commented
that the "Digger Indians" were "a filthy thieving race, and would
not scruple to take a persons life if could be done without risk-
ing their own."[27] Like the Pawnees, the "Digger Indians" of the
Goshute tribe lost their ability to survive in their desert environment as overlanders destroyed their grasslands and seeds.
The "Diggers" found little to dig, so they begged and stole animals to survive. In her diary entry Eliza McAuley mentioned
losing horses, then later "found one horse alive, and the Indians eating another." In western Utah, Ada Millington observed
Indians who "as soon as an ox dies . . . begin to cut his carcass
into suitable pieces to carry home with them."[28]

Of all the young diarists Eliza McAuley spent enough time

---

[25]Murphy, "Virginia," Letter 1: 1; McAuley, Diary, 35; Bender, Typescript, 5; Hassrick, *The Sioux*,
325–327.

[26]Riley, *Women*, 152; Myres, *Ho for California*, 39–40. See Nash, "European Image," 4, 6–11, and
Cawelti, *Adventure*, for information about popular novels about the West during the nineteenth century.

[27]Bender, Typescript, 7–8, 10; Hester, "Diary," 238; Murphy, "Across the Plains Diary," 9; Taylor, "Overland Trip," 177.

[28]Madsen, *Shoshoni*, 9–13; McAuley, Diary, 71; Millington, "Journal," 253. To compare what adult
writers said about the tribes along the trail, see Riley, *Women*, 153, 198–199; Myres, *Westering Women*, 39, 56; and Unruh, *Plains Across*, 183–185.

with Native Americans to learn that many were kind people and not the "ignorant miserable race of beings" Harriet Hitchcock believed they were.[29] Granted, Eliza was writing in 1852 before much retaliation occurred, and Harriet traveled in 1864 when conflict between the cultures had accelerated. Yet Harriet's comments on the way to Colorado were not based on her own experience. Eliza McAuley's negative impression of Pawnees changed when a chief and his braves spent the night. "At break of day the Indians awoke us, singing their morning song. The old chief started the song, and the others chimed in, and it was very harmonious, and musical. After breakfast, when the boys went down to the river, our guests went along and asked to be taken across." Later, the McAuley party "met about a hundred Pawnees returning from a hunt. . . with furs and dried meat." The Indians "passed our little band of two wagons and three young boys with a civil 'how dye do' but meeting the rest of our train three wagons and eight men, they relieved them of most of their clothing, knives, tobacco &c and stampeded a team with Mrs Bollard in the wagon."

When the McAuley train stopped to build a road in Wyoming, they made friends with a man named Poro. He had been "to the Missouri River and seen steamboats, and explained by signs what they are like. He seems to understand the customs of the whites very well." During their two-week reprieve from traveling, the emigrants enjoyed visits from Poro, his small son, and a friend named Pavee. Poro "interpreted a number of Indian words for us" and tried to teach some of his language, for "it pleases him very much to see us try to learn it." After Eliza McAuley asked to buy some moccasins, Poro and his son brought her a neatly made pair. Eliza

> offered a gay plaid shawl in payment for the moccasins. Poro was quite pleased with it, and inclined to accept it, but referred the matter to the boy. He talked to his father, who explained to us that he said it was

---

[29]Hitchcock, "Thoughts," 239. Riley, *Women*, 129, observed that some women writers called Indians "creatures," "which implies something less than a human being."

very pretty, but he could not eat it. He wanted bread and sugar, so we gave him what he wanted.

The next day Poro brought them some service berries. "He has been counting the 'sleeps' before we go away, and regrets our going very much. He said today 'One sleep more, and then wagons go away to California.'"[30]

Although reminiscences provided opinions of Native Americans, most came from "we remember" recollections and did not reflect the child's perspective. Franklin Johnson described Native Americans at the jumping-off place sitting "with their feet hanging over the water, apparently in deep meditation, but probably with minds entirely vacant." Later on the trail, the "half-civilized Indians" used old and poor guns because they were "too lazy to afford the price of good guns." These were not eight-year-old observations. Mrs. M. A. Gentry colored her eleven-year-old recollections with white middle-class attitudes: ". . . these tribesmen of the plains were a cleanly people, and trained from early youth to bathe and swim. Often we would see all the children of a village swimming and sporting in the Platte River." Their clothes were "spotless and beautifully ornamented with fringe," and they "had fine, large wigwams of beautifully dressed buffalo hide." With adult eyes Harvey Cluff wrote, "To look a savage in the face all painted for war, was indeed horrowfying, but a little flour, sugar and coffee made the face of the savage more humanitarian. And he proved a closer friend than our white brother."[31] Yet Harvey Cluff provided no personal experiences to back what he was saying.

A few "I remember" experiences produced several child perceptions. Nearly five years old, Julia Miller noticed a man wearing a linen bedspread covered with clay because he had dug up a body and was wearing the burial shroud. Julia "thought

---

[30]McAuley, Diary, 19–20, 24, 55, 57, 58.
[31]Johnson, "Crossing the Plains," 7, 23, 25; Ross, "Child's Experiences," 301–302; Cluff, "Journal," 17.

that's what they meant when they spoke of Digger Indians. I thought they meant Indians who had dug up the bodies of dead people and wore their clothes." Her recollection fits the developmental pattern of a small child thinking in literal terms. Eight-year-old Florence Weeks (Blacow) was more afraid of soldiers than of Native Americans, and she and her sister "were so fond of babies we even wanted to take the Indian babies whose heads would be alive with creepers." Perhaps her squeamish mother pointed out the creepers, or Florence projected her own adult perceptions. Jean Frederick Loba from Switzerland was "profoundly impressed" by the "wild tribes of Indians" on the trail, while six-year-old Catherine Anderson (Ross) from Denmark was frightened by them.[32]

Through brief associations, curious emigrants and Indians began to learn about each other's ways. Young pioneers entered wigwams and watched women do handiwork. They sat in awe during war dances and stared at skilled young braves shooting coins with their arrows. The adolescent diarists described such experiences in their writings. William Pace wrote, "This night A part of A tribe of Indians Came in to our camp and Had A war Dance." At an Indian town his Battalion enjoyed "melons and green corn." Patrick Murphy reported that a trader, his "squaw" wife, and family joined his stock train for several days on their way to Oregon with their animals. Rachel Taylor visited several wigwams and at one place the women showed "their ornamental work, and seemed very friendly." At a trader's house his "squaw" wife "had just lost a brother killed by the Pawnee Indians and had her hair cut short as is their custom when mourning." These young writers tended not to judge racial intermarriage as adult writers did, although their general opinions implied they still assessed Native Americans according to their own cultural standards.[33]

---

[32]Helm, *Conversations*, 245; Weeks, "Diary," 12, 14; Loba, "Reminiscences," 7; Butcher, *Hakan Anderson*, 416.

[33]Pace, "Diary," 22–23; Murphy, "Across the Plains Diary," 7; Taylor, "Overland Trip," 167. See Riley, *Women*, 128, about imposing standards of one's society upon a different way of life.

Reminiscences also noted children's curiosity about Native Americans. Some pioneers wrote "I remember" experiences, which seems logical as children tend to internalize and remember unique events. As with contemporary writings, reminiscences discussed visiting, watching young braves shoot coins, and observing dances. Mary Creighton entered a home

> and started to sit down on what looked like a big roll of blankets lying before the open fire. Before I could get seated an Indian woman shrieked at me and nearly threw me into a fit, while she gave a vigorous push with her foot to the roll which sent it across the room, and under the bed. There was a baby rolled up in the blankets.[34]

Lucinda Cockrill (Claypool) recalled a chief's daughter coming into camp. "She let me sit on her pony," and seven-year-old Lucinda cried to stay with her that night. When she saw a woman with a hungry papoose, "Mother let me fix some crackers and milk and feed it. Its mother gave me a pair of moccasins." As a small child, Mrs. Lee Whipple-Haslam admired some moccasins being traded, so she stole a pair. "An old squaw howled a long vicious wail, and about forty Indians were after me." The child's father met her at the wagon and spanked her in front of "the train and about a hundred Indians as spectators." After that experience "I had lost all admiration and love for the beautiful things of this world and the world to come." William Colvig described a "we remember" experience his father must have told the six-year-old. "Two ragged-looking Indians" came into camp prepared to spend the night. The captain did not "like the looks of those fellows" and suggested that William's father give the men some food, "then we will order them to move on." When the visitors sat down to their meal, the older one "removed an old, much-worn hat from his head," raised his hands, and offered a prayer in English for the safety of their white friends. These English-speaking "fellows" had come from the Whitman mission and were "all right."[35]

---

[34]Creighton, "To My Grandchildren," 2.
[35]Claypool, "Memory," 39, 40; Whipple–Haslam, *Early Days*, 8; Colvig, "Annual Address," 340–341.

In the early years of travel, curious youngsters remembered peace pipes and dances. These, however, were not mentioned in later years when emigrants flooded the plains. Thomas Belliston from England remembered a time when male emigrants and Native Americans sat in a circle, lit a long-stemmed pipe, and passed it around to puff as a symbol of friendship. A few reminiscences noted that Native Americans were afraid of pioneers taking their land. When the inhabitants learned the overlanders would not harm them, they brought out the peace pipe.[36]

Several early reminiscences noted Native American dances. John McBride watched one in which "the music rose and fell on the mild evening wind in tones of decided melody. I can imitate the music with my voice to this day, so deeply did it impress me" as a boy of fourteen, "but I cannot describe it." In an oral interview as well as her own written reminiscence, Lucy Henderson (Deady) described a war dance she had seen; however, she colored each with different details. In her interview she said,

> While we were stopping at Fort Laramie, the Indians gave a war dance. I was scared nearly to death. They were nearly naked and all painted, and they jumped and yelled and brandished their tomahawks while the fire around which they danced lit up their savage faces. There was one young squaw who was really pretty. She had a shirt and skirt of beautifully beaded and nicely tanned buckskin. It looked very pretty, but I was afraid of Indians so I didn't go very close to her.

Lucy's written recollection contained more elaboration.

> One night while we were there the Indians had what we would call a war dance. They had a great corral with a fire in the center, they were nearly naked, and all painted, and they jumped and yelled and brandished their tomahawks while the fire lit up their savage faces. It was very weird--really a terrible sight. I was scared nearly to death.
>
> Among the Indians was a young squaw who was called Princess Mary, probably named by the trappers. She was very pretty, the only Indian I ever saw that I thought was pretty. She had a most beautiful

---

[36]Belliston, *James Thomas*, 9; Smoot, "Autobiography," 3.

Ft. Laramie by Frederick Piercy. From James Linforth, ed., *Route from Liverpool to Great Salt Lake Valley.*

costume which, curiously enough, was made almost exactly like the Chinese costume, with coat and trousers. It was of buckskin, bleached and very soft. It was most elaborately embroidered with beads, and of course she was quite the thing. But I was afraid of Indians, so I didn't go very close to her.[37]

The interview was published in a 1923 Oregon newspaper, but no date was given for the written account. Either Lucy Henderson referred to the interview while composing the memoir, or she memorized certain phrases after frequent retellings. In two places she used the same words: "I was scared nearly to death" and "but I was afraid of Indians, so I didn't go very close to her." Lucy had more time to think about the written

---

[37]McBride, "Overland, 1846," 24; Helm, *Conversations*, 83; Henderson, "Young Adventure," 77.

piece, while during the interview she said what came to mind. The oral version with its simple wording and description appeared to be a more logical recollection of an eleven year old.

Another curiosity that attracted youngsters was the Native American form of burial. Young diarists sometimes commented about it. Lucy Canfield "discovered a dead Indian in a tree in the morning." Patrick Murphy explained, "When any of the indians die, they are wrapped in their blanket and hung in a tree or on a pole until they fall off or dry up; then their Spirit has departed for their Spirit hunting grounds." Rachel Taylor "passed a place where a dead Indian warrior was placed on a scaffold, their way of burying. A bunch of feathers had fallen down and we took each of us one in memory of the departed *brave.*"[38] Adults also discussed these burial customs. According to Glenda Riley, women either saw burial places as sad sights or they treated them irreverently by collecting the beads to wear. Men, on the other hand, were inquisitive but generally revered the deceased. In reminiscences, most young people respected the dead—or maybe they feared "ghostly" repercussions if they stole from one—and only a few like Emma Shepard (Hill) mentioned taking trinkets.[39]

Even though death was common to nineteenth-century children, Native American burials affected them in different ways. When James Farmer saw one of the graves, he thought he might like to be buried that way. Six-year-old Catherine Anderson (Ross) from Denmark was terrified of live Indians but wanted "to see a dead Indian hanging in a tree." She seemed satisfied to report, "I saw one, he was wrapped in a red blanket." Most children, though, were afraid. Eleven-year-old Lorenzo Hadley from England found a place with "all kinds of Indian bones, fingers, toes, skulls, arms and legs. They had

---

[38]Margetts, "My Journal," Sept. 9; Murphy, "Across the Plains Diary," 4; Taylor, "Overland Trip," 168.
[39]Riley, *Women*, 131, 196; Hill, *Dangerous Crossing*, 16.

evidently been burying their dead for years there and on looking up in the tree we saw a body. It apparently had just recently
been placed there and when we saw it we got scared and ran
back to the wagon." Fifteen-year-old William Hill and his
friends spotted a blanket in a tree. "As I neared it and getting
a whiff of wind from the direction of the tree I stopped and
told the others they could have it." William Pleasants watched
other boys climb "to where these grewsome relics were
deposited to view them more closely, but as for myself I was
as close to them as I desired to be while standing on the
ground."[40]

Native Americans, too, gratified their curiosity of emigrants
by peering into pioneer wagons, tasting their meals, and
occasionally spending the night. One thing they did not understand, according to Harriet Hitchcock, was the telegraph.
"They call it the whispering spirit." In a "we remember" incident, twelve-year-old Mary Powell (Sabin) was helping her
Welsh family pull their handcart when they met a large group
of Native Americans. "Father presented some of them with
beautiful peacock feathers," and they stared at the handcarts.
"Little wagons, little wagons," they said, and their women
laughed. Lorenzo Hadley recalled Indians asking where they
were going. Captain Ricks told them Utah "for the Big
Spirit," and one man said, "Mebbe so he go get Big Spirit."
These Native Americans did not bother their train. Brigham
Roberts wandered into a Sioux encampment near his train.
Earlier, his hair had been practically shaved to rid it of lice.
An Indian saw the bare head, brought "his open hand with
great force on the top," and yelled, "No scalp!" Roberts felt
his "short neck driven hard upon my shoulders, and with an
answering yell to that of the savage's, I bolted for my camp."
The man assumed "not even a scalp lock had been left on my
head at the place where the scalp ought to grow." Roberts'

[40]Giese, *My Life*, 22; Butcher, *Hakan Anderson*, 416; Federal Writers Project, "Lorenzo Hadley,"
5; Hill, "Autobiography," 4; Pleasants, *Twice Across*, 30.

humorous retelling came from an adult perspective, possibly to entertain his readers, but the child Brigham would have recalled it with fear and trembling. In "we remember" incidents Dilius Ward noted that bugle blasts ran off a band of Arapahos, and Mary Jane Long said that curious Indians squatted on the ground and listened to a violinist playing old-fashioned music.[41]

In addition to learning about each other's ways, Native Americans sometimes assisted and traded with overlanders. Especially during the early years, they guided emigrants to the best trails, grass, and water. They transported wagons and animals across rivers and sometimes guarded their stock. Native Americans exchanged moccasins, buffalo robes, and horses for food and other pioneer items. Along the Salmon Falls they bartered fish and fresh vegetables for emigrant goods. A few young diarists touched upon these topics. William Pace's Mormon Battalion company hired Native Americans to pilot them through the California mountains. The Donner party used two guides sent by Captain Sutter from California, but Virginia Reed complained about feeding them when provisions grew scarce. Mary Warner was grateful that "an Indian showed us where to find good feed and guarded the horses until dark." Thomas Griggs and Eliza McAuley mentioned trading, and several individuals came to Flora Bender's camp to trade for biscuits and blankets. "Pa bought a nice large buffalo robe for $3.50." Reminiscences also discussed trading and helping, but most came from "we remember" experiences. In one of the few "I remember" incidents, fifteen-year-old Sarah Davis (Carter) was walking ahead of the train with her sister and friends and got lost. An "old squaw" agreed to help them find their way if the girls gave her a petticoat and stockings, which they gladly did.[42]

[41]Hitchcock, "Thoughts," 241; Sabin, "Mary Powell Sabin," 12; Federal Writers Project, "Lorenzo Hadley," 4; Bergera, *B.H. Roberts*, 30; Ward, *Across the Plains*, 29–30; Long, *Crossing the Plains*, 7.

[42]Pace, "Diary," 21–22; Murphy, "Virginia," Letter 2: 3; Warner, "Diary," 24; Bender, Typescript, 7; Carter, *Pioneer Heritage*, 12: 228–229.

Although the young diarists did not experience major difficulties with Native Americans, they sometimes reported what other travelers told them—or they described tragic scenes that occurred before they arrived. According to David Lewis and Robert Munkres, adult diarists also described second-hand experiences and made it difficult to sift fact from fiction.[43] Rachel Taylor heard that "reports are continually reaching us of Indian depredations," and for a time she was wary and over-cautious. Flora Bender learned that emigrants were attacked and received assistance from soldiers. A stage station near the Nevada border was burned a few nights before the Bender train arrived, and the bones of a man and horses remained as evidence. When a soldier visited their camp with a scalp, he told the Benders he got it two weeks earlier. "During the night ten Indians visited their camp. They were soon surrounded by the soldiers and guarded. When day broke, they were all killed but one squaw. They took her prisoner. She was kept a few days and then shot." Flora Bender gave no explanation for the murders. A year later Mary Warner also mentioned this incident in her diary. Neither girl witnessed the massacre, but both were eager to record it. Flora also included a bit of gossip. The dead men belonged to the "Go Shoot," or Goshute, tribe which was "hostile to soldiers and emigrants but friendly to the Mormons. Old Brigham gives them 300 pounds of flour for every soldier and 100 for every emigrant they kill." Flora had heard rumors that Mormon leaders and Indians collaborated to harass or kill soldiers and emigrants. Happenings like these found their way into diary entries from second-hand reports on the trail, and many emigrants believed such charges.[44]

In addition to tales related by others, a few young diarists mentioned fear of Native Americans. Near Fort Kearny Patrick Murphy wrote,

---

[43]Lewis, "Argonauts," 294; Munkres, *Saleratus*, 112.

[44]Taylor, "Overland Trip," 162; Bender, Typescript, 12, Warner, "Diary," 19. See Unruh, *Plains Across*, 184, 315; Myres, *Ho for California*, 41; and Riley, *Women*, 229.

We started this morning, and five miles from camp, there were about five-hundred indian warriors; met a woman on horse back that the indians chased and stopped their wagon; they stopped us and we were going to fight them; we were all arranged with our guns and pistols; and being surrounded by the indians, we compromised by giving them a little sugar and flour; they took a bowie knife from a man that belonged to another train.

One wonders if Murphy was exaggerating when he stated five hundred warriors, since his train contained only a couple dozen men and hundreds of cattle. This occurred near Fort Kearny, so the company sent word to the fort, "and the captain ordered out a dozen men after them." Glenda Riley suggested that men exaggerated when they wrote about such topics, and "hundreds" of warriors may have really been fifteen. Later, young Murphy saw a dead Indian with six holes in his head, and he was hesitant to stand guard that night. Mary Warner and her aunt were walking ahead of their train when they discovered "fresh tracks of Indian ponies," and they hurried back to the road to safety.[45]

While Mary Warner's fear may have been unfounded, Harriet Hitchcock had reason to be frightened on her return trip from Colorado with a large military train. The 1864-1865 year was one of increasing hostility between white people and Native Americans. Traveling back to the States shortly after the Sand Creek massacre kept everyone in the train on edge. Someone shot at a rabbit, and the advance guard and scouts thought they were being attacked. During the night, a guard fired at Indians prowling near the wagons, and "great excitement prevailed throughout the camp until morning." Harriet Hitchcock saw the American Ranch burning, and "the bodies of two Indians were lying in the fire." Her train "passed a ranch which was burned yesterday." Julesburg had been destroyed the week before. Train members buried the body of a Mr. Andrews who had been killed "in the battle at Valley Station."[46] Being surrounded by death and destruction must

---

[45]Murphy, "Across the Plains Diary," 2, 9; Riley, *Women*, 101; Warner, "Diary," 9.
[46]Hitchcock, "Thoughts," 262–263.

have terrified thirteen-year-old Harriet. Still, she was the only one of nineteen young writers who witnessed such atrocities on the trail.

Eliza McAuley, on the other hand, noted that Native Americans sometimes feared pioneers:

> Our poor little antelope got killed by the Indian's dogs. The Indians were very much frightened, and tried to rescue her. They then offered to pay for her in skins and robes. We told them it was an accident, and they were not to blame, but they immediately packed up to go, saying they were afraid the men would shoot them when they came." [47]

Eliza McAuley crossed the plains in 1852 when Native Americans occasionally attacked single wagons and small groups, usually for plunder and not necessarily to kill. According to John Unruh, emigrants murdered more Indians between 1840 and 1860 than were killed by them. Ninety per cent of pioneer slayings occurred west of South Pass, with the worst stretch along the Snake and Humboldt rivers and on the Applegate route to Oregon. By the late 1850s, the pattern became an "eye for an eye and tooth for a tooth." If a white traveler refused to pay a toll at a bridge, or if a Native American indiscriminately killed a pioneer after losing his family from the white man's measles, one atrocity led to another. Because many pioneers made the trek only once, they often did not consider the repercussions of their hasty or cruel actions to travelers behind them. [48] This was not usually the case with Mormons who knew family, friends, and other church members would be following. Also, Utah teamsters made frequent trips back and forth across the plains, and they were usually careful in their dealings to insure a safe journey.

By the end of the 1850s, the United States Government had made and broken too many promises to the inhabitants of the land. White emigrants and traders often antagonized them, and soldiers and Native Americans treated each other with

[47]McAuley, Diary, 55.
[48]Unruh, Plains Across, 184–189.

hostility for decades following the "Grattan Massacre" in 1854. This incident occurred after soldiers near Fort Laramie ordered the Sioux to surrender a Dakota brave who killed a Mormon's cow when it strayed from the wagon train. Lieutenant John Grattan's men and the Native Americans exchanged fire. An Indian chief was killed, the Indians massacred the small military band sent against them, and later an army of six hundred killed or captured half the Sioux village. This event became the turning point for Indian-white relations on the plains.[49] Soldiers were sent to forts and stations on the trans-Mississippi trail to protect the overlanders, but it appeared that some military men believed the dictum that "the only good Indian is a dead Indian."[50] Flora Bender's story of the soldier with the scalp was an example of how some soldiers treated Native Americans. After the Sand Creek massacre, Harriet Hitchcock wrote,

> At the late battle at Sand Creek Col Shivington destroyed a village of 1000 Cheyennes The next day while the soldiers were burning the wigwams three little Indian children were found hidden under some Buffalo robes. They were nearly frightened to death. The soldiers brought them here and are getting clothes made for them. Bell has made a dress for the little girl and I have made her an apron. She is very shy and afraid of white people but seems much pleased with her new clothes. The man who took her intends sending her to the states to be educated.

Native Americans did their share of killing, but such violence was directed more often to soldiers and station keepers than at emigrants during the 1860s. Flora Bender observed that Indians "are not so hostile to the emigrants as they are to the soldiers and Stage men."[51]

"I remember" reminiscences mentioned terror in their trains when warriors approached in war paint until they

---

[49]Utley, "Indian–United States," 165; Mattes, *Platte River*, 3; and Munkres, "Plains Indians," 29. For information about military and Indian relations on the trail, see Unruh, *Plains Across*, 221–225, and Utley, "Indian–United States."

[50]Munkres, "Indian–White Contact," 455. See White, *It's Your Misfortune*, 337–340, about "Indian hunting" and whites murdering Native Americans.

[51]Hitchcock, "Thoughts," 260; Bender, Typescript, 14.

learned the men were fighting other tribes. Mormon hand-cart pioneers felt especially vulnerable. Ether McBride recalled three thousand Sioux going east to battle the Pawnees. When the warriors saw the frightened handcart emigrants, they jab-bered, laughed, and made signs of friendship. Since the train consisted mostly of "squaws and papooses," the men did not consider it "a brave act" to kill them. Ether McBride was only eight when this happened, so his young mind probably reg-istered three thousand warriors. Children sometimes shivered with fear when Native Americans stampeded their stock or came into camp. Six-year-old Ann Wilden (Johnson) from England hid in her wagon from "an old Indian chief." He "ran his long spear as far into the wagon as he could reach" and terrified the child even more. An inquisitive man sneaked up and peeked inside Sarah Luper's (Douglas) wagon. "Well maybe I did not let out a yell, loud enough to raise the dead on those Plains," but the girl made sure everyone knew she was there. "To this day I have no love for an Indian nor do I like to read 'Indian stories.'"[52]

Youngsters remembered being frightened when they were away from the safety of their wagons. Ten-year-old John Young waited behind his train to bring in a cow that needed to rest. "I saw an Indian just across the creek move from behind a tree. Needless to say I made quick tracks toward camp." The next morning the boy learned that his cow had been killed. Four-year-old Amos Johnson was riding his horse behind the wag-ons when several Native Americans appeared and pretended to capture him. Before a search party arrived, the men put the boy back on the trail and headed him toward his people. Mar-garet Olsen (Atkinson) from Sweden stopped with a friend to pick flowers in a hollow, and several Indians rode toward them. "One shot an arrow at us but it did not hit us. We hid, lying flat under the bushes and grass." The men "looked every-where for us and then rode away." Mrs. John Gowdy had just

[52]Carter, *Heart Throbs*, 7: 80; King, "Long Journey," 9; Douglas, "Memories," 2.

finished gathering "choke berries" with her friends when "an Indian boy about our size" came from behind the brush. "We ran screaming at the top of our voices" back to camp. The boy followed them with "the limbs of cherries on his arms" and offered to trade them "for a needle and thread that my aunt had." Allene Taylor (Dunham) was playing away from the wagons with friends when several Native Americans approached on horseback. Seeing the girls were frightened, one of the men said, "No be fraid. Heap Indians coming, no hurt white pappoose." Along came men, women, children, horses, and dogs. "Some of them stopped and looked us over and talked among themselves" but did not harm the young pioneers. Soon the girls' fathers came and escorted them back to the wagons with a warning to "never to get so far away again."[53]

Of all the reminiscences, only 3% noted attacks that killed family members, and many of these were instigated by white renegades. White men disguised as Indians either provoked assaults or committed crimes for which the land's inhabitants were blamed. Even emigrants knew about the out-cast whites who led marauding, plundering bands to attack innocent overlanders. In 1854, Mary Perry's (Frost) train divided into smaller groups after Native Americans burned the grass along the trail in Idaho. The Ward division moved on ahead and was massacred. The Perrys followed with three other families. Their small party was also attacked, and Mary's father was killed. Mary "never entertained a doubt but that the two men who led the Indians in the attack, were white men as their manner, dress and talk indicated it. They wore good clothes and had their hands and faces and feet painted, which the Indians did not."[54]

In 1860, Emeline Fuller's train separated in Idaho, with some

---

[53]Young, *Memoirs*, 56; Johnson, "Autobiography," 7; Wilson and Cowan, *Descendants*, 63; Gowdy, *Crossing the Plains*, 4; Dunham, *Across the Plains*, 7.

[54]Unruh, *Plains Across*, 193; *Told by the Pioneers*, 1: 103. For information about the Ward massacre, see Unruh, *Plains Across*, 189–190, and Madsen, *Shoshoni*, 57–59.

taking the California Trail and Emeline's party going to Oregon. One day when their small company stopped, "three Indians and two squaws came into camp and all agreed that the leader among them must be a white man, as his dress and appearance was different from the rest. He had a beard, and you could see plainly that he was painted." The wary emigrants continued on the trail until one fateful day Indians descended upon them. Thirteen-year-old Emeline watched part of her family die, then she grabbed her baby sister and told four younger siblings to follow. "I started, I knew not whither, but with the one hope of getting away from the wretches who seemed to thirst for the blood of everyone of us." She and the other survivors "traveled by night and hid in the willows that grew along the river by day." They had no food or clothing and eventually did as the Donner party and subsisted on the bodies of those who died. Finally, a relief party rescued them after a soldier who had been traveling with them earlier reached Fort Walla Walla with the tragic news. "I shall never forget the pitying looks bent on me by those strong men. Tears stood in every eye as one of the officers gave me a part of a buscuit. . . . I could not have lived many days longer if help had not reached us."[55] As Mary Perry and Emeline Fuller said, many attacks on trains were instigated by white men disguised as Indians.[56]

In 1865, a few months after the Sand Creek massacre, Amanda Fletcher's (Cook) wagon was attacked by a small band of Cheyenne Indians, most likely in retaliation for the recent killings. Amanda's mother died, her wounded father escaped, and she and her two-year-old sister Lizzie were captured. Originally from England, the Fletchers were on their way to Cal-

---

[55]Fuller, *Left By Indians*, 12, 18–19, 27, 28, 31. For details about the Otter–Van Orman train massacre, see Unruh, *Plains Across*, 192; Madsen, *Shoshoni*, 115–119; and the entire text of Emeline Fuller's account.

[56]See Unruh, *Plains Across*, 193, 197; Riley, *Women*, 107; and Madsen, *Shoshoni*, 17, 46–47, for information about "white Indians" perpetrating acts which were blamed on Native Americans.

ifornia in a larger company when this occurred. Being the lead wagon, the family kept a few hundred yards ahead of the train. At noon they stopped at Rock Creek in Wyoming, and Indians attacked and captured thirteen-year-old Amanda and her little sister Lizzie. The child cried "first for mother and then for me to take her, till finally she was carried out of my sight." Amanda Fletcher lived with her captors nine months before being rescued. The next year Annie Cottle's family from England got separated from their Mormon train at a river crossing. Indians appeared and shot Annie and her father, killed her grandparents, and took her mother captive. Annie Cottle assumed "the Indians did not capture me . . . because I was dressed like a boy with my hair cut short." She never saw her mother again.[57]

Although most experiences were not so tragic, friction still occurred because the two cultures did not understand each other. Most young diarists complained about Native Americans begging, but the writers probably did not realize that overlanders were part of the cause. Flora Bender noted camps "swarming with red skins all day, begging and stealing when they had a chance." Another day "a number of Indians of the Shoshone nation are around camp, begging for biscuit." Patrick Murphy mentioned giving biscuits to several Paiutes, and Thomas Griggs's and Lucy Canfield's trains fed people as well. Eliza McAuley described an old Indian on an old pony "with a begging letter written by some white man, asking people to treat him well and give him something." Reminiscences also mentioned begging but usually in general "we remember" terms. Thomas Miller recalled that Native Americans sometimes carried begging papers "to prove that they were good Indians," though some of the letters "were very curious. An Indian would gravely hand out a 'recommendation' read-

[57]Cook, "Captured by Indians," 1–3; Trenholm, "Amanda Mary," 6–46; Carter, *Pioneer Heritage*, 2: 240–241.

ing 'This is a bad Indian. Look out for him. He will steal your eyeteeth if you don't watch him.'"[58]

In addition to begging, young pioneers noted when Native Americans stole animals. Again, the children did not understand the other culture or circumstances. Horse stealing was a time-honored custom which increased a tribe's economic wealth and social status and enhanced trade. By mid-nineteenth century, horses had become necessary to the Native American way of life. The animals were obtained in three ways: natural increase, theft, and the capture of wild horses. Most Indians had perfected their horse stealing ability and, according to John Unruh, theft was somewhat of a game to many tribes.[59] Several times William Pace noted the loss of animals. Once he said, "This night we had two horse stolen by the Indians," and later he wrote, "This night Joseph White had a Horse stolen by the snakes." Mary Warner talked about Indians stampeding their animals. The men found their horses "guarded by two Indians who fled as soon as they saw them." At the same time, Native Americans did not understand pioneer ways. When an emigrant family lost its draft animals, the impact was disastrous. Andrew Jenson "passed a number of wagons from which during the night previous the Indians had stolen all the animals and . . . were consequently unable to move till help could be sent." Reminiscences usually described animal thefts through "we remember" or second-hand experiences. John Braley wrote about a band of young Sioux warriors who stole animals and everything else they could take from another train. Finally, an emigrant went to the village and told the chief. "Without saying a word, the chief seized his shotgun, mounted his

[58]Bender, Typescript, 7, 15; Murphy, "Across the Plains Diary," 9; Griggs, "Crossing the Plains," 33; Margetts, "My Journal," Aug. 23; McAuley, Diary, 20; Helm, Voices, 339.

[59]Hyde, *Pawnee Indians*, 251; Moore, *Cheyenne Nation*, 137, 187; Madsen, *Shoshoni*, 52; Munkres, "Plains Indians," 27; Unruh, *Plains Across*, 198.

pony and rode like the wind to the train." Then "he let out a warwhoop," and his warriors fled.[60]

When pioneers and Native Americans treated each other disrespectfully, ill feelings resulted and affected relationships on the trail. In her diary Rachel Taylor explained that a "Digger Indian" approached her father to talk, but "one sight of his revolver however was sufficient to clear the road." Eliza McAuley wrote that "some Pawnee Indians came around, and getting impudent, and toublesome, we pointed empty pistols at them, and told them to 'pucachee', or we would shoot them. The ruse succeeded, and they soon left us." Almost all of the "I remember" reminiscences describing cruel acts between the two cultures came from California and Oregon trail travelers. Al Hawk recalled a drunk Indian dumping his siblings out of a chair. Al's father hit the man over the head with an iron shovel, which frightened the other emigrants because "an Indian never forgets." Native Americans at Salmon Falls stole almost all of the whips in Robert Earl's company. Then a "big Indian" wanted to trade a whip he had taken from another train, and Robert's brother grabbed it and hit the man on the head. Later, a kind Indian helped Robert Earl get his pony across a river and asked for remuneration, but Robert's brother "gave him a good thumping" instead. That night the man took his pay by stealing four horses. One ill treatment deserved another. Other conflicts arose if pioneers did not give tribute for passing through Native American lands or if they refused to pay tolls at bridges or ferries. Since overlanders were killing wild game and destroying grass, timber, and water resources, tribes along the trail believed they should receive renumeration from the trespassers. Also, if Indians built bridges and provided ferries, emigrants should pay as they did to white entrepreneurs who performed similar operations.[61]

---

[60]Pace, "Diary," 28, 29; Warner, "Diary," 20–21; Jenson, "Journals," 80; Braley, *Memory Pictures*, 58–59.
[61]Taylor, "Overland Trip," 178; McAuley, Diary, 18; *Told By the Pioneers*, 1: 159; Earl, "Reminiscences," 2–3; Unruh, *Plains Across*, 169–171.

Some emigrants did not consider Native Americans people and badly abused or killed them. Jesse Applegate remembered a Mexican in his train who chopped off a Native American's hand "and hung it on a stake about three feet high in the encampment. I saw it hanging there myself, and was afraid of it, for I saw it was a man's hand." The Mexican was banished from the train. Benjamin Bonney recorded a "we remember" experience, probably told by his father. A Southerner captured a Native American for a slave, and Bonney's father said, "The first thing you know, that Indian will escape and tell the other Indians and they will kill all of us." But the Southerner refused to listen. He whipped the Indian to "break his spirit," and finally after several weeks the man escaped. The white person's superior attitude often created hostile feelings and contributed to later problems on the trail. These experiences of Robert Earl, Jesse Applegate, and Benjamin Bonney occurred in the 1840s and could have contributed to subsequent animosity. But Native Americans were cruel to white people as well. Amanda Fletcher (Cook) described her experience in captivity as a slave where she prayed to die. Some tribes did participate in slave trade, and this was one cause of Utah's Walker War.[62]

Sometimes pioneers accused Native Americans of acts they did not commit, partly because nerves were taut from tales of capture and plunder. When two horses were missing from their train, Rachel Taylor assumed that "Indians were at the bottom of the affair." The men loaded their guns and went to retrieve the animals. Soon they returned "not having fired a gun," for the horses had strayed during the thunder the night before. After hearing about attacks, Rachel Taylor's mind swam with Indians. She and a friend went for a walk on a bluff

and after rambling around for a while, we looked over to another ridge and saw some living moving objects which we thought could be noth-

[62]Applegate, *Recollections*, 13; Lockley, *Across the Plains*, 6–8; Cook, "Captured by Indians," 2–3; Allen and Leonard, *Story of L.D.S.*, 270–271.

ing but an Indian. After looking at it awhile, and seeing it raise up and then stoop down quickly out of sight, we ran into camp and told the news. Away went the men with their guns to the top of the hill, and saw not a hostile Indian but one of our men, who had been dipping water from a spring with a dipper. We came in for a good share of jokes and there is no end to the fun at our expense.

Poor Phil! what a dangerous situation was his—exposed to the murderous fire of their empty guns.[63]

According to Glenda Riley, false alarms taxed both men and women, but women tended to overreact as Rachel Taylor and her girlfriend did. Traveling ahead of their train, Ada Millington's family panicked when they approached wigwams with Indians milling about. "When they saw us they went into their camp and began to fire guns." The Millington family waited for the train to catch up, then they all moved toward the enemy. To their surprise, the "wigwams" and "Indians" were really tents and soldiers. They all "had a good laugh over our scare." Occasionally adults created similar threats to keep their trains in line. The captain of Flora Bender's train went ahead in search of grass, then returned with news that he had seen forty "redskins." The company

immediately corralled, without a drop of water within three miles, all in the highest state of excitement, and expecting a savage band of Indians to pounce upon us at any minute. But they did not come after all the fuss. I guess it was only a joke of the captains to have an excuse for camping for it was getting late and all the company were dissatisfied.[64]

Sometimes emigrants teased Native Americans. Several diarists wrote about such scenes. When Rachel Taylor's mother was ill, a "Digger Indian" entered her tent. A white traveler "made signs" that the woman had smallpox, and the "dusky guest separated and was seen no more." A Native American came to Ada Millington's camp and saw Ben Freeman washing clothes. "Be you one squaw?" the man asked, and Freeman answered, "Yes, washerwoman." The confused man repeated "washerwoman" to himself. Later, Jake Shontz

---

[63]Taylor, "Overland Trip," 161, 162.
[64]Riley, "Frontierswomen's," 24; Millington, "Journal," 227; Bender, Typescript, 10.

made some bean soup for supper and after peppering some of it very much he gave it to the Indians. They saw us eating ours with such a good will they thought it must be very good so they tried to eat what he gave them. But it was so hot with pepper that with tears standing in their eyes they said, "Whitey man like, Indian no like it," and they gave it up. This was rare fun for Jake.

Mrs. M. A. Gentry's brother-in-law shook hands with several warriors "each in turn till he came to the last warrior in the line. To him he extended only his little finger." The man "drew himself up to his full height and strode away in haughty anger." Although her brother-in-law considered it a joke, the girl was ashamed of his lack of manners. With adult perspective, Mrs. Gentry said, "I have often wondered if much of the trouble between the Indians and white men was not caused by just such foolish and insulting actions."[65]

On the other hand, a Native American's sense of humor could be as inappropriate as a pioneer's. Margaret McNeil's (Ballard) Scottish family settled at Wood River, Nebraska, before continuing to Utah. One day the adolescent and her brother were searching for their cow when three Sioux Indians approached. Margaret "was afraid they would carry us away," and she told her brother to pray and run. The men caught up with them and "tried to pull my brother up on his horse," but the boy slipped away. "The indians laughed and had a good time at our efforts to get away from them." Finally at home, their mother fed the men "a nice warm supper and they went away peaceably." Francis Watkins "got the scare of my life" when he was playing near the camp and several Indians "decked out in their feathers and war paint" rode toward him. The boy thought of his scalp and took off "as fast as my little legs would go." The men followed "laughing their sides off" watching him run.[66]

Youngsters learned that there were "good Indians" and "bad Indians" just as there were good and bad white people, and

[65]Taylor, "Overland Trip," 178; Millington, "Journal," 252, 261; Ross, "Child's Experiences," 302.
[66]Ballard, "Margaret McNeil," 8–10; Milliken, *Crow Emigrant*, 4–5.

individuals in both cultures sometimes provoked each other. But children did not usually harm or annoy. Adults committed the malicious acts, and young people became victims or witnesses. Children considered Native Americans people even though their appearance, lifestyle, and ways were different. Although most young pioneers feared Native Americans, they were equally inquisitive about them. As long as they were protected by their families or trains, they attempted to satisfy their curiosity. Young emigrants learned that Native Americans varied from tribe to tribe and, most importantly, from individual to individual.[67]

Children's perceptions of others on the trail were influenced by family values and society's expectations. Missourians, Mormons, and Native Americans were often stereotyped, mainly because pioneers did not take the time to get to know and understand those who did not fit their own nineteenth-century standards. Yet, young people tended to judge these groups less harshly than did their adult counterparts. They were curious about Native American lifestyles and they saw positive aspects about Mormons in Utah. Other wagon trains on the trail gave children a sense of security because pioneers assisted and socialized with each other in a large traveling community. At her journey's end, Flora Bender observed that the "savage race" was "mostly harmless."[68] Most of the young writers could have said the same about other groups on the trail as well.

---

[67]Riley, "Frontierswomen," 29; see also Williams, "My First Indian," 18.
[68]Bender, Typescript, 18.

CHAPTER VI

Goldilocks Revisited

*Goldilocks was a dimpled darling, three years old. She had
big blue eyes, a fair skin and golden hair with a natural
curl .... Goldilocks was a cheerful, contented child who
laughed easily and frequently at her brother's efforts to
amuse her. Even the hardships of the trail could not curb
her high spirits.*

In the mid-1960s, historian Francis Haines published an
article entitled "Goldilocks on the Oregon Trail" in which he
reported that pioneers told their most colorful stories years
after an actual event. But because Haines did not find similar experiences recorded in trail diaries, he assigned the tales
to folklore.[1] "One such story which crops up again and again
in various reminiscences, but is never found in the journals or
diaries, might be called: GOLDILOCKS ON THE OREGON
TRAIL." In this story, Haines explained, Indians on the trail
were fascinated with Goldilocks, a golden-haired emigrant
child for whom they were willing to trade an "entire herd" of
horses. More often, though, they offered five to twenty animals. Of course, the pioneer mother refused.

From his study of trail diaries and reminiscences—how
many he did not specify—Haines learned that only in reminiscences did "Goldilocks" travel "with many a wagon train."
Sometimes Indians made several attempts to buy the female
child. Other times a train captain teased Native Americans
by agreeing to trade a white child or young woman for ponies.

---

[1]Haines, "Goldilocks," 27–30.

According to Haines, "this joking offer by the captain of the train, or some other man, . . . is a motif which recurs frequently." In fact, about a third of the "Goldilocks" stories contained the joking friend or relative.[2] Haines concluded that these tales were based on two common Anglo-Saxon misconceptions: other people envied white children and Indians bought their wives. Was Haines's assessment of "Goldilocks" stories accurate?

Although Francis Haines identified many "Goldilocks" tales, only one diary and fifteen reminiscences of the 453 young pioneer accounts which I studied noted such an incident. Since the exchange usually involved children or young women, it seems they might have included the experience more frequently in their writings. Fifteen of the sixteen documents involved a female in the trade. Six writers stated the event happened to them, nine mentioned someone else in their train, and one recalled general information about buying a "white squaw." Half of the sixteen accounts described the incident as a joke.

From his unspecified number of diaries, Haines found only two which described Indians bargaining for children. Both were written in 1853 by adult women. Celinda Hines wrote that an Indian woman on her way to the Shoshone country offered to trade her baby for a skirt. Harriet Sherill Ward recorded that an Indian would not sell his pony but would swap it for an emigrant girl of seventeen.[3] Neither account mentioned the exchange as a joke. Of the twenty-three young pioneer diaries, letters, and journals which I analyzed, one diarist did record this type of jesting. Mary Eliza Warner wrote in her 1864 diary, "Uncle Chester traded Aunt Lizzie off for three ponies but she would not go." According to Aunt

---

[2]Haines, "Goldilocks," 28.

[3]Haines, "Goldilocks," 29; Hines, "Life and Death," 120. According to Haines, Celinda Hines said the Indian wanted to trade her baby for a "skirt." In the *Covered Wagon Women* account, the word was "shirt."

Lizzie's trail diary, Indians bargained for her two different times.[4]

John Unruh described the "Goldilocks" theme as "one of the basic components of reminiscent accounts." He reported that reminiscence writers "were fond of magnifying and even inventing such episodes"; however, "not all such incidents can be relegated to the realm of folklore." He referred to a few trail diaries which described the event. In addition to those mentioned by Haines and Unruh, several other adult diarists recorded the experience. In 1850, Indians wanted to buy Angelina Farley's child for ponies, and the same year Sophia Goodridge wrote that a Sioux "wanted to trade a horse for a white woman."[5] On her way to Denver in 1860, Helen Clark made three separate entries about Indians wanting to trade for her. West of Fort Kearny, she wrote,

> This morning we go 3 miles from camp and meet Indians moving— come to the wagon and wanted to give a pony for ME, and Mother guessed as I was the only papoose she had she couldn't spare me. He also wanted to give a pony for Mrs. Wimple & Mr. W. thought as she was the only one, he could not spare her conveniently.

Helen was twenty years old and single; Mrs. Wimple was near her age. In the Cheyenne region Helen said, "We saw some Indians that offered 5, 6, and 10 ponies for me and Mrs. Wimple. One wanted to sell his pony & get her and whisky." Helen's final experience included joking.

> Three Indians passed us today horseback and they stopped as they passed Mr. Kline, Mrs. Wimple and me, and Mr. Kline wanted to know what they would give for ME, and one, the chief, held up all his fingers and Mr. Kline asked him if he had three ponies, he gave assent and made room on behind for me when Mr. K. backed out.[6]

In F.W. Blake's 1861 diary, two Sioux Indians "met our Train yesterday. They were mounted on ponies. one of them enrap-

---

[4]Warner, "Diary," 8; Mattes, *Platte River*, 587.

[5]Unruh, *Plains Across*, 166–167; Mattes, *Platte River*, 251; Goodridge, "Mormon Trail," 223.

[6]Evans, *Two Diaries*, 26, 38, 39.

tured I suppose with the sight of the girls offered to barter his poney away for one of them, he wanted one with dark hair poor chap he was doomed to dissapointment,—he might have struck a bargain with some poor henpecked fellow."[7]

From these contemporary trail accounts, it appears that the "Goldilocks" motif was based on fact, at least in origin. English folklorist George Gomme claimed that folk customs or beliefs had their roots in real historical events. What produced "Goldilocks" roots? Several historians provide possible insight. James Axtell noted that during the colonial period Native Americans sometimes captured and adopted white women and children to replace family members who died. Most of the young captives were carefully chosen to maximize their adjustment into Indian society. According to Peter Stern, Native American raiders of the Southwest wanted women and children, partly to replenish tribal numbers after losing them to war and disease. They knew that children under twelve assimilated more easily into a new culture. John Moore wrote that Cheyennes captured and traded women and children; they also intermarried to improve trade relations and strengthen military alliances. By 1880, adoption and remarriage had formed the bulk of the Cheyenne nation. Royal Hassrick stated that the polygamous Sioux stole wives and adopted children. If a youngster died, parents sometimes took in an orphan or asked to adopt another family's child as a replacement. This adoption was formalized by feasting, performing a give-away ceremony, and presenting a horse to the birth parents.[8] These statements show that some Native American tribes were accustomed to assimilating women and children from other tribes and cultures into their own. As a result, "Goldilocks" incidents could have occurred on the emigrant trail.

---

[7]Blake, "Diary," 10 Aug. 1861.

[8]Montell, *Saga*, xvi; Axtell, *Invasion Within*, 304, 306, 315; Stern, "White Indians," 266, 269, 270, 281; Moore, *Cheyenne Nation*, 186, 189, 262–263, 297; Hassrick, *The Sioux*, 43, 47, 110–111. See also Allen and Leonard, *Story of L.D.S.*, 270–271.

In his essay entitled "Folklore and Reality in the American West," Barre Toelken stated that "Goldilocks" is a widespread legend in the Pacific Northwest and to an extent throughout the West. In fact, families of pioneers have often shared tales about Grandma almost being sold to the Indians. Toelken identified these retellings as "culturally created truth." Legends like these help socialize people and place them in a cultural value system. Toelken wondered if the reality of "Goldilocks" was common or if it only happened to a few families on the trail. Like Francis Haines, Toelken questioned the practice as diaries did not confirm family legends. Since only fifteen of the 430 childhood reminiscences I studied mentioned "Goldilocks" experiences, the actual practice probably occurred less frequently than family legends suggest. Also, according to an L.D.S. Church Historical Department pioneer database search, only one diary and seventeen reminiscences of more than 2,000 first-person accounts described such an incident.[9] The "Goldilocks" story must be more prevalent in second-hand retellings and family legends than in first-person documents.

Of the fifteen reminiscences which I identified, seven "Goldilocks" stories occurred on the way to Oregon, five on the road to Utah, and three on the California Trail. Although there were twice as many total Mormon accounts, a greater percentage of Oregon Trail travelers mentioned "Goldilocks" incidents. Perhaps this corroborates with Haines's assessment of large numbers of Oregonians discussing them. Ten of the fifteen experiences took place before or in Wyoming. Three of these accounts referred directly to the Sioux tribe, and one identified the Cheyennes. This agrees with what the historians said about these tribes wanting to capture or trade for women and children. Almost all fifteen writers were between 63 and 81 years old; the oldest was 87. Yet most were between ten and fifteen when they crossed the plains, and the youngest

[9]Toelken, "Folklore," 18–21; Bashore, Letter, 30 Jan. 1998.

was six years old. The credibility of this motif is affected by who participated as "Goldilocks": the writer of the reminiscence, someone else in the train, a person days ahead on the trail, or a pioneer who did not record the incident but a descendant who did.

The more realistic and unembellished "Goldilocks" reminiscences were the unpublished ones. Of course, writers may have invented or embroidered some of the stories, especially if they reported second-hand information. Eight of the fifteen accounts described the experience happening to someone besides the writer. Harrison Sperry only touched upon the topic when he said, "One day while we were traveling along, there was a large bank of Indians came to our camp and wanted to buy a white squaw. They also wanted whiskey and sugar, but we had no white squaw or whiskey for sale." Mosiah Hancock wrote,

> When we got within about two days travel of Laramie, we just about got into some trouble with a large company of Sioux Indians. John Alger started in fun to trade a 16-year-old girl to a young Chief for a horse. But the Chief was in earnest! We got the thing settled, however, and were permitted to go without the loss of Lovina.[10]

According to the diary of John D. Lee, an adult who traveled in Hancock's train, John Alger was a real member of their company. Lee mentioned Alger's name but did not describe the experience Hancock related. In a diary entry at Ancient Bluff Ruins, Lee noted a band of Sioux camped near them. He wrote that

> visits were made by this band of Sioux. They had a large american Flag which they hoisted. Returned by a Flag of Truce from the cos. who gave them Some litle presants & some thing to Eat. They seemed perfectly Friendly & Harmless, wanted to trade for Some thing to eat. After smoking the Pike by thier request a Letter of commendation was given them.[11]

---

[10]Sperry, "Short History," 4; Hancock, "Life Story," 26.
[11]Cleland and Brooks, *Mormon Chronicle*, 1: 43, 56.

Why did Lee ignore the "Goldilocks" incident in his diary? Was he doing something else when Hancock witnessed the scene, or did Hancock create the tale years later? If John Alger, the story's antagonist, had recorded the experience, its credibility would be more reliable. Even so, Mosiah Hancock did not fictionalize his retelling by adding flowery or unrealistic details.

Several other young pioneers recalled unembellished "Goldilocks" experiences about someone else in their train. In a published interview Mrs. M. A. Gentry remembered hearing "many strange stories of queer bargains made by the travelers with the redmen." But because of what happened to her married sister, she was willing to give credence to them. Mrs. Gentry wrote,

> One day a chief came to our camp with five ponies, which he offered in exchange for my sister. Naturally, she was much frightened, and climbed into the wagon in haste and buttoned down the canvas flaps as tightly as she could. I was asleep at the time, and so have no personal knowledge of the episode, and do not know how the men managed to decline the proposal without giving offense to the old chief.[12]

Mrs. Gentry was honest enough to tell the interviewer she did not know what actually happened when she could have embellished the story with shared or collective memory.

Olive McMillan's (Huntington) experience may have come from shared memory since she did not say what she remembered as an eight-year-old pioneer. The family crossed the Missouri River and fell behind the other wagons. That evening as they set up camp, two Native Americans paid them a visit. One held Olive's one-year-old sister who

> played with his beads. This pleased him so much that he asked to buy her. Mother shook her head but when her attention was taken from him he put sister up behind him and began backing away from the camp. He was within a few feet of some when mother saw him and calling to the other members of the party. He dropped sister and ran into the woods.[13]

---

[12]Ross, "Child's Experiences," 302.
[13]Huntington, "Tells of Experiences," 1.

Annie Taylor (Dee) recalled as an eight year old going to Utah that

> two big Indian chiefs . . . wanted to trade two ponies for my cousin, Annie Maddock. She was a nice looking girl about seventeen years old. Of course father said, "No," and she hid in the wagon and we traveled on. The Indians did not make any trouble for us, however, as we feared they might. That was one ride that Annie got, and maybe the only one, as we were all supposed to walk.[14]

These "Goldilocks" stories involving other individuals seem realistic based on the fact that the pioneers did not make a spectacle of their recollections. Instead of exaggerating and fictionalizing, they stated what happened and moved on with their memories. Annie Taylor Dee's comment about Indians not causing trouble "as we feared they might" may have provided impetus for pioneers to magnify these situations as years went by and tales were told and retold.

While nine of the fifteen pioneers reminisced about "Goldilocks" occurring to someone else, six said it happened directly to them. Because these stories were not second-hand tellings, their credibility increases. Of course, they would be more believable if the youngsters had written diary entries the day the incidents took place. In one reminiscence Belle Redman (Somers) was only six years old, and she did not record what she remembered personally. Most likely her mother kept the story alive, for Belle related the tale from her mother's point of view. Two Sioux Indians begged Belle's mother to swap her daughter for a pony.

> My mother was thoroughly frightened and held me closely to her side. The two Indians then retired to the rear end of the Train, and while one sat on his horse and waited, the other Indian moved forward rapidly to our wagon and reaching forward made a quick movement to grab me. Mother's frightened screams gave the alarm, while at the same time the Indian rapidly joined his companion, swung on his pony and dashed away at top speed. The men of the Train followed in hot pursuit but failed to capture the Indian.[15]

---

[14]Dee, *Memories*, 13.   [15]Somers, "Crossing the Plains," 3.

Belle's trail experience was published in a California newspaper when she was eighty-two years old.

Martha Gay (Masterson) recalled at age thirteen almost being sold to Indians. Her father jokingly asked some men who were selling ponies "how many ponies they would give for Mamie or I." They offered "a number of their best," but Martha's father explained he was only teasing. The Indians "got angry and we got alarmed and ran and hid in the wagons. Father could not make them understand it was a joke. He fed them and tried to talk them into a better humor. He never asked another Indian how many ponies he would give for one of us." Martha's father probably helped supply the details and perpetuate the tale through the years. Elisha Brooks crossed the plains at the age of eleven. At eighty-one he recalled that Native Americans "were anxious to buy white children, offering a pony for a boy and two for a girl; but no mother wished to sell her children at that price, though our teamster tried to dispose of me in this way, claiming that was more than I was worth." His was the only account to mention a boy being offered to the Indians. In her unpublished interview Margaret West (Irvin) recalled that Indians sometimes visited their camp. The eleven-year-old girl was frightened "because the Indians were crazy over my red hair and several times offered to trade a pony for me. When I would see them coming, my mother would hide me in the back of the wagon and throw a shawl over my head."[16] These young people did not embellish the "Goldilocks" experience; instead, it became one of many trail incidents.

Eleven-year-old Ellen Perks (Johnstun) emigrated from England alone in a Mormon handcart company. A Scottish teamster had nothing to trade for a pair of moccasins and, being bothered by Indians, he "thought to get rid of them by saying he would trade me for them. The Indians were very pleased

[16]Barton, *One Woman's West*, 37; Brooks, *Pioneer Mother*, 22; Adams, "Covered Wagon," 21.

and would not change the trade. These Indians followed us for three days and I had to be hidden to keep them from stealing me."[17] One wonders where Ellen was concealed since the group pulled handcarts, and only a few supply wagons traveled with them. Since her family was not with her on the trek, Ellen could not build shared memory with them. When she recorded the incident, she did not embellish it.

In contrast to succinct descriptions, Susan Johnson (Martineau) wrote published and unpublished accounts of almost becoming an Indian bride at the age of fourteen. In the published version she added dialogue, embellishment, flowery description, and extra days to her tale. In her unpublished memoir Susan said,

> One night we camped near a band of Cheyennes. The following day, being rainy, we remained in camp. The Indians, old and young, came into camp trading moccasins and robes. Among the rest was a fine looking young Indian who wanted to buy a squaw. Offering some fine ponies, Andy Kelley asked him who he wanted, and I was pointed out as his choice on account of my dark eyes and rosy cheeks. Kelly finally made a trade for five ponies, a buffalo robe, and the silver ornaments on his hair. In the evening he came with his ponies. Kelley told him it was all a joke – that the girl belonged to another family. This made the Indian mad; he said a trade was a trade. Then Captain Markham came and explained to the Indian that Kelley was no good and had no right to do as he had done. The Indian finally went away very indignant.

By piecing the two stories together, we learn that Kelly was a soldier who had deserted from Fort Kearny and joined the Mormon train. He revealed his true character by stealing some of the emigrants' clothes and later worked on Salt Lake City streets with a ball and chain attached to his leg. Susan continued her unpublished tale with:

> That night there was a high wind which blew down Aunt Sarah's tent. The tent was placed facing our wagon with the back toward a deep ravine full of willows. Aunt Sarah was holding the front tent pole and I the back while two men were driving stakes at the side. The night

---

[17]Clayton, "Biographies," Box 2: 4.

was pitch black, lighted at intervals by flashes of lightening. Suddenly I felt strong arms lift me to the back of a pony. I gave a terrified scream. At that instant a flash of lightening revealed the situation to the men who came to my rescue. I slid off the horse's back which the Indian mounted and escaped. He had been hiding in the ravine waiting his chance for revenge, and but for the flash of lightening I would have been carried off. An extra guard was placed for the night, but when morning came everything that was loose, such as frying pans, skillets, and other cooking utensils which had been put under the wagons, had disappeared, leaving the company short of these articles. The band of Cheyennes disappeared and were seen no more by the company.[18]

According to the story published in the Mormon *Young Woman's Journal*, the Cheyenne was approximately twenty years old. The deserting soldier told the man, "You may have her for five horses, five buffalo robes, and some dried meat, and two antelope skins." The amount bartered was slightly different in the two accounts. After the Cheyenne agreed to the sale, he said,

> he would come "one sleep" and bring the pay. Many were the mock congratulations showered upon the bride-to-be and requests for invitations to the wedding, much to the annoyance of the prospective bride. . . . The next morning affairs assumed a serious aspect. The Cheyenne appeared early in the morning with the horses. . . and demanded his bride.

When informed it was a joke, the man was determined to obtain his bride. He had brought his goods "and would have her, or the company would be sorry." Being "absolutely denied," he "went away in furious rage, with dire threats of revenge." Train members feared attack, and they kept their guns ready. A few days later, "a terrible tempest of rain, hurricane, thunder and lightning came upon us." The darkness was "like that of Egypt," except for intermittent flashes of light. The Cheyenne attempted to steal his bride but was "foiled of his prey." He "dashed down among the willows and was gone in an instant." In this published account Susan added phrases to build suspense and move the plot along, but she ignored details,

---

[18]Johnson, "Record of Susan," 7–8.

such as pans and cooking utensils disappearing from camp. Her purpose and audience for the journal article were to promote faith among young Mormon women. She acknowledged that the Lord saved her "by a single flash of light," and she added, "How wonderful are the ways of the Lord!" These two records of the same incident suggest that memories can change depending upon audience, purpose, and the circumstances under which they are remembered. Two other young people in Susan's company briefly recalled the journey, but neither mentioned associations with Native Americans. Only Thomas Forsyth wrote, "We passed lots of Indians on our way But They never gave us any trouble." Cholera was the main topic of discussion in both documents.[19]

Of the fifteen childhood "Goldilocks" reminiscences, nine were published during the pioneer's lifetime. Five writers, including Susan Martineau, exaggerated their tale. In a published interview Catherine Thomas (Morris) at the age of eighty-seven had quite a yarn to tell. Her father was captain over 100 wagons, twenty-five young drivers, and many children including ten-year-old Catherine. A "young chap, along about 20 or thereabouts," named Steve Devenish traveled with them. He was jolly, likable, and "a great hand at joking." Naturally, all the young ladies liked him. Catherine recalled that

> some Indians came to our wagon train and, like most Indians, they were very anxious to get hold of some of the white girls for wives. When Steve found what the chief wanted he pointed to one of the prettiest girls in the bunch and asked the chief what he would pay for her. The chief offered ten horses. Steve and the chief bargained back and forth and finally the chief raised his bid to 20 horses. Steve said, "Sold. She's yours."

Of course, the young people considered this great fun until the chief returned with the horses and demanded the girl.

Steve explained that he was joking, that white people didn't sell their

---

[19]Martineau, "Almost an Indian Bride," 264–265; Forsyth, "Pioneer Life," 2–3, 25–27; Genealogical Society, *Utah Pioneer*, 7:1.

women for horses, that a white man didn't have to pay anything for a wife and sometimes she was dear at that price. The Indian couldn't see the joke. He became angry and demanded that Steve carry out his bargain. Finally the girl's father and my father, the captain of the train, sent the Indian about his business and we went on.

This was not the end of the story, for Catherine continued, "That night the Indians swooped down on us and stampeded our stock." While the men were searching for the animals, the Indians "met them with a volley of arrows" and badly injured one of them. Unable to recover the stock, the company was forced to abandon half of its wagons. "Mother had to leave all of her treasured possessions" except a flatiron which she received as a wedding gift. The men burned the fifty wagons so the Indians could not take them.

Meanwhile, the girl's father planned to kill Devenish. This practical joke cost him animals, a wagon, and most of the family's heirlooms. The men of the company decided to banish Devenish from the train. Now with fewer wagons every child over ten, including Catherine, was forced to walk to Oregon.[20] This tale fits the exaggerated pattern Francis Haines found common in Oregon Trail reminiscences.

So do three accounts of Oregon pioneers who published childhood memories. Joaquin Miller prefaced his story with preconceived notions. He said that Native American women west of the Missouri River

> were very fond of the white children and all the time wanted to touch and fondle them. Mother seemed afraid they would steal her little girl. She . . . had read a yellow book telling all about how Indians would steal little girls! The Indian women were all the time trying to lay their hands on my little brother Jimmy's great shock of frouzy yellow hair, but he would run away from them and hide under the wagon.

After Miller's train passed Fort Hall and crossed the desert to Oregon, "a friendly Indian chief" on a "fine spotted horse" asked Mr. Wagoner, a member of their train, what he would

---

[20]Helm, *Conversations*, 135–137.

give for his beautiful daughter. "The Indian was told in jest that he would take ten beautiful spotted horses, like the one he rode." So the chief

> dashed off and the same day overtook us with the ten horses and a horde of warriors, and wanted the girl. Of course, everybody protested, but the chief would not be put off. The Oregonians that had been sent out to meet us were appealed to. It was a very serious matter, they said.
>
> The chief was an honest man and meant exactly what he said, and had a right to the girl. The majority agreed, and thought the best way out of it was to let papa marry them. This seems strange now, but it was the Indian custom to buy wives, and as we were in the heart of a warlike people, we could not safely trifle with the chief.
>
> The girl was about to throw herself in the river from the steep bluff where we were, at which the chief, seeing her terror, relented, and led his warriors off, scornfully refusing what presents were offered him for his forbearance.

Miller did not record what he remembered about the encounter or even if he was present. Either his story came from collective memory or he invented it because it contains elements of a folktale. As an adult, Miller became a famous poet and, according to Bret Harte, was "the greatest liar the world has ever known." He "wrote 90% fact and 90% fiction" and perplexed readers, critics, biographers, and historians.[21]

In his published account George Waggoner described a "Goldilocks" story about his sister. Along the Snake River, a "young warrior took a fancy to my sister Frances, and asked father how many horses it would take to buy her." At the time Frances was eighteen years old.

> Father answered, with a laugh, that she was worth ten spotted ponies, as she was a very good cook and had long, beautiful hair, and moreover, already had Indian moccasins on her feet. The young lover took the whole thing in earnest and went away. An hour later he returned with a band of spotted ponies, and, reinforced by a dozen comrades, demanded his bride. His wrath knew no bounds when told that father was only joking. He was a warrior of fame with a battle name a yard long . . . and would stand no such foolishness; he had bought a wife

---

[21]Miller, *Overland*, 73, 77–78; Guilford–Kardell, "Joaquin Miller," 7.

and was going to have her, or his people would murder us all. He gave us until sundown to decide whether we were going to treat him right or not.... [D]uring the evening several hundred of the red rascals came into camp, and all declared we should complete the bargain and give up the girl, or we would all be murdered.

The emigrants begged for time, so the Indians agreed to make the exchange the following evening. Meanwhile, "women and children were in tears" and "the men looked pale and anxious." Other trains joined the frazzled company, and soon fifty-six men with guns were ready to fight. The next evening one hundred warriors in war paint appeared. "The young chief rode forward, and in a loud voice, demanded his bride, on penalty of death" if the emigrants did not meet his terms. But George Waggoner's father was perturbed, and his "Jacksonian blood flashed in his face." With fifty-five rifles backing him, he knocked the brave to the ground "and gave him a most unmerciful kicking and drubbing," yet "not an arrow flew, nor a shot was fired." The Indians went away, but the pioneers prepared themselves for future attacks.[22]

This recollection contains the suspense and detail of sensational fiction. No diary thus far described violence, attack, or retaliation if Native Americans could not buy "Goldilocks." Even when overlanders joked about a trade and backed out, diary accounts did not mention war or the threat of it. Indians did not return with many ponies and "hordes of warriors" to claim their prize. Of fifteen reminiscences, Waggoner's is the only one that included such violence.

One aspect of the "Goldilocks" recollection by Joaquin Miller and George Waggoner needs further research. Did the two families cross the plains in the same company? If so, they probably described the same event. Both pioneers went to Oregon in 1852, and Miller said the experience happened to a "Mr. Wagoner's" daughter. In other words, both writers used the name Waggoner but with slightly different spellings. Miller

---

[22]Waggoner, *Stories*, 12–14.

wrote that "Mr. Wagoner" joked about trading his beautiful daughter to an Indian chief for "ten spotted horses." George Waggoner noted that his father joked to a young warrior about exchanging "ten spotted ponies" for his daughter Frances. In both recollections the young Indian returned the same day with the animals and "a horde of warriors" or "a dozen comrades." In both stories the young Indian was disgruntled when he could not obtain his bride. Yet while Waggoner described physical retaliation by Native Americans, Miller only noted that the girl considered suicide. Although the Waggoner family began their trek on April 21 and Miller's party started on May 15, they may have joined each other along the trail, then separated in Oregon since one crossed the Cascade Mountains and the other traveled along the Columbia River. Perhaps Miller, who published his trail experiences in 1930, borrowed parts of his tale from Waggoner, who wrote in 1905.

Fifty years after going to Oregon as a young boy, George Himes spoke at the annual Oregon Pioneer Association with an embellished "Goldilocks" tale. His company was camped near the Umatilla River, and

> a number of Indians rode up, all well mounted on a number of the most beautiful ponies that I ever saw up to that time, all dressed in gay costume with feathers and fringes abounding. One of the Indians, the leader of the rest, whom we afterwards found out was the noted Walla Walla chief, Peu-Peu-Mox-Mox, came near our camp, and seemed especially interested in my baby sister, then ten months old, who had beautiful golden hair. I was taking care of the little girl at the time and noticed that the Indian eagerly watched every movement I made in trying to amuse the child. Nothing was thought of the Indian's visit that night, but the next morning, in some unaccountable way, hundreds of Indian ponies were found grazing near the camp. . . . The Indians were driving the ponies toward the camp under orders from Chief Peu-Peu-Mox-Mox, who proposed to trade them for the little red-haired girl. This information was conveyed to my mother by Mr. Sarjent, and the offer of the great chief was respectfully declined, much to his apparent sorrow, as he rode away followed by his body guard, meanwhile striking his breast and. . . [m]eaning that his heart was very sick.[23]

---

[23]Himes, "Annual Address," 144–145.

At least George Himes placed himself in the "Goldilocks" scene, which is more than what Miller and Waggoner did in their retellings. Still, this story has the folklore quality noted by Francis Haines.

Was Francis Haines's assessment of "Goldilocks" incidents correct? Such experiences did crop up in reminiscences, frequently with the joking offer, but not to the extent he suggested. One fallacy with Haines's article was the way in which he generalized. He did not specify how many diaries and reminiscences he studied to form his conclusions. Moreover, he said the "Goldilocks" motif did not occur in diaries. A few accounts have been found that mention it, and the diarists did not embellish the incident nor did they elaborate on warring Indians when a trade was not completed. Also, Haines stated that "Goldilocks" stories crop up again and again in reminiscences. From the first-person accounts considered here, they do not seem as common as Haines purported.

Teasing about another culture may have contributed to real or contrived "Goldilocks" stories. Mary Ann Parker (Wilgus) remembered that her older sister "Emaretta had red hair and blue eyes and Father used to tease her by telling her the Indians liked red haired girls, so she always hid when she saw Indians for fear they would steal her."[24] Only thirty to forty years ago on a reservation in Eastern Utah white adults told their children, "If you don't behave, I'll give you to the Indians." But turn-about is fair play. One day a white woman was in a J.C. Penney's store in Roosevelt, Utah, and she overheard a mother from the Ute tribe say to her misbehaving child, "Suh, I give you to white lady."[25] Whether "Goldilocks" stories were real, embellished, or created, one cannot discount them all and relegate them to the realm of folklore. Perhaps Native Americans have their own colorful versions of "Goldilocks" stories—and they may not all be folklore either.

---

[24]"Mary Ann Parker," 112.
[25]Heaton, Telephone interview, 10 February 1998.

CHAPTER VII

What Young Pioneers Did and Did Not Say

Different travelers see the same thing in a different light. What is torment to some is mere sport to others. They may go over together the same ground and see the same sights, yet their account of them would scarcely show a resemblance. Both are equally honest and truthful, but they see entirely different sides. The character of the glass gives color to the object.[1]

After they arrived in Oregon in 1852, Margaret, Catharine, and Harriet Scott sent letters home to relatives in the Midwest. Though the sisters traveled together and shared common experiences, their letters emphasized different aspects of the trail just as the quote above suggests. Age, developmental factors, audience, and purpose colored what they wrote. Six months in Oregon, Margaret Scott, now sixteen, discussed topics that interested relatives or answered questions from letters sent to her. To her Grandfather Scott she wrote, "You wished to know what became of the boys that started through with us," then she explained what happened. She also said, "You have doubtless heard that Pa is married and who he married before this time I will only say that we like the lady very much and she is kind to us as our own mother, could be." Margaret mentioned her father's remarriage in a letter to her Grandfather Roelofson, then added, "We get along very well together as yet and I think we always will, But allthough the

---

[1]McCall, *Great California Trail*, 6.

living has taken the place of the dead the image of my sainted Mother will never be erased from my mind." Audience and purpose influenced what she said.

Thirteen-year-old Catharine wrote to her Grandfather Scott two months after she reached Oregon. The journey and her mother's and brother's sickness and death were still fresh in her mind, so she focused on them. She also noted "a great deal of sickness on the plains this season, we passed as many as 7 new made graves a day along Platte river." Relatives in Oregon brought relief teams and provisions and assisted their family through the Cascade Mountains. The short time span between the event and the writing influenced what Catharine said. Although eleven-year-old Harriet wrote the same day as Catharine, she only spent a portion of her letters talking about the journey. The deaths on the trail of "old Flower," their cow, and "old Suckey," their horse, were important to her. Perhaps she did not mention her mother and brother because Catherine did. Harriet assured her Grandfather Scott, "[W]e have got your likeness and it does me a great deal of good to look at it." She was not impressed with the "continiual rain" in winter which made Oregon "dull and gloomy."[2] Of the three girls, Harriet Scott wrote the shortest letters. Her age, interest, and attention span probably did not keep her at her task very long.

LUCY CANFIELD'S 1862 DIARY

The L.D.S. Church Historical Department has compiled records of emigration companies and individuals traveling in them. As a result, documents for a particular year and company can be studied to ascertain what young people said or left out in their contemporary accounts. The 1862 diary of fifteen-year-old Lucy Canfield provides one example. Although the original diary has not been located, transcripts were donated to the church's historical department and to the DUP;

---

[2]Scott Sisters, "Letters," 157–160, 163, 166–167.

also, one of Lucy's relatives gave me a typescript. One of the three accounts appears to be handwritten by Lucy Canfield (Margetts) as an older woman; perhaps she copied her teenage diary verbatim. Each record differs slightly in mechanics and additions or deletions, but the concepts remain the same. For example, one of Margetts' handwritten entries states, "Another day has passed into eternity and all is well Rose stayed last night with Hattie[.]" The same entry in the DUP transcript says, "Another day has passed into eternity and all is well. Rose stayed last night with Hattie in their wagon. Hattie is going back now to Council Bluffs."[3] What did Lucy Canfield include or ignore in her teenage trail diary? For this analysis I have used Margetts' version of the document.

Lucy, her widowed father Isaac Canfield, and twenty-year-old cousin Rose traveled by train from Livingston County, New York, to Marengo, Iowa. ". . . we stayed a couple of weeks and got a team of oxen and a wagon," then went to Florence, Nebraska. There they joined an independent company to Utah, as her father had the means to pay for the journey. Lucy wrote almost daily on the trail, but she did not allow the reader to jump into her mind for long. Her diary appeared to be meant for her eyes alone. One can get an idea of what Lucy did and did not say by comparing her writings to those of James McKnight who, as chaplain and clerk of the train, kept the camp journal. McKnight jotted down day-to-day details as well as minutes of meetings and church happenings. He also compiled a roster of people, wagons, and animals.[4] Mormon trains were urged to keep rosters, as the *Deseret News* reported: "It is the duty of every captain and clerk of 50, and of all lesser and other companies . . . to make out a full list of every soul that was organized in their company. . . with any observations

[3]Margetts, "My Journal," July 24; Canfield, Diary, July 24. See also Canfield, "My Journal," and Carter, *Pioneer Heritage*, 6: 27–30.

[4]Canfield, "My Journal," 1; Carter, *Pioneer Heritage*, 6: 27; Journal History, 16 Oct. 1862, 1–12. This account is an edited version of McKnight's original diary in the L.D.S. Church Archives. For the train roster, see Journal History, 16 Oct. 1862, 13–16.

concerning the situation of their companies they may think proper" and forward them to Willard Richards, editor of the *Deseret News* and general historian and recorder of the church.[5] The Isaac Canfield train roster, writings by members of their company, and accounts of others who traveled west the same season provide insight into what Lucy did and did not say.

What did Lucy write about the company in which she traveled? She noted that Mr. and Mrs. Neal, their daughter, and eighteen wagons joined them at Florence, Nebraska. Their company left the end of July and arrived in the Salt Lake Valley in mid-October, 1862. According to the train roster, Lucy left out some important details. Her company consisted of thirty-one wagons, not eighteen as she stated, and 118 people, which included sixteen one- and two-parent families. Perhaps her train traveled in two divisions, although James McKnight mentioned men in both groups throughout his diary. The train roster showed that children sixteen years old and under comprised 43% of the train; this included five infants. Thirty-five percent of the emigrants were between the ages of seventeen and thirty-nine, and 22% were forty or older. Mr. and Mrs. Bloomfield, ages sixty-two and sixty-one, made the long journey from England. A fourteen-year-old girl traveled alone as did several adults, including a sixty-year-old man. One-third of the emigrants left from Great Britain: twenty-five from England, seven from Scotland, and six from Wales. Others came from states in the Northeast and Midwest as well as Utah. William Dallin was returning from a mission to England. The *Deseret News* reported that Isaac Canfield's train "had an exceedingly prosperous journey; that there was but little sickness and no deaths in the company, and their losses in cattle were inconsiderable."[6]

[5]"List of Mormon Emigrants," *Deseret News Extra*; Jenson, *Biographical Encyclopedia*, 1: 55.
[6]Canfield, Diary, 1; Journal History, 16 Oct. 1862, 1, 3, 13–16. Jenson, "Latter–day Saints Emigration," 118, reported that the Canfield company consisted of 211 passengers. The 1997–1998 *Deseret News Church Almanac*, 174, noted that the train contained 120 people and 18 wagons.

In his account James McKnight often included Lucy's father. Once the company agreed to purchase a riding animal for Captain Canfield. At camp meetings the captain made frequent remarks. During one such gathering, he "earnestly requested the guard to refrain from sleeping or lying down while on duty." At other times he counseled the saints to "cherish the spirit of peace," avoid killing snakes, and have camp prayers.[7] Yet Lucy hardly discussed her father in her diary. She mentioned him in Iowa and Florence, Nebraska, but said nothing more until near the end of the journey. When they reached Weber Canyon, Lucy stayed with relatives while her captain-father led the emigrants to the Salt Lake Valley via Emigration Canyon, then returned for his daughter. On October 21, Lucy wrote, "Father came about 3 o'clock."

From her diary entries, Lucy seemed more interested in her cousin Rose, her peers including young males, and train members other than her father. What concerned adults on the overland trek did not necessarily impress a fifteen-year-old girl whose father was busy being captain and probably relying on others to look after his daughter. One of Lucy's main concerns was Rose. At the Missouri River, Rose grew homesick and wanted to return to New York but was afraid, so she continued on to Utah. Occasionally the girls rode horses together. One evening "Rose got supper all alone. I fell asleep just before we camped."[8] Did Lucy remain asleep while her cousin fixed supper?

Lucy mentioned other young people in her company, but she did not elaborate or explain who they were. The train roster, however, provides additional information. For example, one day Lucy wrote, "Bell was quite sick." According to the roster, "Bell" probably was fourteen-year-old Isabella Gray who emigrated to Utah alone. Knowing that the girl was traveling

---

[7]Journal History, 16 Oct. 1862, 1, 2, 5.
[8]Margetts, "My Journal," July 25, Sept. 26, Oct. 21.

alone provides insight to the statement that she was "quite sick." Lucy frequently mentioned Albert Stickney. From her early entries at Florence, Nebraska, one wonders if the young man had taken a liking to Rose. "We . . . spent the evening" with Al and "had a good time." Al brought them perfume and fans from Omaha, and he and Rose "went for a ride and got back just [before] dark." After they began the journey west, Al "was up twice today. his Co [of ten] is 2 miles from us." Later, Al "over took us just as we were ready to start out in the afternoon. Rose stayed with them all night." On the trail, though, Lucy talked about Al without including Rose. One day his wagon got stuck and another day he went hunting.[9] Lucy also associated with Damie Stickney. The train roster listed Al and Deidamia as nineteen- and sixteen-year-old children of Joseph Stickney, a captain of ten who probably worked closely with Lucy's father.

Besides being friends with the Stickneys, Lucy rode horses with Ruth and Mary. According to the roster, they may have been the fifteen- and ten-year-old daughters of Christopher Dixon, another captain of ten. The Dixons emigrated from Ohio with eight children. Mary more likely was sixteen-year-old Mary Wightman. The Wightmans and their eight children left from the same town in Ohio as the Dixons. Both families had an infant and youngsters ages six and four.[10] Did Ruth, Mary, and Lucy help care for the six small ones? Lucy never said. In fact, she never mentioned younger children in her diary.

Traveling together for nearly three months, Lucy must have known Emily Butler, Henry Minkler, John Pickett, and Fanny Wagstaff who were sixteen years old; but she said nothing about them. She also overlooked fifteen-year-old George Isom and his three siblings. When she noted youthful activities, she mentioned no names. Her company stopped near a military

[9]Margetts, "My Journal," July 1, 2, 8, 10, 11, 30, Aug. 4, 25, Sept. 20; Journal History, 16 Oct. 1862, 16.

[10]Margetts, "My Journal," July 27, Aug. 21, Sept. 11, 30, Oct. 5, 19; Journal History, 16 Oct. 1862, 13, 14.

station, and "some of the girls took dinner with the soldiers." Near Echo Canyon her train "camped opisite some very high bluffs Went up on them & the boys rolled some rocks down." Mormons, particularly young people, often sang and danced on the trail, but Lucy did not mention these entertainments. Yet, that same year Ada Millington wrote about singing and playing dulcimer music around the campfire. Louisa Cook's company "danced cotillions till 10 oclock." Louisa Mills (Palmer) danced to the fiddles played by teamsters in her train, while teamsters in William Lindsay's church train played violins, accordions, and concertinas to help the Saints forget the troubles of the day.[11]

In addition to naming a few peers, Lucy occasionally noted adults in her train. Sometimes she rode with James McKnight or Mr. and Mrs. Neal. When Mr. McKnight and Mr. Minkler went to "Kearney," the company waited for their return. Again, the roster provides details Lucy did not put in her diary. Minkler emigrated from Ohio with his wife and two children, one of whom was approximately Lucy's age. Later, "Mr. McFarlin broke a single tree" on his wagon. The roster tells us he came from Scotland with his wife and four children. European emigrants, like the McFarlins, usually lacked knowledge about oxen, trail travel, and outdoor living.[12] One wonders how Mr. McFarlin dealt with wagon repairs and if the foreign-born Saints in this company experienced other problems on the trail. Did the Welsh converts speak English? How much did Lucy associate with the foreign emigrants? Were they being assimilated into L.D.S. culture?

In his trail diary, James McKnight wrote about incidents Lucy ignored. For example, Mary Wightman's father set up a forge to mend tires, and the men repaired a bridge across a

---

[11]Journal History, 16 Oct. 1862, 13–16; Margetts, "My Journal," Sept. 28, Oct. 11; Millington, "Journal," 220; Cook, "Letters," 43; Carter, *Pioneer Heritage*, 13: 456; Lindsay, "Autobiography," 12.

[12]Margetts, "My Journal," Aug.11, 12, 14, 15, Sept. 2, 10; Journal History, 16 Oct. 1862, 13, 15; Taylor, *Expectations*, 225.

river. Lucy noted friendship with the Neals, but James McKnight reported a problem. Mr. Neal, "a gentile merchant" and sergeant of the guard, refused to pay an assessment on his mules, so "a poor pedlar, not really a camp member," paid it. While Lucy only wrote that "Mr. McNight and Minkler went to Kearney," James McKnight explained that three hub boxes on the Minkler wagon had broken, so they went to Fort Kearny and Kearney City to obtain replacements. It appears that Lucy did not go inside the settlements, or she might have described them as Louisa Cook did in her diary that year. Fort Kearny contained barracks, a garrison house, and government stables, while Kearney City had groceries, grog shops, cobbler and blacksmith shops, and twelve families. The houses were made of adobe and sod with whitewashed or cloth walls and carpets on dirt floors. The male residents were of a rough sort who drank, gambled, cursed, and fought.[13]

In her diary Lucy hardly mentioned daily devotions and Sabbath worship. Yet, James McKnight frequently discussed them. One Sunday Lucy wrote, "Travelled 4 miles had a splendid sermon in the afternoon by Elder McNight[.]" On the same date McKnight noted morning and evening meetings and discussions about Sabbath observance, "prompt attendance at camp devotions," and obedience to God and His servants. Another Sunday did not seem like the Sabbath to Lucy because they "travelled about 15 1/2 miles to day without stoping." On the other hand, McKnight talked about camp devotions, evening songs, prayer, and remarks. Before reaching Salt Lake City, Lucy attended church services in a Utah settlement where she heard Brigham Young speak. Later, the *Deseret News* reported that "the immigrants in this company were more strict in their devotional exercises than some others have been, and generally held meetings every evening during the entire journey.[14] One could not tell from Lucy's writings.

---

[13]Margetts, "My Journal," Aug. 14; Journal History, 16 Oct. 1862, 4, 8, 11; Cook, "Letters," 35.
[14]Margetts, "My Journal," Aug. 3, 10, Oct. 18; Journal History, 16 Oct. 1862, 1, 2, 3.

While James McKnight made observations which Lucy overlooked, Lucy recorded her own discoveries. This was her first trip west, and the girl was intrigued by the scenery. At Chimney Rock she wrote, "Tis a wild & romantic country round this rock," and Scottsbluff had "very romantic looking Bluffs." West of Fort Bridger Lucy "went on the summit . . . and had a most beautiful view of the surounding country." Weber Canyon was the "most romantic road we have had yet. Would not have missed coming this way for anything. I never saw such rocks they beat all that I saw in Echo Kanyan." In his camp journal McKnight omitted scenery, but he had made other trips across the plains and did not see the trek as a first-time traveler. Both writers, however, talked about thunder-storms and pleasant days. Neither mentioned prickly pear cacti or prairie dog towns. Yet on her trip to California that year, Ada Millington saw prairie dogs stand on their mounds and bark at emigrants, then jump in their holes and hide.[15]

Lucy also included topics which involved her personally, such as female duties. She sewed, made buffalo pie, ground coffee, washed clothes in the river, and emptied wet trunks to dry their contents. But she did not write about obtaining wood and water for cooking or making molasses candy on bright moonlight nights as fourteen-year-old Louisa Gittens (Clegg) did on her way to Utah that year. In an adult diary that sea-son, Louisa Cook described leaving the "land of buffalo chips" and burning wild sage two feet tall, and Lucy mentioned "a fine fire" made from sagebrush.[16]

Both Lucy Canfield and James McKnight observed other travelers on the trail, particularly the Mormon down-and-back trains which began running the year before. During the 1862 season, seven church trains made the journey from Salt Lake City to Florence, Nebraska, to transport thousands of Mormons

---

[15]Margetts, "My Journal," Sept. 1, 2, Oct. 9, 14; Millington, "Journal," 211.

[16]Margetts, "My Journal," July 4, Aug. 11, 18, Sept. 8, 19, 24, 26, Oct. 1, 10, 16; Clegg, "Life of Louisa," 14–15; Cook, "Letters," 51.

to Zion. For the first three weeks on the trail Lucy and McKnight observed Ansel P. Harmon's large company traveling near them. They also acknowledged an intermingling between the camps. Lucy noted that "two boys from Church train stayed all night with us," which must have intrigued the fifteen-year-old girl, and James McKnight wrote that Brother Davis from Harmon's camp offered morning prayer. With 650 emigrants and only thirty-six wagons, those in the Harmon train who could walk did so. In contrast, Lucy's independent company had more wagons per person and, as a result, individuals could choose to walk or ride. Yet Harmon's church train arrived in Utah almost two weeks earlier than Canfield's.[17] Church trains were usually better organized than independent groups.

Freighting firms also used the trans-Mississippi route. West of Fort Laramie, Lucy and James McKnight noted several freight trains going their way. According to Lucy, "Hamptons train crossed the river before we started," and McKnight wrote that "Godbe's Company crossed river about noon, including the Bates wagons." A few days later the Bates brothers nooned near them. One day the Canfield company recovered fifty head of wandering cattle, and Hampton and Bates lost stock in the same vicinity. A *Deseret News* article later reported that Canfield lost only three or four cattle during the entire trek "and those mostly belonging to a small train, freighting merchandise, which travelled with the company part of the way." Perhaps this was the incident to which the newspaper referred. While Lucy only mentioned a few small freighting companies, Ada Millington observed twenty-five large wagons loaded with provisions heading to Denver and sixty or seventy wagons returning.[18] By 1862, freighting had become an important business from the Missouri River to the new city of Denver.

[17]Margetts, "My Journal," Aug.10, 12, 13, 22; Journal History, 16 Oct. 1862, 2, 4, 6; *Deseret News Church Almanac*, 174–175. See also Hulmston, "Mormon Immigration," 32–48.

[18]Margetts, "My Journal," Sept. 13, 18, 20; Journal History, 16 Oct. 1862, 1, 9, 10; Millington, "Journal," 207, 208.

Other evidences of civilization could be seen along the western trail as well: improved roads and bridges, stage stations fifteen to twenty miles apart, coaches with passengers or mail, road ranches, trading posts, government forts, and telegraph lines. Yet Lucy did not record many impressions of people and buildings along the way. At Fort Kearny she bid farewell to civilization, then reported a stage station at Chimney Rock, "the first house we have seen for a long time." Between Fort Laramie and Fort Bridger she noted a few stations and a stagecoach. West of Fort Bridger some Utah boys arrived with peaches and flour, and Mormon settlements appeared in Weber Canyon. Traveling through Nebraska, James McKnight observed signs of civilization—Reed's Ranch, the towns of Fremont and Columbus, and Western Stage station—which Lucy ignored in her diary. According to McKnight, near Columbus a guard from Canfield's train left his post, and the animals "damaged a farmer's corn, melon, and broom patches." The company paid for damages but charged the amount to the guard. In central Nebraska McKnight noted Grand Island, Fort Kearny, and Johnson's and Tom Keeler's places.[19]

A more accurate account of stage stations and ranches between Fort Kearny and western Wyoming that year appeared in Ada Millington's journal. Sometimes Ada described the places. A stage station at Mud Springs, Nebraska, had twenty men staying at it. Thirty-five miles east of Fort Laramie a man and his wife took care of a ranch or station, and closer to the fort was a ranch with "a very nice store or trading post." Two days west of Fort Laramie a station or ranch was "kept by a family who seem so nicely fixed." A plank fence enclosed a grassy yard and whitewashed house. "The walls of the house are papered the floors carpeted and furnished to correspond." Although families lived away from "civilization," they took

---

[19]Margetts, "My Journal," Aug. 14, Sept. 1, 15, 22, 26, 28, Oct. 3, 5, 7, 8, 12, 14, 15; Journal History, 16 Oct. 1862, 1–4.

mid-nineteenth-century culture to the desert. Ada Millington continued to notice stations or ranches almost daily to Fort
Bridger.[20] Needless to say, this adolescent made longer entries
than did Lucy.

Throughout her terse writings Lucy Canfield generally
ignored three important but related aspects of travel that season: the Civil War, soldiers on the trail, and Indian problems.
During the 1850s, the U.S. Army had been assigned to posts
in the West to quell conflicts with Indians. By 1862, settlers
and travelers demanded visible protection from marauders, and
telegraph lines which now spanned the continent needed
guarding. Because of the Civil War, most of the regular soldiers returned east to fight, and Western volunteers and ex-
Confederate soldiers replaced them at frontier posts.[21] In spite
of the war, westward migration continued, particularly with
draft-evaders and Southerners escaping the conflict, Mormons
moving to Zion, and miners going to Idaho and other new
regions of the West.

Even before she arrived at the Missouri River, Lucy Canfield gave no indication that the United States was deep in
the throes of the Civil War. Yet sixteen-year-old Thomas
Griggs who traveled to Utah the year before noted evidence
of hostilities. In New Jersey, a regiment of soldiers "displayed
their civilization by endeavoring to force themselves into the
room where the sisters were, but failing in the attempt used
the most obscene language." Traveling by rail near Chicago,
Thomas saw a pole with a noose hanging from it and the
words, "Death to traitors." At Hannibal, Missouri, the home
guards kept a cannon confiscated from the South, and a secessionist leader was being held prisoner. Inside the state "much
excitement existed here in consequence of large bodies of Rebel
Troops" who were "burning bridges firing into trains &c."

---

[20]Millington, "Journal," 219, 221, 224.
[21]See Unruh, *Plains Across*, 201, 227, and Munkres, "Plains Indians," 29.

Chilicothe "presented the appearance of a captured city." Business was "entirely suspended and the streets patroled by armed men of every conceivable character and drunkeness profanity and obscene songs seemed to be the order of the day." Rebels fired at railroad cars, and a secessionist flag was pulled down at St. Joseph.[22] Obviously, Thomas Griggs went through a state where war was raging, while Lucy Canfield traveled farther north to reach the jumping-off place.

On the trail Lucy said little about soldiers and nothing about the war. In Wyoming soldiers visited Canfield's camps at the Upper Platte Bridge and the Sweetwater River. Near Pacific Springs, her train stopped by a military station where some of the girls ate with the soldiers. But other diarists provided additional pieces of information. On the Sweetwater, McKnight reported soldiers "of thirty or more distributed along at different stations." Louisa Cook complained to relatives back home that she had received "no news about the war or the country." Fort Laramie contained six hundred troops, and an Ohio Calvary unit occupied the Sweetwater Bridge Station. Ada Millington saw two companies of Kansas Home Guards at Fort Kearny, Nebraska, and seven regiments had been sent to the Sweetwater River. Twice in June soldiers passed Ada's group on their way back east. She also noted soldiers at stations near Independence Rock, South Pass, and Pacific Springs.[23]

According to McKnight, "straggling members" of the Sixth Ohio Cavalry were sent to the Sweetwater "to quell Indian disturbances." Indian problems were a major concern in 1862, for Native Americans were no longer passive to emigrant invasion and treatment. They destroyed stage stations, attacked stagecoaches, killed drivers and others, and scattered mail. In April near South Pass, the Pacific Springs agent refused to let

[22]Griggs, "Crossing the Plains," 5, 11, 14, 15, 17, 20.
[23]Margetts, "My Journal," Sept. 17, 23, 28; Journal History, 16 Oct. 1862, 11; Cook, "Letters," 46, 48, 53; Millington, "Journal," 212, 219, 227, 229, 230, 233.

mail coaches move through the area unless troops were there to protect them. By the end of May, stage stations had been abandoned and burned and mail sacks torn open, not only by Native Americans but also by white outlaws who put the blame on Indians. Members of the Sixth Ohio Volunteer Calvary unit, led by Lieutenant Colonel William Collins, finally arrived to protect the most dangerous part of the mail route from the Upper Platte Bridge through South Pass.[24] Many stations along the trail contained telegraph offices which required protection as well.

In the early 1860s, Ben Holladay's stage line boasted five hundred coaches, five freight wagons, five thousand horses and mules, and several thousand oxen. Changing drivers every ten to twelve hours and animals every other station shortened travel time to the Pacific Coast. In July 1862, however, Ben Holladay's mail service between St. Joseph, Missouri, and Salt Lake City was moved to another route via Denver and southern Wyoming to Fort Bridger, rather than along the well-traveled but now dangerous Oregon Trail. Lucy Canfield and James McKnight each mentioned abandoned stations. Lucy ate at an empty building, and McKnight noted deserted spots west of Fort Laramie since mail was being routed through Denver.[25]

While traveling near South Pass, Ada Millington's party encountered problems with Native Americans. Two men and a boy near Ada's age had moved ahead of the train, and an Indian approached, pushed the boy off his horse, and tried to take it. The boy's father ordered the Indian to give the animal back, but the man refused. Soon other warriors appeared with bows and arrows, but the emigrant ox teams also came in sight. Then the Indians stole four stage mules, and gunfire was

---

[24]Journal History, 16 Oct. 1862, 11; Josephy, *Civil War*, 244–248.

[25]Dawson, *Pioneer Tales*, 76–77; Josephy, *Civil War*, 249; Margetts, "My Journal," Sept. 15; Journal History, 16 Oct. 1862, 9.

exchanged. "So many Indians kept coming in sight," that Ada's company was "afraid the whole 500 would attack us. So the train concluded it was best to go on." Ada obviously exaggerated when she wrote that 500 might attack. She then reported that a telegraph dispatch was sent to Pacific Springs for additional soldiers, and the next day the soldiers recovered the stage mules. Ada also learned that at Warm Springs Station two men fell behind their company and were killed.[26] In her diary Louisa Cook wrote that she heard "many reports about Indians & some of the ladies are very much frightened." Near South Pass she "passed the graves of 2 white men who were killed by the Indians about a week ago. They had fallen behind the train when the Indians attacked & murdered them taking their teams & whatever of value they had in their wagons."[27]

What did Lucy Canfield write about Native Americans? She noted them camped on the Platte; another time her company gave flour and meat to individuals on horseback—and her train did not build a fire. James McKnight provided additional details about Lucy's second entry: "We were visited by several Sioux Indians with their squaws. We gave them some 50 pounds of flour, sugar and traded flour for moccasins." Later on the trail Lucy saw two women and discovered a dead Indian in a tree. But when her train passed South Pass, Lucy said nothing. Did she hear about troubles between emigrants and Native Americans that season? It would be difficult to believe that she had not. The company was reminded more than once of dangers. West of Fort Kearny, McKnight summarized a camp meeting in which precautions were taken before they reached the more dangerous part of the trail. Captain Canfield "gave some general instructions and warnings against Indian and

---

[26]Millington, "Journal," 232–233; Clark, Millington Journal, 180. In an earlier article I published about Lucy Canfield, I assumed that this experience near South Pass resulted in the station burning down. But it did not occur in 1862. See Palmer, "Lucy Canfield, 6–7, and Guenther, "Burnt Ranch," 16–17.

[27]Cook, "Letters," 47, 49–50.

other assaults. He recommended that two at a time instead
of one be placed on camp guard. Four at a time are called for
cattle guard." Perhaps Lucy felt comfortable in her train of
118 people and thirty-one wagons. After all, Isabel Price
Kunkel, who also made the trek in 1862, remembered being
told that Native Americans did not attack Mormon groups
who traveled in large numbers.[28]

By comparing Lucy Canfield's diary to the company roster and to the writings of other travelers that year, it is obvious that the young girl diarist left out more than she said. In
fact, much more was not said than was written. One wonders
why she chose to write, for Lucy gave no indication, and many
of her entries contain little substance. Some days she seemed
compelled to put something down just to get the job done.
For example, one day all she wrote was, "Nothing of importance transpired today." One wonders what Lucy did when
nothing important transpired. Did she walk ahead of the train
with friends? Was the weather hot? Did she contend with
pesky insects? On the day that Lucy found so unremarkable,
McKnight noted that the train "nooned at Great Papillion"
where "the creek banks were steep and the water bad, but grass
was abundant." They camped at Reed's Ranch and during the
night experienced a severe rainstorm.[29]

Lucy Canfield was not purposefully writing for historical
reasons, or her entries no doubt would have contained more
depth. The adolescent seemed to write for herself, and some
days she did not strain her brain but put something down to
complete the task she had assigned herself. Travel diaries were
popular during her time; and diary-keeping and letter writing were common activities in a society without telephones,
televisions, computers, and other technologies that presently

---

[28]Margetts, "My Journal," Aug. 5, 23, Sept. 9; Journal History, 16 Oct. 1862, 2, 5, 6; Carter, *Pioneer Heritage*, 7: 265.
[29]Margetts, "My Journal," Aug. 1; Journal History, 16 Oct. 1862, 1–2.

monopolize a person's day. Even with terse entries, one can get an idea of this fifteen-year-old girl's perspective of the journey. Lucy probably felt secure in her extended home environment in spite of the Civil War and Indian threats along the trail. She did not appear to have taxing responsibilities or trying experiences, and the *Deseret News* reported that her company had an "exceedingly prosperous" journey with "little sickness and no deaths."[30] Keeping a record of these three months of her life denotes the importance this young pioneer placed upon it.

YOUNG EMIGRANTS OF 1866

European children, too, had stories to tell about crossing the plains. Unfortunately, no original diaries were located from those who left their native lands and went directly to Utah. Thomas Griggs lived in Boston before going west and probably became familiar with American ways. Andrew Jenson kept a diary from Denmark to Nebraska and across the plains in 1866, but his original teenage writings have not surfaced. Similar in content and writing, Jenson's 1895 journal, his published autobiography, his Journal History account, and a chapter in his *History of the Scandinavian Mission* offer insights into European emigration.[31] To begin to understand a young European's perceptions of the journey, one might consider Andrew Jenson's journal, childhood reminiscences of other youngsters who crossed that year, and historical documents describing the 1866 travel season.

By 1866, the war had ended and the church's down-and-back system was working systematically. Most of the trains en route kept church headquarters aware of their progress via the over-

---

[30]Journal History, 16 Oct. 1862, 1.

[31]Jenson, "Journals," 68–90; Jenson, *Autobiography*, 20–26; Journal History, 8 Oct. 1866, 2–14; Jenson, *History of Scandinavian*, 189–195.

land telegraph. The *Deseret News* published these telegrams, and settlers of Utah kept abreast of those on the trail as well. This year's emigration was one of the largest conducted by the Mormon church, with ten trains led by Thomas Ricks, Samuel White, William Chipman, John Holladay, Daniel Thompson, Joseph Rawlins, Horton Haight, Peter Nebeker, Andrew Scott, and Abner Lowry. Andrew Jenson crossed the plains in Andrew Scott's company, one of the later groups to arrive in the Salt Lake Valley. This was the last season church trains departed from eastern Nebraska, for the Union Pacific Railroad expanded to North Platte in 1867 and to Laramie City and Benton, near present-day Rawlins, Wyoming, in 1868.[32] During 1866, emigration agent Thomas Taylor arranged a different route from New York to Nebraska. Emigrants traveled by rail from New Haven, Connecticut, through Massachusetts, Vermont, and across part of Canada. "This route, although longer, proved healthier than that usually traveled by our immigration, while the cost of transportation was $5 per head cheaper than by any other line." According to Andrew Jenson, railways in the eastern United States hoped to profit from the Mormon migration by asking unfair prices, so Taylor looked elsewhere.[33] Also in 1866, several emigrants kept visual accounts of the trek west. Sixteen-year-old Alfred Lambourne made drawings, Charles Savage photographed, and William Henry Jackson sketched scenes and events in his non-Mormon caravan. Later, Jackson took pictures of the trail when he joined a geological survey as government photographer. Few photographs of the overland experience exist, for photography then was a cumbersome process. Charles Savage said, "To photograph successfully on the Plains, you must be perfectly safe from Indians. . . . [Y]ou must have plenty of time at your disposal,

[32]*Deseret News Church Almanac*, 176; Jenson, *History of Scandinavian*, 195; Taylor, "Mormon Crossing," 320–321.
[33]Journal History, 11 Sept. 1866, 2; Jenson, *History of Scandinavian*, 192.

a strong party well armed with good Henry rifles, and good animals."[34]

The first 1866 church trains included mostly British travelers. The later companies—particularly the Rawlins, Nebeker, Scott, and Lowry—contained Scandinavians who crossed the ocean aboard the ships "Kenilworth," "Humboldt," and "Cavour." Twelve-year-old Evan Stephens's family from Wales had planned to sail with English Saints until a mistake was made at Liverpool. As a result, the family joined a Scandinavian group. Evan Stephens enjoyed walking with two to three hundred Danish girls, but "I couldn't talk anything but Welsh, one thing I missed by not coming over with the English Company. Coming over with Scandinavians, I learned more of their language than English."[35]

In his published autobiography Andrew Jenson noted that "several companies of British Saints preceded our company and were already on the plains when we arrived." According to Jenson, "the total number of emigrating saints from Europe in 1866 was 3,327, of whom 1,213 were from the Scandinavian countries. All of the companies came by way of Wyoming [Nebraska] and most of them crossed the plains with Church teams." Almost all of these trains contained between 230 and 520 people with forty-six to eighty-four wagons. They reached Utah in approximately two months.[36] The first company, a mule train led by Thomas Ricks, left Nebraska around July 10 and arrived in Salt Lake City on August 29. Samuel White's mule train pulled in a week later after "a very pleas-

[34]Lambourne, *Old Sketch Book*, 1–3 ; Lambourne, *Pioneer Trail*, 48; Jackson, *Pageant of the Pioneers*, 3; Carter, "Photographing," 60–63. Besides making sketches, Alfred Lambourne kept a diary on the way to Utah, but he subsequently lost his writings "perhaps fed to the flames." Twenty years later he published a reminiscence with what might be embellishments of his original drawings. See Lambourne, *Pioneer Trail*, 48.

[35]Jenson, *History of Scandinavian*, 193–194; Stephens, "A Talk," 1, 3. The roster of the Rawlins train in Journal History, 1 Oct. 1866, 1, lists Evan Stephens as a passenger.

[36]Jenson, *Autobiography*, 20. The *Deseret News Church Almanac*, 176, approximates the L.D.S. emigrants in 1866 as 3,109.

ant trip" of fifty-three traveling days with "only one shower and a rain on Bear River." Earlier departures from Nebraska implied less chance of snow in Wyoming. But down-and-back trains could not begin the trek too soon, for they had to travel the thousand miles from Utah first. Also, moving in large groups necessitated sufficient forage for animals.[37]

On their eastward trip to Nebraska in 1866, church teams "each deposited 1200 sacks of flour on the journey" with "300 sacks at the crossing of the Sweetwater or at Sweetwater Bridge; 300 sacks at Bissonetts, Deer Creek; 300 sacks at Mud Springs; and 300 sacks at Pyper and Robinson's, Kearney City." Andrew Jenson reported that some of the provisions which Captain Scott cached along the way had been stolen. Jenson blamed Indians or renegade whites for making his company be placed on half rations, "and I, who was a robust and growing boy with a good appetite, could at times think of nothing more desirable than to live long enough to enjoy a square meal, or to have my appetite satisfied."[38]

The third church train led by William Chipman left the Midwest on July 11 or 12 with approximately 354 emigrants and sixty wagons and arrived in Salt Lake City September 15 or 16.[39] Among the passengers were Charles Savage, photographer, and nine-year-old Brigham Henry Roberts from England with his nineteen-year-old sister Mary. Roberts was prolific in describing his experiences in Captain Chipman's train. He remembered himself as

> rather heavy, such as is described for lads as 'chunky.' My hair was of light mouse-colored hue, ill kept, slightly wavy and unruly of management... [At Castle Garden] I was a boy evidently who was accustomed to being alone—apart from the throng. I was not restless, but rather solemn and gloomy.

---

[37]Journal History, 29 Aug. 1866, 1; Journal History, 5 Sept. 1866, 1.

[38]Journal History, 22 Oct. 1866, 8; Jenson, *Autobiography*, 24.

[39]*Deseret News Church Almanac*, 176. The *Deseret News* account in Journal History, 15 Sept. 1866, 1, states that Chipman's company left July 13 and arrived September 15.

Four years earlier Brigham's mother took two children to Zion and left Mary with distant relatives and four-year-old Brigham with a couple who treated him poorly. The gospel "had not been altogether a happy circumstance to the Roberts family." Brigham's father accepted the church with reservation, and this reluctance along with "certain unconquered intemperate habits and wild craving for independence began to suggest the possibility of a family rupture." Brigham remembered "family misunderstandings, my father coming home and no supper prepared—perhaps no food in the house— my father standing at the pantry door and twirling the plates across the room to the table." Mrs. Roberts left her husband and emigrated to Utah.

After four lonely years in England, Brigham and Mary journeyed to Utah in Captain Chipman's train. They were assigned to a wagon with two other families; the women slept inside, and the men and boys made their beds under or beside the wagon. Although Mrs. Roberts had sent clothing and quilts for her children, they never received them. Consequently, young Brigham shivered across the plains with his sister's petticoat as a blanket. At times this inquisitive lad found himself in curious predicaments. When his train neared the Platte River, Brigham wanted to cross first, so he arose early in the morning and walked the long distance by himself. While waiting for the others to arrive, he crawled in some willows and feel asleep. By the time he awoke, the last wagon had crossed the river. Brigham called to the captain who yelled back and asked if he could swim. After replying that he could, the boy plunged into the water but struggled to reach the shore. So Captain Chipman rescued him, then gave him several swats for leaving the train. Another time young Roberts fell asleep in a barrel of molasses. The next morning when he climbed out "with molasses dripping from my trousers, I was greeted by some of the teamsters and emigrants who caught sight of me with yells and laughter." The boy had no change of clothes, so he scraped at the sticky substance. Being separated from his mother and sometimes fending for himself in England may have provoked young Roberts to be independent during the overland trek. But one wonders why his sister did not supervise him more.

Brigham Roberts also remembered that the Chipman train had its cattle "stampeded by the Indians at a noon encampment, and something over a hundred head of stock were permanently lost." The *Deseret News* also reported this incident. Roberts added a personal memory in which he and a friend were playing in a swimming hole when three Native Americans appeared, frightened the animals, and caused them to stampede. The little boys, "naked as when born," rushed to tell their captain who laughed "and advised that we had better find our clothes before we went into camp." Then the captain ordered the wagons into "solid corral formation" and sent men after the herd. Caroline Hopkins Clark, also a member of the Chipman train, reported in her diary, "Today we had trouble with the Indians. We suppose they followed us. We had just corralled, and begun to cook our dinners, when the alarm came that the Indians were driving our cattle. The boys followed them, but they got away with ninety-one head and wounded three." Two days later, "we passed Deer Creek. The same day the Indians took our cattle, they took all the possessions of two homes, killed the people and burned their homes. A telegraph message has come to tell us Brigham Young is sending us some mule teams and provisions to help us." Roberts said nothing about this, but he noted that relief wagons "came in time to rescue the train from absolute starvation."

According to Roberts's autobiography, when the night guards found two mountaineers secretly guarding a cattle herd, Captain Chipman arrested the strangers and confiscated the animals. Soon the company met a camp of soldiers, learned that the cattle belonged to them, and returned the stock. Caroline Clark described this same event in her diary: "This morning we were just starting when four of our men drove in about one-hundred cattle that they had taken from the Indians. We found the train they belonged to and we gave them back." Her story was somewhat different from Roberts's retelling. The men retrieved the cattle from Native Americans, not mountaineers, and Clark said nothing about soldiers owning the animals.[40] Time may have altered the childhood recollection.

Passengers in the fourth church train led by Captain Holladay were the Lambournes and Cottles from England. Alfred Lambourne, a sixteen-year-old artist, sketched such scenes on the trail as a prairie fire, an overlander's grave, and a night watchman. In a published reminiscence he recalled how the captain warned the girls about being "led too far by their passion for the gathering of flowers." A year earlier a train had crossed the Black Hills, and

> a band of five Sioux suddenly dashed out from amid a clump of trees on the [LaBonte] river bank, and carried away, beyond all hope of rescue, one of two girls who had rashly gone too far down the stream. The train remained at the river for a period of three days, the Indians were pursued for many miles, but it was all in vain. The young husband never saw his young wife again. One of the young women was slightly in advance of the other, and those few steps made this difference, that one was lost, the other saved. And the young woman who escaped was the writer's sister.[41]

Yet neither Lambourne nor others that year, according to the documents I studied, discussed the tragedy of the Cottle family. Fourteen-year-old William Cottle, his ten-year-old sister Anne (Robenson), and their family went to Colorado from England and, according to William Cottle, in 1866 joined a Mormon train to Utah

---

[40]Bergera, *B. H. Roberts*, 3, 6–8, 25, 27–28, 31–33, 37–38; Journal History, 15 Sept. 1866, 1; Clark, "Liverpool to Utah," 160.

[41]Lambourne, *Pioneer Trail*, 55–56; Journal History, 25 Sept. 1866, 2.

at big larmmey river and there was a tole brige and father payed the tole and went over and started a head as we ust [used] to travel a little a head of the train to keep out of the dust. the wagon master and the tole man got into a dispute about the amount tole so the wagon master would not pay the tole witch was 2 dollars.

The Cottles got separated from the Holladay train, and Anne remembered her father seeing

> a large cloud of dust, thinking this was the wagon train . . . . But to our sorrow it was Indians. Father tried to treaty, but they whirled around & started to shout and shot father. He fell & we thought he was dead. The team ran away. One terrible looking Indian picked my mother up as I was holding to her skirt & lifted her on a horse and rode away with her. We never saw her again.

The Native Americans shot Anne and killed the grandparents. William and Anne ran back to their train, who "picked us up & father also." The family returned to Denver to begin an unsuccessful search for their mother, then the next year migrated to Utah.[42]

Athough Captain Holladay sent periodic telegrams to Salt Lake City about his company's progress, he said nothing about the Cottles. The *Deseret News* noted the train's arrival and its "fine trip across the plains." There were eight deaths, "the last one of whom died the night before reaching the city." The clerk of the train provided a list of deaths, but no Cottle was listed. Yet "H. Cottle, wife and 5 children" were on the roster.[43] Why was this incident not reported? Since the family had just joined the Holladay train, the other emigrants probably did not know them, but the excitement must have unnerved the travelers. Still, sixty-year-old memories are easily forgotten. If Alfred Lambourne had preserved the teenage diary he wrote on the trail, might he have mentioned the Cottle tragedy? One can only wonder.

---

[42]Cottle, Account, 2; Robenson, Letter, 1. Two other versions of Anne's letter are found in Carter, *Pioneer Heritage*, 2: 240–241, and a typescript, "Indian Attack," from Elva C. Fletcher in my possession. This version spelled Anne Cottle Robenson's name Ann Cottle Robson.

[43]Journal History, 25 Sept. 1866, 1.

Andrew Jenson's family crossed the plains in Andrew Scott's church train with approximately three hundred British and Scandinavian Saints and forty-nine wagons. The *Deseret News* observed, "This company of people is reported as one of the finest that has got in for a long time. They are mostly from Norway, in Europe, from a highly respectable class of society, and have a fine choir of 25 voices." Yet Jenson did not mention these melodious voices in his journal. Did his family join in singing around the campfire? Captain Scott's company left Nebraska August 8 or 9 and arrived in Salt Lake City on October 8.[44] Since they traveled later in the season, they and the two church trains behind them experienced Wyoming snowstorms. Periodic telegrams to Utah provided details about this. On September 20, Horton Haight telegraphed from the Sweetwater: "I pass here this morning; All well, Snow all day yesterday." On September 21, Captain Scott wrote from South Pass, "Encountered a very severe snow and wind storm for 12 hours; while passing from Sage Creek over the Rocky Ridge. Some cattle were badly frozen. Eight head died and 50 more are disabled. The snow was six inches deep; feed covered up, heavy wind from northwest; very cold. Today fine weather, cattle looking better, Camp in good condition." On September 23, Captain Haight said, "Camp in a snow storm, all well. Total loss of stock seven head."[45]

In his journal Andrew Jenson kept track of the inclement weather. On September 18, "the weather was cold and the roads uneven and rocky. In the evening before we camped for the night it commenced to snow and blow furiously." The next day when

> we awoke this morning the ground was covered with about six inches of snow, and it continued to snow all forenoon. It was very cold indeed, and we all suffered in consequence severely, especially when we were making the morning camp fires. . . . the teamsters kept up courage, and

---

[44]Journal History, 8 Oct. 1866, 2; *Deseret News Church Almanac,* 176.
[45]Journal History, 20 Sept. 1866, 1; 21 Sept. 1866, 1; 23 Sept. 1866, 1.

it only took them a few minutes to get an immense sagebrush campfire under way. . . The snow, however, continued to fall all forenoon,
and we made no attempt to move. It was truly the coldest and most
unpleasant day on the whole journey.

Jenson noted on September 20 that "eight of our oxen were
left in a dying condition on last night's camping ground, and
about fifty others were so cold and benumbed that they could
scarcely drag themselves along. Later in the day the sun peeped
through the clouds and most of the snow melted before its
warming touch." On September 21, Jenson's company encountered a severe snowstorm, then two days later, "it snowed again
last night and this afternoon, owing to which the roads
became muddy and heavy." How did the adolescent respond
to these conditions? Did he have warm clothing? What did
he do to help? No more bad weather hindered the Scott train,
but according to a young member of Abner Lowry's company,
their group experienced "a snowy blizzard on the divide in Par-
leys Canyon, which lasted for three days. The wind blew so
hard that it was impossible to make a fire, – the wind swept
it right off the ground."[46]

Besides discussing the weather in his journal, Andrew Jenson described his company's food allowance and cooking skills:

> 1 1/2 lbs of flour and 1 lb. of bacon per day for each adult, besides sugar,
> molasses, coffee, dried fruit etc., all of which we were to cook and pre-
> pare to suit our respective tastes. Some of us found the baking of bread
> and the cooking of meals in the open air a very difficult task, but after
> a few day's experience, we mastered the situation quite satisfactorily.

In her diary Caroline Clark confirmed and added to what Jenson wrote about the food:

> We do not get any fresh meat or potatoes, but we get plenty of flour
> and bacon. We have some sugar, a little tea, molasses, soap, carbonate
> of soda, and a few dried apples. We brought some peas, oatmeal, rice,
> tea, and sugar, which we had left from the vessel. We bought a skillet
> to bake our bread in. Sometimes we make pancakes for a change. We
> also make cakes in the pan, and often bran dumplings with baking pow-

---

[46]Jenson, "Journals," 86–88; Hansen, "History of Jorgen," 2.

der. We use cream of tartar and soda for our bread, sometimes sour dough. At times Roland goes to the river and catches fish and sometimes John shoots birds. We get wild currants and gooseberries to make puddings.

Andrew Jenson remembered "howling wolves, which approached our camp in large packs" west of Devil's Gate station. Was the Danish boy frightened? He noted river crossings, travelers on the road, soldiers, Native Americans, relief parties, daily routine, and chores but seldomly involved himself personally. His impression of walking nearly all the way across the plains was, "I rather enjoyed it." Jenson learned to understand English by mingling with British emigrants, but he did not describe these associations nor ones with his peers. Entering the Salt Lake Valley "I obtained my first view," and "with my companions I almost shouted with joy . . . As long as I can remember I had prayed and hoped for this opportunity."[47] But who were the adolescent's companions?

During the 1866 emigration season, all of the L.D.S. church trains suffered disease and death. In his journal Andrew Jenson noted that Jens Christensen from Denmark died and was buried without a coffin. With the burial customs of the nineteenth century, this troubled many travelers, but what could they do? Jenson also reported two other emigrants who succumbed. "As they were English I did not learn their names; yet it cast a gloom over us all." The language barrier may have created casual relationships with some train members. Jenson explained in his autobiography, "Quite a number of the people in our company died on the plains, but I failed to make a record of them, as I as yet was an amateur in record-keeping." Jenson's family completed the journey intact, but others in his train did not. Eleven-year-old Marie Neilson (Robins) remembered, "Just as Mother was preparing the meal my older brother called, 'Oh, Mother, Ditlow is dying.' He was the first of the

---

[47]Jenson, "Journals," 72–73, 75, 79, 81, 85, 90; Jenson, *Autobiography*, 22; Clark, "Liverpool to Utah," 160.

company to be left by the side of the trail." Laura Swenson's (Fowers) father died from a wagon accident, then "seven days later my mother died after giving birth to a premature baby. She was buried on Big Mountain.... Our grandmother cared for us and we reached Salt Lake City" where eight-year-old Laura and her siblings were adopted by an English family.[48]

Of all the 1866 church trains, Abner Lowry's company experienced the most illness and death. The *Deseret News* reported,

> This is the last immigrant train of the season. They encountered some severe weather on the latter part of the trip; but the immigrants stood it very well. We are glad that this train has got in and that all the immigration is safe in the territory as early as it is. There was more mortality than ordinary in Capt. Lowry's train, in consequence of the malignant form of dysentery which afflicted many on the first part of the journey across the plains."[49]

The trouble began when a group of Scandinavian Saints were aboard the ship *Cavour* and cholera broke out, then leaving the East, they "were overtaken by cholera." When they stopped at St. Joseph, Missouri, for two nights and two days, "the plague made a deadly attack upon the company. During our sojourn in St. Joseph we buried thirty-three Saints . . . and left others dying." On the Missouri River "the cholera continued its ravages, and at Wyoming we buried eight more of the emigrants." Weakened by the disease, the people traveled slowly across the plains. On September 1, emigration agent Thomas Taylor telegraped Utah: "The companies we have passed are all doing well, except Capt. Lowry who, when we last heard from him, was detained at Kearney through sickness."[50]

Andrew Jenson mentioned the Lowry company several times in his journal. On August 8, he wrote,

> With our departure from Wyoming [Nebraska] that village again

---

[48]Jenson, "Journals," 75, 77; Jenson, *Autobiography*, 23–24; Carter, *Treasures*, 3: 123; Carter, *Pioneer Heritage*, 12: 95.

[49]Journal History, 22 Oct. 1866, 1.

[50]Journal History, 11 August 1866, 4–5; Journal History, 1 September 1866, 1.

assumed its normal condition, being left with its own very limited number of inhabitants, save a few emigrants and Elders who were waiting for the last company of Saints from Europe to arrive. Capt. Abner Lowry's company of Church teams was kept back to bring this last company across the plains. This last company of Church teams was known as the Sanpete train, as most if not all the teams composing it hailed from Sanpete Valley, Utah.

Emigration agents who stopped at Jenson's camp on August 19 said that several pioneers had died in the Sanpete train "and others were sick and dying." On September 14, "a small mule-train [passed us] en route from Salt Lake City to meet . . . the so-called Sanpete train – which was said to be in a suffering condition, and their animals getting poor." Church leaders sent Arza Hinckley's relief party to assist these last emigrants to the Valley. Hinckley traveled approximately 450 miles to reach the suffering people. On October 7, Andrew Jenson's company "passed over the summit into Parley's Canyon. The mule-train which met us Sept. 14th to meet the last train overtook and passed us to-day, bringing quite a number of the emigrants from that train with them. The ox-train itself, they reported, was two weeks' journey behind us."[51]

Several young people from the Lowry train remembered the sick and dying. Their memories contained common elements, possibly because the journey affected them personally or they shared stories as the years passed. Ten-year-old Charles Anderson from Sweden recalled leaving some behind at St. Louis. Going up the Missouri River "we buried four and the next [day] five. . . . I could not help but feel sad," for death was "daily sweeping young and old into a premature grave." The cholera continued until the weather turned cool. Anderson "never heard how many died but at least one third, perhaps more. One family from Denmark of thirteen all died but one, another from Sweden of five, only one remained." Anderson himself "was sick across the Atlantic, through the States, and did not gain strength until the cool weather on the latter

---

[51]Jenson, "Journals," 72, 77, 84, 90; Bergera, *B. H. Roberts*, 23.

part of the journey across the plains." Almost fourteen, Jorgen Hansen from Denmark recalled the death of his mother and three brothers. "Some families were completely wiped out (no one left to tell the tale). My father and myself were the only ones left out of a family of six."[52]

Also in the Lowry train, eight-year-old John Nielsen from Denmark remembered walking to Utah. "Many times I felt as if I could not go another step, I was so tired but the Lord gave me strength to go on." Captain Lowry "had a large tent which he had pitched every evening and had his teamsters assist in carrying the sick into it in the evening and back into the wagons in the morning." The camp sang and prayed each day. Finally a relief party came. "As we neared the mountains the disease abated, but it left practically every family broken up. My mother took two families of children into her care" after the parents died. "One day as we were traveling along I noticed the head team stop and the next and so on till an irregular circle was formed. I learned that we had just crossed the line into Utah and the company all bared and bowed their heads, and Niels Nielsen the Presiding Elder, offered up a prayer of thanksgiving after which we proceded on our journey." Twelve-year-old Niels Rasmussen from Denmark said, "During the early part of that journey, the mortality continued among us at a fearful rate, until about one hundred persons out of a total of between two and three hundred, who left Scandinavia in the spring, had perished by the wayside. My own brother and mother fell victims to the terrible disease." But Captain Lowry "will ever be held in affectionate remembrance ... especially by those who recovered from their sickness through his untiring efforts in alleviating their sufferings." A relief train "met us about four hundred miles east of Salt Lake City. All the orphans, of which there were many in our company, were taken by that train. This included our family, which now had been reduced to five in number." Ras-

---

[52]Anderson, *Charles P.*, 2; Hansen, "History of Jorgen," 2.

mussen's family reached the Valley on October 7, but "the main company, which lost nearly half their cattle in the snows in the mountains," arrived two weeks later.[53]

From Andrew Jenson's revision of his original teenage diary, it appears that this church historian did not value his youthful writings, for he "was yet an amateur in record-keeping." His journal provides information about the Mormon emigration of 1866, but it tantalizes the reader to delve into the original writings to see a young European's perspective. Perhaps his diary lacked these perceptions as well. Yet the letters of Margaret, Catharine, and Harriet Scott provide adolescent insights. Reminiscences of Brigham Roberts and William and Anne Cottle suggest that individuals and families had their own unique experiences, and what was traumatic to one may have been unknown or ignored by others in their train. Also, discrepancies crept into retellings of the same event. William and Anne Cottle's stories did not always coincide. Both agreed that their wagon was alone when it was attacked, but they disagreed about their grandfather's death. William said, "The indians kild my granmother and strok [struck] my granfarther over the head with the but of a pistel and he dide [died] in six weeks after thrue [through] the affects of it." Anne remembered, "They killed my Grandmother Ann Adams out right, but Grandfather died the next day from the wounds." William continued his story:

> My father was not ded [dead] as we first thought he was but he had only got a skelp [scalp] wound the bullet just grase his skull and nocked him senceless for a wile futher and my sister and myself run fore miles back my sister being shot fore times in the back with arrows when we had run a bout fore miles we met the stage wich turn around and took us back to big larmmey river station-when we got back to big larmmey every boddy was excited and Capten Smith was there with one company of a bout 75 men and he started after the indians and follard them three days and knights and had a fight with the indians but thay could not get my mother back all throw [although] thay seen her the government then took us back to forte Camp Collens.

---

[53]Nielsen, "Biographical Sketch," 22–23; Jenson, *Biographical Encyclopedia*, 1: 597.

William Cottle noted that the family went to Denver two months later.

Anne Cottle's version of the story was:

> The Indians mocked me and shot me & I fell senseless as I saw them ride off with my mother. When I came to my brother (William) took me by the hand & said let us run, and as we looked around we saw that father was not dead, but was bleeding terrible. . . . My brother and I ran on & on finely we got back to the wagon train they picked us up & father also.
>
> My wounds were only flesh wounds and were not poisoned. The Dr. took me home to his wife & treated father. We went back to Denver in the fall to the Indians to find my mother.[54]

Anne recalled details about herself which her brother did not, which is logical because they happened to her, and William's retelling was longer than his sister's. Perhaps the four-year age difference allowed him to process and store more of the incident in his memory. Or, maybe he was a better storyteller. Edmund Bolles reminds us that "memory is so subjective that two people can sit side by side through an event and produce widely differing accounts of what happened. . . . We remember things according to our understanding of what happened, not according to the way something really occurred."[55] Even in contemporary writings of young pioneers like Lucy Canfield or Margaret, Catharine, and Harriet Scott, what they wrote depended upon their ability to see, comprehend, and interpret an incident, for "the character of the glass gives color to the object."

---

[54]Cottle, Account, 3; Robenson, Letter, 1.
[55]Bolles, *Remembering*, 66, 72.

CHAPTER VIII

Conclusion

*This story will be told by many firesides long after these
pioneers have been gathered to their fathers. And with
intensest interest will those who come after you listen to
the story of how grandly you performed your part in the
brave days of old.*

Thus the myth of the overland trek evolved. J. C. Moreland, who emigrated to Oregon as a child, celebrated this myth
in an annual address to the Oregon Pioneer Association. In
addition to his quote above, Moreland believed that pioneer
experiences "will live in song and story, history and legend, as
long as the human race shall love to hear of and honor deeds
of daring and heroism."[1] Yet young people writing diaries and
letters on the trail did not see the journey as a myth; instead,
it was life with its ups and downs. The legend was created later
by sharing, selecting, and editing individually and in groups,
like the Oregon Pioneer Association and Daughters of Utah
Pioneers, as J.C. Moreland suggested.

Young pioneers from Europe and America were part of a
nineteenth-century culture, and they carried its various codes
of conduct, etiquette, and conventions with them as their
diaries and letters suggest. Many middle-class overlanders, like
the Millingtons, hired extra hands to make their journey less
tedious; others went by less expensive means, such as pulling
handcarts. Whichever way they traveled, nineteenth-century
parents believed in a strong work ethic, and they expected chil-

---

[1]Moreland, "Annual Address," 26.

dren to pitch in and help on the trail. Most families adhered to separate gender roles as they were accustomed to doing at home; boys assisted fathers and girls helped mothers, but when circumstances required it, they assumed the other's place. Separate gender emotions filtered into young people's diaries and letters as well.

Young writers took their prejudices and Victorian attitudes with them on the trail. How they perceived others depended upon family values and society's views; consequently, they expressed mixed feelings about "Missourians," Mormons, and Native Americans. Their writings were colored by prejudices at the time of travel and later as they reminisced. They acquired these preconceived notions from popular novels of the day, newspaper and periodical accounts, others on the trail, and family and train members. Most youngsters had superficial contact with others on the trail and did not get to know them as individuals. Young female diarists portrayed Victorian attitudes as they cultivated friendships, went "calling" to neighboring wagons, and helped family and train members. If they attended dances in other trains or walked around towns like Salt Lake City, adult escorts accompanied them. Father was the patriarch of the home and wagon, and children obeyed and respected him. Ethics, values, and religion were common to American and European pioneers. Most believed in God and observed the Sabbath as best they could; some companies held Sunday religious services which young people attended. When family or train members died, young writers expressed trust in a Higher Being. Diaries and letters disclosed literacy skills and nineteenth-century culture with terms and phrases like "romantic" and "I take my pen in hand." Some reminiscences, particularly the published ones, reflected the society in which the young pioneers were born, even though the writing occurred at a later time. Memoirs were sometimes didactic and included such virtues as obedience, faith, patience, and endurance. But these writings did not view the world through young people's eyes.

Diaries and letters written during or soon after an event are the most reliable documents to study since the value of a piece of writing increases the closer it is to the event. Contemporary accounts portray the thoughts and feelings of a writer, even though much is left out and the author does not see the overall picture. Diarists, as on-the-spot witnesses, describe immediate experiences, events, behaviors, and impressions but in a random way; often they do not see the reality before them or consider the normal chaos of a day. Diarists may write about personal concerns and perceptions and ignore what might have lasting significance to certain historians, but to researchers who want to delve into documents preserved at the age of writing and pull out youthful perceptions, moods, and thoughts, such diaries are gold mines. Letters also provide glimpses into a writer's personality and thoughts as well as literacy and writing style. Since writers assume their letters will be read, they may be less inclined to reveal personal thoughts and more selective in what they discuss. Letters composed soon after an event can present a narrative of the experience, for the writer knows the beginning, middle, and end of the story. Journals are less authentic than diaries and letters but more reliable than reminiscences because they are revisions of contemporary documents. But they do not give the original writer's personality, perspective, or writing style.

Reminiscences recorded years after an event are definitely not as reliable as a diary entry or letter written the day of the happening since credibility decreases as time increases between the event and the writing. Also, the circumstance under which a reminiscence is written affects the way it is remembered. Most child pioneer recollections came from individuals who were between sixty and ninety years old. These informants could not describe the journey as youngsters would, neither could they express their childhood opinions, feelings, and personalities because they were no longer children. They could, however, remember certain experiences which left impressions on their minds. Precise information about the trail, forts, landmarks, and other aspects of the journey can provide today's trail analysts more data to study, but such material cannot be used when searching for the child's mind. Placing Fort Bridger before Independence Rock on the trail may make researchers squirm and discredit an account, but when one is searching for the child's perspective, this error puts flesh on a youngster's viewpoint. True "I remember" memories should fit the age and developmental pattern of those who experienced them, usually without rich and precise details. These documents may enrich and complement the actual writings of young pioneers. Even if reminiscences are written in first person, one cannot be sure if those submitted to historical repositories are first-hand primary documents. With oral histories one takes the chance that transcripts of pioneer interviews might have been altered by the interviewer.

Family memories across generations create shared memory, and recollections within a community form a group identity. The past we remember is both individual and collective, and many events when told and retold become our own until it is difficult to distinguish between primary and secondary memories or if they happened at all. Children on the three trails described general and generic experiences, such as gathering buffalo chips or singing and dancing around the campfire. These generic topics were much the same for all age groups, perhaps because they were produced from collective memory. "We remember" recollections often resulted from shared or collective memory, adult research in secondary or other published accounts, and adult perceptions from years of living. Hindsight expanded the view of the trail but distorted the child's short vision. Although "we remember" happenings occurred in reminiscences of all ages of children, they were easier to detect in youngest and middle-year recollections. Older children with expanded knowledge, experience, and ability to remember tended to elaborate on experiences.

Why should we bother to look at young pioneers' accounts? What do they contribute to the westward experience? Young pioneers' writings may not be historically significant for some scholars who want explicit facts and descriptions of the trail. But these contemporary accounts paint an authentic picture of a child's persective, and they help readers today learn about a young literate class who crossed the plains. Original documents present the lifestyle, culture, personality, language, and mechanics of the writer. Diaries and letters reveal how nineteenth-century conventions, values, and attitudes influenced young people's thoughts and writing. Such documents portray pieces of who they were and what they thought. These writings contain life and optimism, youth and confidence, sadness and grief. They offer opinions, perceptions, and personality through less experienced eyes. We can see how happenings on the trail affected what they wrote. By comparing their writings to those in their company or others traveling during the same season, we can identify what young writers chose to include or leave out.

We can collate what youngsters said to the writings of adult diarists according to what historians like John Mack Faragher and Lillian Schlissel identified. Young people noted health and safety, practical aspects of the trail, and landscape, but their interpretation of the landscape came through their keen senses and a literal lens. Lillian Schlissel observed that "the landscape appeared far more magnificent when one was not searching for a lost child or carrying a babe in arms as she walked."[2] This was true for many young contemporary writers who seemed to ignore little children. But some reminiscence writers like Margaret McNeil (Ballard) did carry babes in arms, and perhaps that is why they wrote reminiscences instead of diaries. Young female diarists revealed social needs similar to adult women, and some displayed "adolescent poutings," impressions, and poignant feelings. Others shared

---

[2]Faragher, *Women and Men*, 12; Schlissel, *Women's Diaries*, 150.

descriptions and topics unique to their youthful years, such as flooding a prairie dog out of its burrow or climbing Devil's Gate, a feat too dangerous for children under fourteen.

Some individuals in trains were sources of support to children, and young people built relationships with them. But trains had their problems, and individual wagons, particularly on the California and Oregon trails, joined and separated from each other. Adult diaries noted this discord; so did young people in diaries and reminiscences. But they were observers and reporters, although some young diarists like Flora Bender had definite opinions about people in their trains. Women and girls were concerned when trains divided and female friends departed. Even though Mormon trains were organized with many men, women, children, and older folks who usually remained together, members of religious trains had disagreements.

According to Faragher, "the concerns of the everyday predominate" in adult diaries. But young contemporary writers like Lucy Canfield did not discuss many of the mundane details which adults like James McKnight included. For example, they mentioned but brushed off chores, such as washing clothes, yet adult diarists like Helen Carpenter, Charlotte Pengra, and Rebecca Ketcham recorded in detail what washing clothes and other tedious tasks entailed.[3] Consequently, adult records can flesh out what young people did not discuss, but young writers can present another point of view, the pleasure/play, youthful sensory experiences, or drama of the trail. Young pioneer reminiscences can also fill in what contemporary accounts overlooked. All of these pieces fit together to make a more complete picture of the westward trek.

Faragher and Schlissel observed that adult male emigrants fulfilled dreams of camaraderie, action, and achievement while women wanted familiar home routines and worked to keep the family intact as they endured the journey. What did children see? Young writers described sibling rivalry and

---

[3]Faragher, *Women and Men*, 13; Schlissel, *Women's Diaries*, 78, 81, 82, 102.

friendships. They went on hunting expeditions and assisted around camp, and they felt trauma or sadness, but usually as helpers and followers. Women with young offspring marked the dangers of the trail and with feeling noted inscriptions on children's graves. The adolescent writers which I studied did not. Adults talked about youngsters crying and complaining, but they did not explain from a child's viewpoint why they shed tears or grumbled. Parents fretted over children getting lost, and youngsters were afraid of being lost. Adults attempted to contain their fears, and young pioneers revealed them. According to Faragher, adult diaries and reminiscences hardly mentioned their small charges and children were allowed to fend for themselves.[4] Although the young diarists did not explain how children were looked after on the trail, reminiscence writers did because they watched young siblings. But to be accurate in comparing contemporary writings and reminiscences of pioneer men, women, and children, researchers must make a side-by-side analysis of actual documents.

What was included or overlooked when comparing contemporary and reminscent accounts of young pioneers? Reminiscences did not reveal the child's personality and adolescent poutings, although some tried to remember childhood feelings. Accuracy of the experience tended to improve if reminiscences captured childhood feelings and understandings, not adult ramblings. Age and developmental characteristics influenced "I remember" happenings, and developmental principles and memory research validated what the three age groups might remember. Young diarists noted practical aspects of the trail—place, time, road conditions, grass, fuel, and water—and the landscape because they were experiencing them. Yet most reminiscences generalized practical topics and briefly mentioned the landscape when youngsters reached a landmark like Independence Rock and climbed it. Most diarists focused on other aspects of the trail rather than family relationships, but

---

[4]Faragher, *Women and Men*, 59, 79, 136–137, 170, 176; Schlissel, *Women's Diaries*, 14–15, 30, 49, 111.

"I remember" recollections provided a picture of families in the trail experience.

Themes important to young pioneers emerged in contemporary and reminiscent accounts, and both types of documents considered trail reponsibilities high on the list. While teenage diaries emphasized pleasure or play with family and train members, only middle-year reminiscences valued this topic; however, most of these young people did not assume heavy responsibilities. Diaries and reminiscences both mentioned childhood fears, although the contemporary accounts I analyzed did not describe terrifying river crossings or animal stampedes. Death was a common and frightening experience to children, and the majority of accounts mentioned some contact with death. Occasionally parents died before reaching the jumping-off place. Even if children started the journey with one or both parents, some of them lost family members along the way and were at the mercy of relatives or train members to get them to their journey's end. If California and Oregon trail companies did not have the support system to send youngsters across the plains alone, they developed it on the trail if both parents, like those of the Sager children, died. The sense of loss deepened as the child experienced the absence of family members. But young pioneers adapted to trying or new situations.

Researchers who want to learn about children on the trail from their perspective should first look at diaries and letters, then journals and "I remember" oral and written reminiscences with the knowledge that some writings produce a child's viewpoint better than others. According to both contemporary and reminiscent accounts, the lens through which young emigrants looked when they described their journey depended on what they experienced. As John Unruh observed, "The overland trip was unique to each individual traveler." Comments "about the ease or difficulty of the venture were invariably based upon what they themselves were experiencing."[5] This was true with children also. Preparations made by parents or church trains, trail conditions, traveling companions, age of traveler, personal and family constitution, and individual train circumstances influenced how young people considered the trip west. Many Mormon children experienced trying circumstances before they reached the jumping-off place and, as a result, the rest of the journey was affected by what had already occurred. Children on the California and Oregon trails found their greatest trials near the end of the trail. Whether or not youngsters described the trek as "fun" depended upon age, responsibilities, health or the health of others, treatment by others, feelings of security, and other factors.

Most of the twenty-three contemporary diarists and letter writers were optimistic in spite of the challenges they faced on the trail. Reminiscences, on the other hand, displayed a variety of emotions. Children crossing the plains saw a new world of people and relationships. They were intrigued by families in neighboring wagons and by friendships they could make. But sometimes they were bored with the journey and frustrated with people in their trains. A train acted like one big family, and this included jealousy, quarrels, and separations as well as kindnesses and loving relationships. Some children went west alone; others became orphans along the way. These youngsters relied on train members for support, and they obtained it in varying degrees. Little children were completely dependent upon adults for safety and security. Their sense of trust, lack of understanding, and ability to endure often pulled them through tough moments. In spite of setbacks, loss of family members and friends, and arduous responsibilities, older children fought back with resiliency. They adapted to what life offered them and moved on. Their attitudes reflected the idea that "this

---

[5]Unruh, *Plains Across*, 382.

too shall pass" because something better is around the cor-
ner, up the steep hill, or at one's destination.[6]

Adults then and now who view children's trail experiences
as a pleasure trip may be looking at childhood through nostalgic eyes. They should dispel the myth of childhood as the
best time of life and examine individual cases. Of course, children had happy, giggly, curious, and wonderful times; but they
had sad, bored, fearful, guilt-ridden, demanding, angry, and
sorrowful ones as well. Some youngsters had few responsibilities; others were assigned tasks far beyond their years. Many
felt secure in their extended home environment, and others
longed for love from adults who cared. The lenses through
which adults see childhood are not the ones children use when
they look at their own lives. After arriving in Oregon, eleven-
year-old Harriet Scott wrote to her grandfather, "A very small
part of the journey I enjoyed very well but the greater part of
it is very tiresome and hard to get along." She added, "I rode
on horse back most of the way but I got very tired of it there
was some places on the road that is almost Impossible to
travel."[7]

Although various attitudes can be inferred from their
accounts, many young pioneers did not express either joy or
sorrow about their journey. A small number of reminiscences
made such statements as: "It was a long trip," "I kept a good
heart," "Every journey has its ups and downs," "I had a splendid time because I trusted in my parents," "It was a journey
with great hardships," "It was not a hardship," "Nothing
important happened," and "It was a hard journey but no one
complained." But the majority of reminiscences did not ver-
balize any attitude. They just described what happened.

What future studies can researchers make to learn more
about children and the Westward Migration? Greater num-

---

[6]See also Schlissel, *Women's Diaries*, 150; Werner, *Pioneer Children*, chapter 9; West, *Growing
Up*, chapter 2; and Baur, *Growing Up*, 2.
[7]Scott Sisters, "Letters," 159.

bers of actual documents written by young people, especially boys and children younger than thirteen years old, need to be analyzed to increase our understanding of the pioneer child's personality and point of view. Almost all of the research about pioneer children have come from the white child's perspective, and we need to see black, Hispanic, Asian-American, and Native American viewpoints. Children on the southern trails as well as those who went by ship might be studied and compared to those on northern trails. No one has made a detailed analysis of the diaries and letters of pioneer men, women, and children to compare what they said about family and train relationships or about themes they emphasized. How did their personalities, grammar and mechanics, and other aspects of their writing compare to one another? How were adult perceptions alike or different from young emigrants? In addition to diaries and letters, reminiscences of adults and children might be considered together. Although Faragher observed that children were hardly mentioned in adult diaries and reminiscences, an intensive study might be made about this, and researchers could analyze what parents and train members observed about children from an adult viewpoint. "Different travelers see the same thing in a different light" and from "entirely different sides. The character of the glass gives color to the object."[8] Consequently, we need to study the westward trek from as many perspectives as we can.

---

[8]McCall, *Great California Trail*, 6.

APPENDIX

TABLE I. PLACES OF BIRTH AND DESTINATION OF YOUNG PIONEERS

Place of Birth	CA/NV	OR/WA	Other	UT
Missouri	11	41	6	17
Illinois	12	30	1	36
Wisconsin	1	2	3	5
Michigan	2	1	1	1
Iowa	8	20		25
Indiana	2	10	1	3
Ohio	2	7	1	16
Minnesota		1		
Kansas			3	
Nebraska			1	8
Delaware				3
New York	1	1		16
Connecticut				2
Maryland	1			
Vermont				1
New Hampshire	1			1
New Jersey				3
Massachusetts				10
Pennsylvania		3	1	11
Mississippi	1			1
Kentucky	1	7		
Arkansas	1	3		
Tennessee	1	1		4
Alabama				2
Texas				1
Louisiana			1	
The South	1	1		
Trail (OR/WY)		1		4
Total USA	46	129	19	170

Place of Birth	CA/NV	OR/WA	Other	UT
England	I			144
Ireland				3
Wales				13
Scotland	I	I		24
Isle of Jersey				2
Isle of Mann				I
Denmark				60
Sweden				15
Norway				5
Germany/Prussia	I			2
Switzerland				7
South Africa				3
Canada	I			9
Nova Scotia				I
Total Foreign	4	I	0	289
Birthplace not listed	17	27	4	6
Total	67	157	23	465

Total diaries, letters, journals, oral and written reminiscences = 712

Table II. Age of Young Male Pioneers When They Began The Trek

Age	CA/NV	OR/WA	Other	UT
child (no age)	3	6		2
infant—2	1	5	1	30
3		2		15
4		1		10
5		2		15
6	3	4		9
7	3	2		10
8	3	3		10
9	1	12	1	25
10		8		19
11	6	5		17
12	1	4	1	30
13	2	6	2	19
14	4	9	1	15
15	3	4	2	30
16				
Total Males	30	73	8	256

Total male diaries, letters, journals, oral and written reminiscences = 367

Table III. Age of Young Female Pioneers When They Began the Trek

Age	CA/NV	OR/WA	Other	UT
child (no age)	2	8	2	5
infant—2	2	8		35
3	2	7	1	10
4	2	6	2	8
5		2	2	10
6	4	4		15
7	1	3	1	14
8	3	9		15
9	1	6		11
10	5	6	1	16
11	1	9		12
12	4	3		18
13	2	8	4	16
14	2	3		13
15	4	2	2	11
16	2			
Total Females	37	84	15	209

Total male diaries, letters, journals, oral and written reminiscences = 345

TABLE IV. YEAR OF CROSSING

Year	CA/NV	OR/WA	Other	UT
Did not say	2	7	1	9
1841				
1842				
1843		5		
1844		6		
1845	1	10		
1846	9	11		
1847	1	19		34
1848	2	2		30
1849	12	1		11
1850	2	5		29
1851	1	7		16
1852	13	46	1	32
1853	3	17		18
1854	5	3		10
1855	2			13
1856	1			45
1857	2		1	13
1858			1	4
1859	2	1	1	14
1860		2		21
1861	1			21
1862	1	3	1	31
1863	3	1	3	28
1864	2	6	8	23
1865	2	4	4	4
1866			2	35
1867				4
1868		1		20
Total	67	157	23	465

Total diaries, letters, journals, oral and written reminiscences = 712

Selected Bibliography

NOTES ON BACKGROUND TO RESEARCH

Only first-hand accounts written by individuals who crossed the plains as children were sought for this study. Many of the primary accounts appeared in printed sources, some were typescripts, and a limited number were original documents or microfilm copies of originals. Many of the known primary documents were identified in Merrill J. Mattes's *Platte River Road Narratives*, Melvin L. Bashore's and Linda L. Haslam's "Mormon Pioneer Companies Crossing the Plains (1847–1868)," Davis Bitton's *Guide to Mormon Diaries and Autobiographies*, Utah State Historical Society's *Guide to Archives and Manuscript Collections in Selected Utah Repositories*, and Kris White's and Mary-Catherine Cuthill's *Overland Passages: A Guide to Overland Documents in the Oregon Historical Society*. Other accounts were found in the eleven volumes of Kenneth L. Holmes' *Covered Wagon Women* and the bibliography sections of books and articles by Judy Allen, Lyndia McDowell Carter, Mary Bywater Cross, John Mack Faragher, Julie Roy Jeffrey, Susan Arrington Madsen, Dale Morgan, Ruth Barnes Moynihan, Robert L. Munkres, Sandra Myres, Georgia Willis Read, Lillian Schlissel, John Unruh, Emmy E. Werner, and Elliott West. Since many of the sources did not specify which authors were young when they journeyed west, each entry was checked for age and year of crossing. After young emigrants were identified, an attempt was made to locate each document either by searching in person, writing personal letters to the repositories, or using interlibrary loan through the University of Wyoming.

Other searches for printed or manuscript documents included leafing page by page through professional journals on Western American history at the University of Wyoming; historical and genealogical journals in the Family History Library of the L.D.S. Church in Salt Lake City, Utah; and records of handcart pioneers at Riverton Wyoming Stake of the L.D.S. Church in Riverton, Wyoming. Additional searches were made on ERIC, CARL, and RLIN computer databases as well as library and special collections computer database catalogs for the University of Wyoming,

Brigham Young University, University of Utah, Weber State University, Utah State University, and University of California at Berkeley (GLADIS). A search was also made through the Utah Historical Society's *Guide to Archives and Manuscript Collections in Selected Utah Repositories*. Volumes of *Dissertations Abstracts* were searched for dissertations on the subject. Personal letters were written to all museums and historical societies in Oregon to identify documents in their archives and special collection departments. Copies of many of the documents were obtained through personal correspondence, interlibrary loan, and a visit to the Oregon Historical Society in Portland. Also, to locate records from private collections, advertising was done on radio stations throughout Wyoming; written ads were placed in *Pioneer Magazine* and *Utah Historical Quarterly*; and flyers were distributed at a Willie handcart monument dedication site at Rock Creek, Wyoming, in July, 1995.

Sources that were searched in depth for primary and secondary materials included the American Heritage Center and Coe Library at the University of Wyoming; museums and historical societies in Oregon; the Bancroft Library at the University of California at Berkeley; the Utah State Historical Society in Salt Lake City, Utah; Brigham Young University in Provo, Utah; the University of Utah; and the Church of Jesus Christ of Latter-day Saints Historical Library and Archives in Salt Lake City. All of the Daughters of Utah Pioneers volumes—*Heart Throbs of the West, Treasures of Pioneer History, Our Pioneer Heritage, An Enduring Legacy*, and *Chronicles of Courage*—were searched page by page for first-hand accounts of Mormon pioneer children who went to Utah. The pioneer data base at the Church Historical Library was only beginning to be developed at the time of this research; therefore, names, ages, and primary documents of Mormon youngsters had to be accessed by hand. Sources searched to a limited extent were Weber State University in Ogden, Utah; Utah State University in Logan, Utah; and references cited in Merrill Mattes's *Platte River Road Narratives*, such as the California State Library; the Huntington Library in San Marino, California; the California State Historical Society; and Denver Public Library.

Locating primary documents of children younger than sixteen or who turned sixteen on the trail as well as secondary materials relating to the subject was the first step of data analysis. Because only a few diaries and letters written by children younger than sixteen were found, contemporary documents written by sixteen-year-olds were also included. The time frame set for the study was any year before the transcontinental railroad was completed in 1869. Once gathered and catalogued, the next step of data analysis was identifying each pioneer's place and date of birth, age at the time of crossing, and destination; noting which were male and female; and marking crossing-the-plains data in each account. Oral and written reminiscences were categorized according to those that explained the trip in detail, those that described it briefly, and those that did not talk about it at all. The records that provided little or no information were eliminated from the study. The remaining documents were then analyzed for examples and details that gave children's perceptions. Of 712 total documents, 453 were studied. The documents were placed in the context of secondary materials to present a more authentic picture of mid-nineteenth century westward migration. To try to extract the child's perspective in reminiscences, concepts were borrowed from child development, child psychology, and theories and research on American and European children and childhood. Being a professional educator and a mother gave the author insights into young people and their thought processes. Learning about the remembered past and shared/collective memory and studying memory research and the new historicism point of view helped link reminiscences to children's viewpoints. This study, however, has only scratched the surface as far as connecting children's perceptions to the historical moments in which they lived.

Unpublished Primary Sources

Adams, Myra Abbott. "Covered Wagon Days As Related By Margaret Elizabeth Irvin to Myra Abbott Adams." MS 1508. Oreg. Hist. Soc., Portland.

Alston, Christopher. "Biographical Sketch of Christopher Alston, Pioneer." Photocopy of typescript in the author's possession from Robert A. Cloward, Cedar City, UT.

Alston, Ray L., comp. "Thomas Alston and Mary Ellen Holt Alston: Book of Remembrance." Utah State Hist. Soc., Salt Lake City.

Armstrong, Isabella Siddoway. "Sketch of Life of Isabella Siddoway Armstrong." MS 804. The Church of Jesus Christ of Latter-day Saints, Family and Church Hist. Dept., Church Archives (hereafter Church Archives), Salt Lake City, UT.

Ballard, Margaret McNeil. "Recollections." MS 484. Harold B. Lee Library, Brigham Young Univ., Provo, UT.

Bender, Flora Isabelle. "Autobiography of Flora Isabelle Bender from Ohio to Virginia City to Sacramento." Photocopy in author's possession from Frank Bender, Reno, NV.

Bender, Flora Isabelle. Typescript of Diary. Photocopy in author's possession from Frank Bender, Reno, NV.

Berrett, Ivan J. "Journal of Heber Robert McBride." Harold B. Lee Library, Brigham Young Univ., Provo, UT.

Blake, F. W. "Diary, 1861 April–Dec." MS. Church Archives, Salt Lake City, UT.

Boatman, Mary L. "Crossing the Plains to Montana in 1865." Small Collection no. 444, Montana Hist. Soc. Archives, Helena.

Bond, John. "Handcarts West in 56." MIC A–235, Item 7. Utah State Hist. Soc., Salt Lake City.

Bowers, Jacob. "History of Jacob Bowers." MS A 1687. Utah State Hist. Soc., Salt Lake City.

Campbell, S. W. "Over the Oregon Trail Year of 1857." MS. Western History Collections, Univ. of Oklahoma, Norman.

Canfield, Lucy. Diary. MS 8795, reel 11, no. 6. Church Archives, Salt Lake City, UT.

Canfield, Lucy. "My Journal—Lucy Canfield." Photocopy of typescript in author's possession from Julia Carver, Salt Lake City, UT.

Christensen, C. L. "Leaves from the Journal of C. L. Christensen." MS A 228. Utah State Hist. Soc., Salt Lake City.

Clayton, Roberta, comp. "Biographies of 195 Pioneer Arizona Women." MS 715, box 2. Harold B. Lee Library, Brigham Young Univ., Provo, UT.

Clegg, Hazel Jane Billman. "Life of Louisa Gittens Clegg, Utah Pioneer of 1862." MS. Riverton Wyoming Stake, The Church of Jesus Christ of Latter-day Saints, Riverton, WY.

Cluff, Harvey H. "Journal of Harvey H. Cluff, 1836–1868." Harold B. Lee Library, Brigham Young Univ., Provo, UT.

Cook, Amanda Fletcher. "Captured by Indians." MS 323, box 7, Morrison Collection. American Heritage Center, Univ. of Wyoming, Laramie.

Cottle, William Henry. Account. Photocopy of handwritten account in author's possession from Elva C. Fletcher, Salt Lake City, UT.

Creighton, Mary E. "To My Grandchildren, Laura Lee Owen, Robert Dale Owen." MS. Capt. Alfred King Collection, film 593 K39. Bancroft Library, Univ. of Calif., Berkeley.

Davies, J. Kenneth. "George Beard: Mormon Pioneer Artist with a Camera." Harold B. Lee Library, Brigham Young Univ., Provo, UT.

Davis, Thomas "Ap." "Handwritten Autobiography." MS A 2543. Utah State Hist. Soc., Salt Lake City.

Douglas, Sarah Jane Luper. "Memories of the Trip Across the Plains." Box 4, Henderson Collection. American Heritage Center, Univ. of Wyoming, Laramie.

Dudley, Susan. "Dudley Family Correspondence." MS SC 449. Harold B. Lee Library, Brigham Young Univ., Provo, UT.

Dunlap, Caroline Cook. "Ancotty (Long Ago)." MS 657. Oreg. Hist. Soc., Portland.

Earl, Robert. "Robert Earl Reminiscences." MSS 793. Oreg. Hist. Soc., Portland.

Federal Writers Project. "James Herman Tegan." MS B 289, box 10. Utah State Hist.Soc., Salt Lake City.

Federal Writers Project. "Lorenzo Hadley." MS B 289, box 4. Utah State Hist. Soc., Salt Lake City.

Federal Writers Project. "Mary Ann Chapple Warner." MS B 289, box 11. Utah State Hist. Soc., Salt Lake City.

Finley, Newton Gleaves. "Memories of Travel." MSS C–D 5182. Bancroft Library, Univ. of Calif., Berkeley.

Flake, Lucy Hannah White. "To the Last Frontier: Autobiography of Lucy Hannah White Flake." MS A 284. Utah State Hist. Soc., Salt Lake City.

Forsyth, Thomas R. "Pioneer Life of T. R. Forsyth." MS 1969. Church Archives, Salt Lake City, UT.

Garrison, Abraham H. "Reminiscences of A. H. Garrison, His Early Life and Across the Plains and of Oregon from 1846 to 1903." MS 874. Oreg. Hist. Soc., Portland.

Gay, William. "An Extract from the Life of Bill Gay." Small Collection no. 52, Willliam Gay Papers, Montana Hist. Soc. Archives, Helena.

Genealogical Society, comp. *Utah Pioneer Biographies*. 44 vols. Family History Library of The Church of Jesus Christ of Latter-day Saints, Salt Lake City, UT.

Gibson, James. "From Missouri to Oregon in 1847." MS 141. Oreg. Hist. Soc., Portland.

Greer, Catherine Ellen Camp. "Anecdotes and Reminiscences of Her Life As Related By Grandma Ellen C. Greer." MS 671. Harold B. Lee Library, Brigham Young Univ., Provo, UT.

Griggs, Thomas Cott. "Crossing the Plains from Boston, Massachusetts, to Great Salt Lake City Utah Territory." MS 1593, book 1. Church Archives, Salt Lake City, UT.

Hancock, Mosiah. "The Life Story of Mosiah Lyman Hancock." Harold B. Lee Library, Brigham Young Univ., Provo, UT.

Hansen, Jorgen. "History of Jorgen Hansen, 1852–1932." Church Archives, Salt Lake City, UT.

Henderson, John H. "Life of John H. Henderson." MIC A–344, Joel Ricks Collection. Utah State Hist. Soc., Salt Lake City.

Hill, William John. "Autobiography of William John Hill." MS B 289, box 4. Utah State Hist. Soc., Salt Lake City.

Hockett, W. A. "Experiences of W. A. Hockett on the Oregon Trail, 1847." MS 1036. Oreg. Hist. Soc., Portland.

Holdaway, Lydia Thrower. "Life Story of Mrs. Lydia Thrower Holdaway." MS 2050, reel 3 (4:5:2). Church Archives, Salt Lake City, UT.

Howard, Sarah Alice Zaring. "Crossing the Plains." MS. Eastern Wash. Hist. Soc., Spokane.

Howe, Charles Ross. Letter. Photocopy in the author's possession from Margaret M. Cannon, Provo, UT.

Humphrey, Edith A. Lockhart. "Original Diary." MS. Nev. State Hist. Soc., Reno.

"Indian Attack on Henry Cottle's Family." Photocopy of typescript in the author's possession from Elva C. Fletcher, Salt Lake City, UT.

Jenson, Andrew. "Autobiography and Journals, 1864–1941." MS. Church Archives, Salt Lake City, UT.

Johnson, Amos Partridge. "Autobiography of Amos Partridge Johnson." MS 1271, folder 1. Harold B. Lee Library, Brigham Young Univ., Provo, UT.

Johnson, Franklin. "Crossing the Plains, 1845." MS 1508. Oreg. Hist. Soc., Portland.

Johnson, Susan Ellen. "Record of Susan Ellen Johnson." Harold B. Lee Library, Brigham Young Univ., Provo, UT.

Journal History. Church Library/Archives, The Church of Jesus Christ of Latter-day Saints, Salt Lake City, UT.

Judd, Mary Minerva Dart. "Sketch of the Life of Mary Dart." MS A 461. Utah State Hist. Soc., Salt Lake City.

Larsen, Hans S. "Autobiographical Sketch of Hans S. Larsen." Photocopy of typescript in the author's possession from Jane Gibson, Rock Springs, WY.

Lindsay, James. "History of James Lindsay, (1849–1938)." MS A 729. Utah State Hist. Soc., Salt Lake City.

Lindsay, Willliam. "Autobiography of William Lindsay." Harold B. Lee Library, Brigham Young Univ., Provo, UT.

Loba, Jean Frederick. "Reminiscences of Jean Frederick Loba." Kansas State Hist. Soc., Topeka.

Margetts, Lucy Marie Canfield. "My Journal." MS 1850, submitted by Lucy B. Roach. Church Archives, Salt Lake City, UT.

McAuley, Eliza Ann. Diary. Thomas Macaulay, Reno, NV.

McBride, John Rogers. "Overland, 1846." MS 458. Oreg. Hist. Soc., Portland.

Millington, Ada. "Journal Kept While Crossing the Plains." MSS C–F 11, BNEG box 1046:3. Bancroft Library, Univ. of Calif., Berkeley.

Mitton, William C. "A Sketch of My Life." MS A 708. Utah State Hist. Soc., Salt Lake City.

Murphy, Mary. Letter. MS 72–29. Tennessee State Library and Archives, Nashville.

Murphy, Mary. "Three Letters Written to Dear Uncles, Aunts and Cousins." MS. Covilland Family Files. Yuba County Library, Marysville, CA.

Murphy, Patrick Henry. "Across the Plains Diary (1854)." MS F593M85. Bancroft Library, Univ. of Calif., Berkeley.

Murphy, Virginia E. "Letters to McGlashan." MS C–B 570, box II, folders 48–55, April 18, 1879. Bancroft Library, Univ. of Calif., Berkeley.

Murphy, Virginia E. B. Reed. "Virginia E. B. Reed Murphy." 2 letters. MS A 949.Utah State Hist. Soc., Salt Lake City. Letter 1. MS 543, folder 2, Virginia Elizabeth B. Reed Manuscript Collection. Southwest Museum, Los Angeles, CA. Letter 2. BANC MSS 89/127c. Bancroft Library, Univ. of Calif., Berkeley.

Neilsen, Christian Emil. "Autobiography of C. E. Neilsen, 1839–1907." Daughters of Utah Pioneers Museum Library, Salt Lake City.

Nielsen, John. "Biographical Sketch of John Nielsen." Harold B. Lee Library, Brigham Young Univ., Provo, UT.

Pace, William B. "Diary of William B. Pace, 1847, and Autobiography, 1847–1852." Harold B. Lee Library, Brigham Young Univ., Provo, UT.

Pence, Mrs. Anna. "Pioneer Hardships." Western History Department, Denver Public Library, Denver, CO.

Pendleton, Daniel S. "Autobiography of Daniel S. Pendleton." MS B 289, box 8. Utah State Hist. Soc., Salt Lake City.

Pringle, Catherine Sager. "Account of Overland Journey to Oregon in 1844; Life at the Whitman Mission at Waiilatpu; the Whitman Massacre." MS. The Huntington Library, San Marino, CA.

Pulsipher, Elizabeth. "Life History of Elizabeth Isabelle Jacobson Pulsipher." MS 715, box 3, folder 130. Harold B. Lee Library, Brigham Young Univ., Provo, UT.

Robenson, Anne Cottle. Letter. Photocopy of typescript in possession of the author from Alice Hulse, Jerome, ID.

"Robert Sweeten Family Reunion Held in the Mission Home in Salt Lake on May 5, 1961." Church Archives, Salt Lake City, UT.

Robinson, William S. "Biographical Sketch of William S. Robinson." Film 920, no. 51: 188–192. Harold B. Lee Library, Brigham Young Univ., Provo, UT.

Rowley, Richard. "Richard Rowley." MS 1150. Harold B. Lee Library, Brigham Young Univ., Provo, UT.

Rowley, Samuel. "A Biographical Sketch of the Life of Samuel Rowley, Son of William and Ann Jewell Rowley." MS 1150. Harold B. Lee Library, Brigham Young Univ., Provo, UT.

Sabin, Mary Powell. "Mary Powell Sabin." MS 3203. Church Archives. Salt Lake City, UT.

Schenck, Naomi Pike. "Letters to McGlashan." BANC MSS C–B 570, April 23, 1879. Bancroft Library, Univ. of Calif., Berkeley.

Sharp, Sarah Bethula Palmer. "Autobiography of Sarah Bethula Palmer Sharp." MS 4188. Church Archives, Salt Lake City, UT.

Smith, Harriet A. L. "My Trip Across the Plains in 1849." MS. Calif. State Library, Sacramento.

Smith, John. "Autobiography of John Smith, Patriarch to the Church of Jesus Christ of Latter-day Saints." BANC MSS P-F 60. Bancroft Library, Univ. of Calif., Berkeley.

Smoot, Diana Eldredge. "Autobiography of Diana Eldredge Smoot." MS SC 1587. Harold B. Lee Library, Brigham Young Univ., Provo, UT.

Sperry, Harrison. "A Short History of the Life of Harrison Sperry Sr." MS 722. Church Archives, Salt Lake City, UT.

Squires, John Paternoster. "Notes of Interest to the Descendants of Thomas Squires By His Son." MS. Harold B. Lee Library, Brigham Young Univ., Provo, UT.

Stephens, Evan. "A Talk Given By Prof. Evan Stephens Before the Daughters of the Pioneers, Hawthorne Camp, Feb. 5, 1930." MS A 2163. Utah State Hist. Soc., Salt Lake City.

Stevens, Augusta Dorius. "Autobiography of Augusta Dorius Stevens, A Pioneer of 1852." MS A 322. Utah State Hist. Soc., Salt Lake City.

Sweetland, Louisa. "Across the Plains." MS. Calif. State Library, Sacramento.

Terry, Susan Zimmerman. "The Garden Grove Company." Letter in "Church Emigration Book, 1850–1854." Church Archives, Salt Lake City, Utah.

Utah Works Progress Administration Historical Records Survey. "Pioneer Personal History Questionnaire." Utah HRS no. 314 (Revised 3/9/37). Utah State Hist. Soc., Salt Lake City.

Warner, Mary Eliza. "Diary of Mary Eliza Warner, 1864." BANC MSS C-F 66. Bancroft Library, Univ. of Calif., Berkeley.

Weeks, Lovina Walker. "Diary of Lovina Walker Weeks of Her Trip Across the Plains, with Notes By Her Daughter Florence Weeks Blacow." MS. Univ. of Nevada, Reno.

Wilder, Francis Evetis Donner. "Letters to McGlashan." BANC MSS C–B 570, box II, folder 54. Bancroft Library, Univ. of Calif., Berkeley.

Woodson, Rebecca Hildreth Nutting. "A Sketch of the Life of Rebecca Hildreth Nutting (Woodson) and Her Family." BANC MSS C–D 5140. Bancroft Library, Univ. of Calif., Berkeley.

Wright, Angus Taylor. "Autobiography of Angus Taylor Wright." MS A 1421. Utah State Hist. Soc., Salt Lake City.

Young, John Ray. "John Ray Young, 1837–1931." MS 1180 2. Church Archives, Salt Lake City, UT.

PUBLISHED PRIMARY SOURCES

Anderson, Charles P. *Charles P. Anderson Journal.* N.p.: Gilbert Publ. Co., 1975.

Applegate, Jesse. *Recollections of My Boyhood.* Roseburg, Oreg.: Press of Review Publ. Co., 1914.

Bagley, Will, ed. *The Pioneer Camp of the Saints: The 1846 and 1847 Mormon Trail Journals of Thomas Bullock*. Spokane, WA: The Arthur H. Clark Co., 1997.

Barton, Lois, ed. *One Woman's West*. Eugene, OR: Spencer Butte Press, 1986.

Belliston, Lester H. *James Thomas Belliston and Louisa Miller, Their Forebears and Descendants*. N.p.: James Thomas Belliston Family Organization, 1976.

Bender, Flora Isabelle. "Notes by the Way: Memoranda of a Journey Across the Plains." *Nev. Hist. Soc. Qtly.* 1 (July 1958): 144–173.

Bergera, Gary James, ed. *The Autobiography of B. H. Roberts*. Salt Lake City: Signature Books, 1990.

Bidwell, John. "Life in California Before the Gold Discovery." *Century Magazine* 61 (December 1890): 174.

Braley, John Hyde. *Memory Pictures: An Autobiography*. Los Angeles: Neuner Co., 1912.

Brooks, Elisha. *A Pioneer Mother of California*. San Francisco: Harr Wagner Publ., 1922.

Butcher, Marie Ross. *Hakan Anderson and Mariane Marie Nielsen, Progenitors and Descendants*. Provo, UT: J. Grant Stevenson, 1972.

Campbell, Remembrance Hughes. *A Brief History of Our Trip Across the Plains with Ox Teams in 1853*. N.p., 1905.

Carter, Kate B., comp. *Heart Throbs of the West*. 12 vols. Salt Lake City: Daughters of Utah Pioneers, 1939–1951.

Carter, Kate B., comp. *Our Pioneer Heritage*. 20 vols. Salt Lake City: Daughters of Utah Pioneers, 1958–1977.

Carter, Kate B., comp. *Treasures of Pioneer History*. 6 vols. Salt Lake City: Daughters of Utah Pioneers, 1952–1957.

Clark, Caroline Hopkins. "Liverpool to Utah in 1866 by Sailing Ship and Prairie Schooner." In *Covered Wagon Women*, edited by Kenneth L. Holmes, 11 vols. (Spokane, WA: The Arthur H. Clark Co., 1990) 9: 151–162.

Clark, Wanda. "History of Nirom Hawley." *Lane County Historian* 14 (Fall 1969): 51–63.

Clarke, Charles G., ed. "Journal Kept While Crossing the Plains By Ada Millington." *So. Calif. Qtly.* 59 (1977): 13–48, 139–184, 251–269.

Claypool, Lucinda Ellen Cockrill. "Memory of My Childhood." *Lifeliner* 10 (December 1974): 37–40.

Cleland, Robert Glass, and Juanita Brooks, ed. *A Mormon Chronicle: The Diaries of John D. Lee, 1848–1876*. 2 vols. San Marino, CA: The Huntington Library, 1955.

Clinkinbeard, Anna Dell. *Across the Plains in '64 By Prairie Schooner to Oregon*. New York: Exposition Press, 1953.

Coburn, Catherine Scott. "Old Pioneer Days." *The Morning Oregonian*, 20 June 1890, 16.

Colvig, William. "Annual Address." *Trans. of the Oreg. Pioneer Assoc.* (1916): 333–350.

Cook, Louisa. "Letters from the Oregon Trail, 1862–1863." In *Covered Wagon Women*, edited by Kenneth L. Holmes, 11 vols. (Spokane, WA: The Arthur H. Clark Co., 1989) 8: 27–57.

Cummins, Flora Violet Pitman. "Crossing the Plains in 1852." *Genealogical Soc. of Siskiyou Co.* (Fall 1975): 23–25.

Currey, Colonel George B. "Occasional Address." *Trans. of the Oreg. Pioneer Assoc.* (1887): 32–47.

Decker, Louisa. "Reminiscences of Nauvoo." *Woman's Exponent* 37 (April 1909): 49–50.

Dee, Annie Taylor. *Memories of a Pioneer.* N.p., n.d.

Delaney, Matilda J. Sager. *A Survivor's Recollections of the Whitman Massacre.* Spokane, WA: Daughters of the American Revolution, 1920.

Dickson, Arthur Jerome, ed. *Covered Wagon Days.* Cleveland: The Arthur H. Clark Co., 1929.

Donner, Tamsen, and Virginia E. B. Reed. "The Donner Party Letters." In *Covered Wagon Women*, edited by Kenneth L. Holmes, 11 vols. (Glendale, CA: The Arthur H. Clark Co., 1983) 1: 65–82.

Drumheller, "Uncle Dan." *"Uncle Dan" Drumheller Tells Thrills of Western Trails in 1854.* Spokane, WA: Inland-American Printing, 1925.

Dunham, E. Allene. *Across the Plains in a Covered Wagon.* N.p., n.d.

Egan, Howard R. *Pioneering the West, 1846 to 1878.* Richmond, UT: Howard R. Egan Estate, 1917.

Evans, John R. ed. *Two Diaries: The Diary and Journal of Calvin Perry Clark . . . Together with the Diary of His Sister Helen E. Clark.* Denver: Denver Public Library, 1962.

Fox, Ruth May. "From England to Salt Lake Valley in 1867." *The Improvement Era* 38 (July 1935): 406–409, 450.

Fuller, Emeline L. *Left By the Indians. Story of My Life.* Mt. Vernon, IA: Hawkeye Steam Print, 1892.

Giese, Dale F., ed. *My Life with the Army in the West: The Memoirs of James E. Farmer, 1858–1898.* Santa Fe: Stagecoach Press, 1967.

Giles, Daniel. "Indian Wars, A Pioneer Struggles As Told By the Late Daniel Giles." In *Pioneers and Incidents of the Upper Coquille Valley, 1890–1940*, edited by Alice H. Wooldridge. Myrtle Creek, OR: Mail Printers, 1971.

Godfrey, Kenneth W. *Charles Shumway, A Pioneer's Life.* Provo, UT: J. Grant Stevenson, 1974.

Goodridge, Sophia Lois. "The Mormon Trail, 1850." In *Covered Wagon Women*, edited by Kenneth L. Holmes, 11 vols. (Spokane, WA: The Arthur H. Clark Co., 1990) 2: 207–235.

Gowdy, Mrs. J. T. *Crossing the Plains: Personal Recollections of the Journey to Oregon in 1852*. McMinnville, OR: n.p., 1906.

Hale, Heber Q., ed. *Memoirs of Anna Clark Hale*. N.p., 1965.

Hamilton, Mrs. S. Watson. *A Pioneer of Fifty-three*. Albany, OR: The Herald Press, 1905.

Hansen, Rev. H. N. "An Account of a Mormon Family's Conversion to the Religion of the Latter Day Saints and of Their Trip from Denmark to Utah." *Annals of Iowa* 41 (Summer, Fall 1971): 709–728, 765–779.

Haskin, Leslie L., et. al. *Pioneer Stories of WPA Interviews*, vols. 4, 5. Albany, OR: Richard R. Milligan, 1989.

Helm, Mike, ed. *Conversations with Pioneer Women by Fred Lockley*. Eugene, OR: Rainy Day Press, 1981.

Helm, Mike, ed. *Voices of the Oregon Territory: Conversations with Bullwhackers, Muleskinners, Pioneers, Prospectors, '49ers, Indian Fighters, Trappers, Ex-Barkeepers, Authors, Preachers, Poets & Near Poets & All Sorts & Conditions of Men*. Eugene, OR: Rainy Day Press, 1981.

Henderson, Lucy Ann. "Young Adventure." *Nev. Hist. Soc. Qtly.* 16 (Summer 1973): 67–99.

Hester, Sallie. "The Diary of a Pioneer Girl." In *Covered Wagon Women*, edited by Kenneth L. Holmes, 11 vols. (Glendale, CA: The Arthur H. Clark Co., 1983) 1: 231–246.

Hill, Emma Shepard. *A Dangerous Crossing and What Happened on the Other Side*. Denver: Smith-Brooks Co., 1914.

Hill, Ivy Hooper Blood, ed. *Jane Wilkie Hooper Blood Autobiography and Abridged Diary*. N.p., 1965.

Himes, George H. "Annual Address." *Trans. of the Oreg. Pioneer Assoc.* (1907): 134–152.

Hines, Celinda. "Life and Death on the Oregon Trail." In *Covered Wagon Women*, edited by Kenneth L. Holmes, 11 vols. (Spokane, WA: The Arthur H. Clark Co., 1994) 6: 77–134.

Hitchcock, Harriet. "Thoughts By the Way, 1864–1865." In *Covered Wagon Women*, edited by Kenneth L. Holmes, 11 vols. (Spokane, Wash.: The Arthur H. Clark Co., 1989) 8: 232–264.

Hixon, Adrietta Applegate. *On to Oregon! A True Story of a Young Girl's Journey into the West*. Weiser, ID: Signal-American Printers, 1947.

Holmes, Kenneth L., ed. *Covered Wagon Women: Diaries and Letters from the Western Trails, 1840–1890*, 11 vols. Glendale and Spokane: The Arthur H. Clark Co., 1983–1993.

Huntington, Mrs. Olive. "Tells of Experiences Crossing the Plains." *Cowlitz Co. Hist. Qtly.* 12 (February 1971): 1–2.

Jenson, Andrew. *Autobiography of Andrew Jenson*. Salt Lake City: Deseret News Press, 1938.

"Jonathan Stout Family's Oregon Trail Experiences." *Timber Trails* 14 (July 1993): 7–8.

Keegan, Elizabeth. "A Teenager's Letter from Sacramento." In *Covered Wagon Women*, edited by Kenneth L. Holmes, 11 vols. (Spokane, WA: The Arthur H. Clark Co., 1991) 4: 21–31.

King, Mike. "The Long Journey of a Mormon Girl." *Frontier Times* (September 1975): 8–40.

Krenkel, John H., ed. *The Life and Times of Joseph Fish, Mormon Pioneer.* Danville, IL: Interstate Printers and Publ., Inc., 1970.

Lambourne, Alfred. *An Old Sketch Book.* Boston: Samuel E. Cassino, 1892.

Lambourne, Alfred. *The Pioneer Trail.* Salt Lake City: The Deseret News, 1913.

Lesson Committee, comp. *An Enduring Legacy.* 12 vols. Salt Lake City: Daughters of Utah Pioneers, 1978–1989.

Lesson Committee, comp. *Chronicles of Courage.* 8 vols. Salt Lake City: Daughters of Utah Pioneers, 1990–1997.

"Letters of S. H. Taylor to the Watertown [Wisconsin] Chronicle." *Oreg. Hist. Qtly.* 22(June 1921): 117–160.

Linforth, James, ed. *Route from Liverpool to Great Salt Lake Valley.* Liverpool: Franklin D. Richards, 1855.

"List of Mormon Emigrants from 1852." *Deseret News Extra*, 1852 broadside. Salt Lake City: The Deseret News, 1852.

Lockley, Fred. *Across the Plains by Prairie Schooner.* Eugene, OR: Koke-Tiffany Co., 1923.

Long, Mary Jane. *Crossing the Plains in the Year of 1852 with Ox Teams.* McMinnville, OR: n.p., 1915.

Martin, Raymond R., and Esther Jenkins Carpenter, eds. *The Samaritans.* Bountiful, UT: Carr Printing Co., 1968.

Martineau, Susan E. J. "Almost an Indian Bride." *Young Woman's Journal* 18 (June 1907): 264–265.

"Mary Ann Parker, Reynolds, Van Norman, Wilgus." *Sutter-Yuba Diggers Digest* 5 (July–December 1978): 111–114.

McAuley, Eliza Ann. "Iowa to the 'Land of Gold.'" In *Covered Wagon Women*, edited by Kenneth L. Holmes, 11 vols. (Spokane, WA: The Arthur H. Clark Co., 1991) 4: 33–81.

McCall, A.J. *The Great California Trail in 1849, Wayside Notes of an Argonaut.* Bath, NY: Steuben Courier Print, 1882.

Miller, Joaquin. *Overland in a Covered Wagon.* New York: D. Appleton and Co., 1930.

Milliken, Ralph LeRoy. *Story of the Crow Emigrant Train of 1865.* 1935. Reprinted from *The Livingston Chronicle*, January 1935.

Moreland, J. C. "Annual Address." *Trans. of the Oreg. Pioneer Assoc.* (1900): 26–34.

Mumford, Violet Coe, and The Royal Family Association, Inc. *The Royal Way West Volume II: Crossing the Plains, 1853*. Baltimore: Gateway Press, Inc., 1988.

Murphy, Virginia Reed. *Across the Plains in the Donner Party (1846–1847)*. Olympic Valley, CA: Outbooks, 1977.

Nibley, Charles W. *Reminiscences of Charles W. Nibley (1849–1931)*. Salt Lake City: Stevens and Wallace, 1934.

Palmer, Harriet Scott. *Crossing Over the Great Plains By Ox-Wagons*. N.p., n.d., 9 pp.

Parker, Inez Eugenia Adams. "Early Recollections of Oregon Pioneer Life." *Trans. of the of the Oreg. Pioneer Assoc.* (1928): 17–36.

Payne, Wilford H. *The Harry M. Payne Family History*. Bountiful, UT: Horizon Publ., 1974.

Peabody, Francis Clelland. "Across the Plains DeLuxe in 1865." *The Colorado Magazine* 18 (1941): 71–76.

Pettit, Edwin. *Biography of Edwin Pettit, 1834–1912*. Salt Lake City: Arrow Press, 1912.

Pleasants, William J. *Twice Across the Plains, 1849 & 1856*. Fairfield, WA: Ye Galleon Press, 1981.

Pringle, Catherine Sager. *Across the Plains in 1844*. Fairfield, WA: Ye Galleon Press, 1989.

Pringle, Catherine Sager. "Letter of Catherine Sager Pringle." *The Oreg. Hist. Qtly.* 37 (December 1936): 354–360.

Pringle, O. M. *Magic River Deschutes and Experience of an Emigrant Boy in 1846*. Fairfield, WA: Ye Galleon Press, 1970.

Purcell, Polly Jane. *Autobiography and Reminiscences of a Pioneer*. Freewater, OR: n.p., 192–?.

Reed, Virginia E. B. "Deeply Interesting Letter." *Illinois Journal*, 16 December 1847, 17, no. 19.

Rogers, Aurelia Spencer. *Life Sketches of Orson Spencer and Others and History of Primary Work*. Salt Lake City: Geo. Q. Cannon & Sons Co., 1898.

Ross, Jennie E. "A Child's Experiences in '49 As Related by Mrs. M. A. Gentry of Oakland, Cal." *Overland Monthly* 63 (1914): 300–305.

Riddle, George W. *History of Early Days in Oregon*. Riddle, OR: The Riddle Enterprise, 1920.

Samuels, Rachel Regina Zimmerman. "Some Early Humboldt County Memories of Rachel Regina Zimmerman Samuels." *Redwood Researcher* 12 (May 1980): 18.

Scott, Abigail Jane. "Journal of a Trip to Oregon." In *Covered Wagon Women*, edited by Kenneth L. Holmes, 11 vols. (Spokane, WA: The Arthur H. Clark Co., 1991) 5: 21–138.

Scott Sisters. "Scott Letters to Illinois and a Poem." In *Covered Wagon Women*, edited by Kenneth L. Holmes, 11 vols. (Spokane, WA: The Arthur H. Clark Co., 1991) 5: 139–172.

Sexton, Lucy Foster. *The Foster Family, California Pioneers, 1849.* N.p., 1925.

Skov, G. A. "From Handcart to Airplane." *The Deseret News,* 4 April 1931, Church Department.

Smith, Joseph Fielding. "True Pioneer Stories." *Young Woman's Journal* 30 (March 1919): 165, 171.

Somers, Mrs. Belle Redman. "Crossing the Plains in a Covered Wagon in 1949." *The Argonaut,* 29 August 1925, 3.

Stokes, George. *Deadwood Gold.* New York: n.p., 1927.

Stucki, John S. *Family History Journal of John S. Stucki.* Salt Lake City: Pyramid Press, 1932.

Sutton, Sarah. "A Travel Diary in 1854." In *Covered Wagon Women,* edited by Kenneth L. Holmes, 11 vols. (Glendale, CA: The Arthur H. Clark Co., 1988) 7: 15–25.

Swingley, Upton. "Gold Rush Fever Hits Mount Morris." *Jnl. of the Illinois State Hist. Soc.* 42 (1949): 457–462.

Taylor, Rachel. "Overland Trip Across the Plains." In *Covered Wagon Women,* edited by Kenneth L. Holmes, 11 vols. (Spokane, WA: The Arthur H. Clark Co., 1994) 6: 149–182.

Told by the Pioneers. 2 vols. N.p.: Washington Pioneer Project, 1937–1938.

Tribble, George. "Autobiographical Sketches of George William Tribble." *Oreg. Genealogical Qtly.* 33 (Fall 1994): 3–5.

Waggoner, George A. *Stories of Old Oregon.* Salem, OR: Statesman Publishing Co., 1905.

Ward, D. B. *Across the Plains in 1853.* Seattle: n.p., 1911.

Webb, Catherine J. *A Family History of California.* Berkeley: Type-Ink-Berkeley, 1975.

Weech, Hyrum. "Autobiography of Hyrum Weech." In *Our Pioneer Parents.* Hollywood, CA: Lee Printing, n.d.

Whipple–Haslam, Mrs. Lee. *Early Days in California: Scenes and Events of the '50s As I Remember Them.* Jamestown, CA: n.p., c 1925.

Williams, Velina A. "Diary of a Trip Across the Plains in 1853." *Trans. of the Oreg. Pioneer Assoc.* (1919): 178–240.

Wilson, Lois Christensen, and Helen Atkinson Cowan. *Descendants of Charles John Atkinson and Ann Smith.* Provo, UT: J. Grant Stevenson, n.d.

Wonderly, Mrs. Pauline. *Reminiscences of a Pioneer.* Placerville, CA: El Dorado Co. Hist. Soc., 1965.

Young, John R. Memoirs of John R. Young, Utah Pioneer 1847. Salt Lake City: Deseret News, 1920.

SECONDARY SOURCES

Crossing the Plains and the West

Allen, Judy. "Children on the Overland Trails." *Overland Journal* 12 (Spring 1994): 2–11.

Andros, Jill Jacobsen. "Are We There Yet? The Story of Children on the Mormon Trail." *Beehive History* 22 (1996): 5–10.

Bashore, Melvin L. Letter to author, 30 January 1998.

Bashore, Melvin L. "Pioneer Companies (1847–1868)—Statistics." The Church of Jesus Christ of Latter-day Saints, Family and Church History Dept., Church Library, Salt Lake City, UT.

Bashore, Melvin L. Telephone interview with author, 15 April 1997.

Bashore, Melvin L., and Linda L. Haslam. "Mormon Pioneer Companies Crossing the Plains (1847–1868) Narratives: Guide to Sources in Utah Libraries and Archives." The Church of Jesus Christ of Latter-day Saints, Family and Church History Dept., Church Library, Salt Lake City, UT.

Baur, John E. *Growing Up with California: A History of California's Children.* Los Angeles: Will Kramer Publisher, 1978.

Bitton, Davis. *Guide to Mormon Diaries and Autobiographies.* Provo, UT: Brigham Young Univ. Press, 1977.

Buchanan, Frederick S. "Imperial Zion: The British Occupation of Utah." In *Peoples of Utah*, edited by Helen Z. Papanikolas. Salt Lake City: Utah Hist. Soc., 1976.

Carter, John E. "Photographing Across the Plains: Charles R. Savage in 1866." *Nebraska History* 71 (Summer 1990): 58–63.

Carter, Lyndia McDowell. "The Mormon Handcart Companies." *Overland Journal* 3 (Spring 1995): 2–15.

Carter, Lyndia McDowell. Telephone interview with author, 18 January 1997.

"Collections." *Oreg. Hist. Qtly.* 94 (Summer 1993): 246–253.

Cross, Mary Bywater. *Treasures in the Trunk: Quilts of the Oregon Trail.* Nashville: Rutledge Hill Press, 1993.

Dawson, Charles. *Pioneer Tales of the Oregon Trail and Jefferson County.* Topeka: Crane, 1912.

Douglas, Mrs. Thurlow. "Bender Family Contributed Much to Nevada Culture, Business." *Nevada State Journal*, 6 April 1941, 14.

Faragher, John Mack. *Women and Men on the Overland Trail.* New Haven: Yale Univ. Press, 1979.

Faragher, Johnny, and Christine Stansell. "Women and Their Families on the Overland Trail to California and Oregon, 1842–1867." *Feminist Studies* 2 (1985): 150–166.

Grant, Carter E. "Robbed By Wolves." *The Relief Society Magazine* 15 (July 1928): 355–364.

Guenther, Todd. "The Burnt Ranch Saga: A History of the Last Crossing of the Sweetwater." *Overland Journal* 17 (Winter 1999–2000): 2–32.

Guide to Archives and Manuscript Collections in Selected Utah Repositories. Salt Lake City: Utah State Hist. Soc., 1991.

Guilford–Kardell, Margaret. "Joaquin Miller: Fact and Fiction." *The Californians* 9 (Nov./Dec. 1991): 6–13.

Hafen, LeRoy R., and Ann W. Hafen. *Handcarts to Zion.* Glendale, CA: The Arthur H. Clark Co., 1960.

Haines, Francis, Sr. "Goldilocks on the Oregon Trail." *Idaho Yesterdays* 9 (Winter 1965–1966): 26–30.

Hartley, William G. "Down–and-Back Wagon Trains: Travelers on the Mormon Trail in 1861." *Overland Journal* 11 (Winter 1993): 23–34.

Hartley, William G. "The Great Florence Fitout of 1861." *BYU Studies* 24 (Summer 1984): 341–371.

Hassrick, Royal B. *The Sioux: Life and Customs of a Warrior Society.* Norman: Univ. of Oklahoma Press, 1964.

Hoig, Stan. *The Sand Creek Massacre.* Norman: Univ. of Oklahoma Press, 1961.

Horton, Loren N. "The Victorian Era in the American West: An Introduction." *Journal of the West* 33 (January 1994): 8–9.

Hulmston, John K. "Mormon Immigration in the 1860s: The Story of the Church Trains." *Utah Hist. Qtly.* 58 (1990): 32–48.

Hyde, George E. *The Pawnee Indians.* Norman: Univ. of Oklahoma Press, 1974.

Jackson, Clarence S. *Pageant of the Pioneers: The Veritable Art of William H. Jackson.* Minden, NE: Harold Warp Pioneer Village, 1958.

Jeffrey, Julie Roy. *Frontier Women: The Trans-Mississippi West, 1840–1880.* New York: Hill and Wang, 1979.

Jenson, Andrew. "Latter-day Saints Emigration from Wyoming, Nebraska—1864–1866." *Nebraska History* 17 (1936): 113–127.

Josephy, Alvin M., Jr. *The Civil War in the American West.* New York: Alfred A. Knopf, 1991.

Kimball, Stanley B. *Historic Resource Study Mormon Pioneer National Historic Trail.* United States Dept. of the Interior/National Park Service, 1991.

Kimball, Violet T. *Stories of Young Pioneers: In Their Own Words.* Missoula, MT: Mountain Press, 2000.

Lamar, Howard R. "Rites of Passage: Young Men and Their Families in the Overland Trails Experience, 1843–69." In *"Soul-Butter and Hog Wash" and Other Essays on the American West,* edited by Thomas G. Alexander. Provo, UT: BYU Press, 1978.

Lewis, David Rich. "Argonauts and the Overland Trail Experience: Method and Theory." *The Western Hist. Qtly.* 16 (July 1985): 285–305.

"List of Mormon Emigrants from 1852." *Deseret News Extra*, 1852 Broadside. Salt Lake City: Deseret News, 1852.

Macaulay, Thomas. Letter to author, 22 September 1999.

Madsen, Brigham D. *The Shoshoni Frontier and the Bear River Massacre*. Salt Lake City: Univ. of Utah Press, 1985.

Madsen, Susan Arrington. *I Walked to Zion: True Stories of Young Pioneers on the Mormon Trail*. Salt Lake City: Deseret Book, 1994.

Mattes, Merrill J. *The Great Platte River Road*. N.p.: Nebraska State Hist. Soc., 1969.

Mattes, Merrill J. *Platte River Road Narratives*. Urbana: Univ. of Illinois Press, 1988.

McGlashan, C. F. *History of the Donner Party: A Tragedy of the Sierras*. Truckee, CA: Crowley & McGlashan, 1879.

Moore, John H. *The Cheyenne Nation: A Social and Demographic History*. Lincoln: Univ. of Nebraska Press, 1987.

Morgan, Dale, ed. *Overland in 1846: Diaries and Letters of the California–Oregon Trail*. 2 vols. Lincoln: Univ. of Nebraska Press, 1963.

Moynihan, Ruth Barnes. "Children and Young People on the Overland Trail." *The Western Hist. Qtly.* 6 (July 1975): 279–294.

Mulder, William. *Homeward to Zion: The Mormon Migration from Scandinavia*. Minneapolis: Univ. of Minnesota Press, 1957.

Mulder, William. "Mormons from Scandinavia, 1850–1900: A Shepherded Migration." *Pacific Hist. Review* 23 (August 1954): 227–246.

Mulder, William. "Scandinavian Saga." In *The Peoples of Utah*, edited by Helen Z. Papanikolas. Salt Lake City: Utah Hist. Soc., 1976.

Mulder, William. "Utah's Ugly Ducklings: A Profile of the Scandinavian Immigrant." *Utah Hist. Qtly.* 23 (July 1955): 233–259.

Munkres, Robert L. "Indian-White Contact before 1870: Culture Factors in Conflict." *Journal of the West* 10 (July 1971): 439–473.

Munkres, Robert L. "The Plains Indians." *Overland Journal* 7 (Summer 1989): 24–32.

Munkres, Robert L. *Saleratus and Sagebrush*. N.p.: Wyoming State Archives and Hist. Dept., 1974.

Munkres, Robert L. "Wives, Mothers, Daughters: Women's Life on the Road West." *Annals of Wyoming* 42 (October 1970): 191–224.

Myres, Sandra L., ed. *Ho for California! Women's Overland Diaries from the Huntington Library*. San Marino: The Huntington Library, 1980.

Myres, Sandra L. *Westering Women and the Frontier Experience, 1800–1915*. Albuquerque: Univ. of New Mexico Press, 1982.

Nash, Gerald D. "European Image of America: The West in Historical Perspective." *Montana The Magazine of Western History* 42 (Spring 1992): 2–16.

O'Brien, Mary Barmeyer. *Toward the Setting Sun: Pioneer Girls Traveling the Overland Trails*. Helena, MT: Falcon Publ., Inc. 1999.

Olson, John Alden. "Proselytism, Immigration and Settlement of Foreign Converts to the Mormon Culture in Zion." *Journal of the West* 6 (April 1967): 189–204.

Palmer, Rosemary G. "Lucy Canfield's Diary: What a Young Pioneer Did and Did Not Say." *Overland Journal* 16 (Fall 1998): 2–9.

Peavy, Linda, and Ursula Smith. *Frontier Children*. Norman: Univ. of Oklahoma Press, 1999.

Purdy, John R., Jr. "Isaac Owen—Overland to California." *Methodist History* 11 (July 1973): 46–54.

Read, Georgia Willis. "Women and Children on the Oregon-California Trail in the Gold Rush Years." *Missouri Hist. Review* 39 (October 1944): 1–23.

Rieck, Richard L. "A Geography of Death on the Oregon-California Trail, 1840–1860." *Overland Journal* 9 (Spring 1991): 13–21.

Riley, Glenda. "Frontierswomen's Changing Views of Indians in the Trans-Mississippi West." *Montana The Magazine of Western History* 34 (Winter 1984): 20–35.

Riley, Glenda. *Women and Indians on the Frontier, 1825–1915*. Albuquerque: Univ. of New Mexico Press, 1984.

Schlissel, Lillian. "Mothers and Daughters on the Western Frontier." *Frontiers* 3 (Summer 1978): 29–33.

Schlissel, Lillian. *Women's Diaries of the Westward Journey*. New York: Schocken Books, 1982.

Schlissel, Lillian, Byrd Gibbens, and Elizabeth Hampsten. *Far From Home: Families of the Westward Journey*. New York: Schocken Books, 1989.

Scott, Bob. *Blood at Sand Creek: The Massacre Revisited*. Caldwell, ID: Caxton Printers, Ltd., 1994.

Smith, Shirley Macaulay. Letter to author, 3 October 1999.

Solberg, Winton U. "The Sabbath on the Overland Trail to California." *Overland Journal* 8 (Winter 1990): 20–27.

Stefoff, Rebecca. *Children of the Westward Trail*. Brookfield, CT: Millbrook Press, 1996.

Stegner, Wallace. *The Gathering of Zion: The Story of the Mormon Trail*. New York: McGraw-Hill, 1971.

Stern, Peter. "The White Indians of the Borderlands." *Journal of the Southwest* 33 (1991): 262–281.

Taylor, P. A. M. *Expectations Westward: The Mormons and the Emigration of Their British Converts in the Nineteenth Century*. Ithica: Cornell Univ. Press, 1966.

Taylor, Philip A. M. "The Mormon Crossing of the United States, 1840–1870." *Utah Hist. Qtly.* 25 (October 1957): 319–337.

Taylor, Philip A. M. "Why Did British Mormons Emigrate." *Utah Hist. Qtly.* 22 (July 1954): 249–270.

Thompson, Erwin N. *Shallow Grave at Waiilatpu: The Sagers' West.* Portland: Oregon Hist. Soc., 1969.

Toelken, Barre. "Folklore and Reality in the American West." In *Sense of Place: American Regional Cultures*, edited by Barbara Allen and Thomas J. Schlereth. Lexington: Univ. of Kentucky Press, 1990.

Trenholm, Virginia Cole. "Amanda Mary and the Dog Soldiers." *Annals of Wyoming* 46 (Spring 1974): 6–46.

Unruh, John D., Jr. *The Plains Across: The Overland Emigrants and the Trans-Mississippi West, 1840–60.* Urbana: Univ. of Illinois Press, 1979.

Utley, Robert M. "Indian-United States Military Situation, 1848–1891." In *History of Indian-White Relations.* 4 vols., edited by Wilcomb E. Washburn. (Washington, D.C.: Smithsonian Institution, 1988) 4: 163–182.

Watson, Jeanne H. "'Cult of Domesticity' versus 'Real Womanhood' on the Overland Trails." *The Californians* 12, no. 2 (1992): 25–33.

Watson, Jeanne H. "'A Laughing, Merry Group': Women Triumphant Over Travail on the Overland Trails." *The Californians* 12, no. 2 (1992): 10–19.

Watson, Jeanne H. "Traveling Traditions: Victorians on the Overland Trails." *Journal of the West* 33 (January 1994): 74–83.

Werner, Emmy E. *Pioneer Children on the Journey West.* Boulder, CO: Westview Press, Inc., 1995.

West, Elliott. *Growing Up with the Country: Childhood on the Far Western Frontier.* Albuquerque: Univ. of New Mexico Press, 1989.

West, Elliott. "The Youngest Pioneers." *American Heritage* 37, no. 1 (1986): 90–96.

White, Kris and Mary-Catherine Cuthill, eds. *Overland Passages: A Guide to Overland Documents in the Oregon Historical Society.* Portland: Oregon Hist. Soc. Press, 1993.

White, Richard. *"It's Your Misfortune and None of My Own": A New History of the American West.* Norman: Univ. of Oklahoma Press, 1991.

Williams, Carol. "My First Indian: Interaction Between Women and Indians on the Trail, 1845–1865." *Overland Journal* 4 (Summer 1986): 13–18.

Winn, Norma B., and Emma R. Olsen. "Daughters of Utah Pioneers Through the Years." *An Enduring Legacy* 12 (1989): 93–99.

Children and Child Development

Aries, Philippe. *Centuries of Childhood: A Social History of Family Life.* New York: Vintage Books, 1962.

Berger, Kathleen Stassen. *The Developing Person Through the Life Span.* 2nd ed. New York: Worth Publ., Inc., 1988.

Berk, Laura E. *Child Development.* 2nd ed. Boston: Allyn and Bacon, 1991.

Boylan, Anne M. "Growing Up Female in Young America, 1800–1860." In *American Childhood: A Research Guide and Historical Handbook*, edited by Joseph M. Hawes and N. Ray Hiner. Westport, CT: Greenwood Press, 1985.

Bryant, Peter. *Perception and Understanding in Young Children: An Experimental Approach*. New York: Basic Books, Inc., 1974.

Burnett, John, ed. *Destiny Obscure: Autobiographies of Childhood, Education and Family from the 1820s to the 1920s*. N.p.: Allen Lane, 1982; London: Routledge, 1994.

Child, Mrs. L. Maria. *The Girls' Own Book*. Boston: Carter, Hendee & Babcock, 1834; Bedford, MA: Applewood Books, n.d.

Donaldson, Margaret. *Children's Minds*. New York: W. W. Norton & Company, 1978.

Dudycha, George J., and Martha M. Dudycha. "Childhood Memories: A Review of the Literature." *Psychological Bulletin* 38 (1941): 668–682.

Gillis, John R. *Youth and History: Tradition and Change in European Age Relations 1770-Present*. New York: Academic Press, 1974.

Hall, G. Stanley. "Note on Early Memories." *Pedagogical Seminary* 6 (1899): 485–512.

Hampsten, Elizabeth. *Settlers' Children: Growing Up on the Great Plains*. Norman: Univ. of Oklahoma Press, 1991.

Heininger, Mary Lynn Stevens, Karin Calvert, Barbara Finkelstein, Kathy Vandell, Anne Scott MacLeod, and Harvey Green. *A Century of Childhood, 1820–1920*. Rochester, NY: Margaret Woodbury Strong Museum, 1984.

Hernandez, Donald J. *America's Children: Resources from Family, Government, and the Economy*. New York: Russell Sage Foundation, 1993.

Irwin, Donald B., and Janet A. Simons. *Lifespan Developmental Psychology*. Madison, WI: Brown & Benchmark, 1994.

Kett, Joseph F. *Rites of Passage: Adolescence in America, 1790 to the Present*. New York: Basic Books, Inc., 1977.

MacLeod, Anne Scott. *A Moral Tale: Children's Fiction and American Culture, 1820–1860*. Hamden, CT: Archon Books, 1975.

Mechling, Jay. "Oral Evidence and the History of American Children's Lives." *The Jnl. of American Hist.* 74 (1987): 579–586.

Norton, Donna E. *Through the Eyes of a Child: An Introduction to Children's Literature*. 3rd ed. New York: Macmillan Publ. Co., 1991.

Owens, Karen. *The World of the Child*. New York: Macmillan Publ. Co., 1993.

Powell, Barbara. "Nineteenth-century Young Women's Diaries." *Canadian Children's Literature* 65 (1992): 68–80.

Santrock, John W. *Children*. 5th ed. Madison, WI: Brown & Benchmark, 1997.

Stearns, Peter N. "Girls, Boys, and Emotions: Redefinitions and Historical Change." *The Jnl. of American Hist.* 80 (June 1993): 36–74.

Wishy, Bernard. *The Child and Republic: The Dawn of Modern American Child Nurture*. Philadelphia: Univ. of Penn. Press, 1968.

Wood, David. *How Children Think and Learn: The Social Contexts of Cognitive Development*. Oxford, UK: Blackwell Publishers, 1988.

Yamamoto, Kaoru. *Their World, Our World: Reflections on Childhood*. Westport, CT: Praeger, 1993.

Young, Leotine. *Life Among the Giants*. New York: McGraw-Hill, 1966.

Theses and Dissertations

Burgess, Barbara MacPherson. "Migrant Women to Oregon, 1836–1860." Ph.D. diss., Univ. of Kansas, 1989.

Palmer, Rosemary Gudmundson. "Voices from the Trail: Young Pioneers on the Platte River Road Between 1841 and 1869." Ph.D. diss., Univ. of Wyoming, 1997.

Other

Allen, Barbara, and William Lynwood Montell. *From Memory to History: Using Oral Sources in Local Historical Research*. Nashville: American Assoc. for State and Local History, 1981.

Allen, James B., and Glen M. Leonard. *The Story of the Latter-day Saints*. Salt Lake City: Deseret Book, 1976.

Arrington, Leonard J. *Great Basin Kingdom: An Economic History of the Latter-day Saints, 1830–1900*. Cambridge: Harvard Univ. Press, 1958.

Arrington, Leonard J., and Davis Bitton. *The Mormon Experience: A History of the Latter-day Saints*. New York: Alfred A. Knopf, 1979.

Arskey, Laura, Nancy Pries, and Marcia Reed. *American Diaries: An Annotated Bibliography of Published American Diaries and Journals, Vol. 1: Diaries Written from 1492 to 1844*. Detroit: Gale Research Co., 1983.

Axtell, James. *The Invasion Within: The Contest of Cultures in Colonial North America*. New York: Oxford Univ. Press, 1985.

Bartholomew, Rebecca. *Audacious Women*. Salt Lake City: Signature Books, 1995.

Barzun, Jacques, and Henry F. Graff. *The Modern Researcher*. 5th ed. Fort Worth: Harcourt Brace Jovanovich College Publ., 1992.

The Bible. King James Version. Salt Lake City: The Church of Jesus Christ of Latter-day Saints, 1981.

Blodgett, Harriet. *Centuries of Female Days: Englishwomen's Private Diaries*. New Brunswick: Rutgers Univ. Press, 1988.

Bolles, Edmund Blair. *Remembering and Forgetting: An Inquiry into the Nature of Memory*. New York: Walker and Co., 1988.

Buchanan, Frederick S. "The Ebb and Flow of Mormonism in Scotland, 1840–1900." In *Coming to Zion*, edited by James B. Allen and John W. Welch. Provo, UT: BYU Studies, 1997.

Burstyn, Joan N. *Victorian Education and the Ideal of Womanhood.* London: Croom Helm, 1980.

Cawelti, John. *Adventure, Mystery, and Romance.* Chicago: Univ. of Chicago Press, 1976.

Church Educational System. *Church History in the Fulness of Times.* Salt Lake City: The Church of Jesus Christ of Latter-day Saints, 1989.

Coben, Stanley. *Rebellion Against Victorianism: The Impetus for Cultural Change in 1920s America.* New York: Oxford Univ. Press, 1991.

Cogan, Frances B. *All-American Girl: The Ideal of Real Womanhood in Mid-Nineteenth-Century America.* Athens: Univ. Of Georgia Press, 1989.

Cott, Nancy F. *The Bonds of Womanhood.* New Haven: Yale Univ. Press, 1977.

Cranston, Maurice. *The Romantic Movement.* Oxford, UK: Basil Blackwell Ltd., 1994.

Cronon, William. "A Place for Stories: Nature, History, and Narrative." *The Jnl. of American Hist.* 78 (March 1992): 1347–1376.

Culley, Margo, ed. *A Day at a Time: The Diary Literature of American Women from 1764 to the Present.* New York: Feminist Press, 1985.

Deseret News 1997–98 Church Almanac. Salt Lake City: Deseret News, 1996.

Dickinson, George, and Michelle Leming. *Understanding Dying, Death, and Bereavement.* New York: Holt, Rinehart and Winston, 1994.

The Doctrine and Covenants of The Church of Jesus Christ of Latter-day Saints. Salt Lake City: The Church of Jesus Christ of Latter-day Saints, 1981.

Emerson, Ralph Waldo. *The Conduct of Life.* New York: A. L. Burt Company, n.d.

Flanders, Robert Bruce. *Nauvoo: Kingdom on the Mississippi.* Urbana: Univ. of Illinois Press, 1975.

Gardner, Howard. *Frames of Mind: The Theory of Multiple Intelligences.* New York: Basic Books, Inc., 1983.

Grele, Ronald J. "On Using Oral History Collections: An Introduction." *The Jnl. of American Hist.* 74 (September 1987): 570–578.

Gutek, Gerald L. *A History of the Western Educational Experience.* Prospect Heights, IL: Waveland Press, Inc., 1972.

Gutek, Gerald L. *An Historical Introduction to American Education.* 2nd ed. Prospect Heights, IL: Waveland Press, Inc., 1991.

Hallwass, John E., and Roger Lanius. *Cultures in Conflict: A Documentary History of the Mormon War in Illinois.* Logan: Utah State Univ. Press, 1995.

Harrison, J. F. C. *The Early Victorians, 1832–1851.* New York: Praeger Publ., 1971.

Harrison, John F. C. "The Popular History of Early Victorian Britain: A Mormon Contribution." In *Mormons in Early Victorian Britain*, edited by Richard L. Jensen and Malcom R. Thorp. Salt Lake City: University of Utah Press, 1989.

Heaton, Karen S. Telephone interview with author, Rock Springs, Wyoming, 10 February 1998.

Hefner, Loretta L. *The WPA Historical Records Survey: A Guide to the Unpublished Inventories, Indexes, and Transcripts*. Chicago: The Soc. of American Archivists, 1980.

Horton, Loren N. "The Victorian Era in the American West: An Introduction." *Journal of the West* 33, no. 1 (January 1994): 8–9.

Howe, Daniel Walker, ed. *Victorian America*. N.p.: Univ. of Pennsylvania Press, 1976.

Hufford, Mary, Marjorie Hunt, and Steven Zeitlin. *The Grand Generation: Memory, Mastery, Legacy*. Washington, D. C.: Smithsonian Institution, 1987.

Huyghe, Patrick. "Voices, Glances, Flashbacks: Our First Memories." *Psychology Today* 19 (September 1985): 48–52.

Jensen, Marvin D. "Memoirs and Journals As Maps of Intrapersonal Communication." *Communication Education* 33 (July 1984): 237–242.

Jenson, Andrew. *History of the Scandinavian Mission*. Salt Lake City: Deseret News Press, 1927.

Jenson, Andrew. *Latter-day Saint Biographical Encyclopedia*. 4 vols. 1901–1936. Salt Lake City: Western Epics, 1971.

Johnson, Allen and Dumas Malone. *Dictionary of American Biography*. Vol. 4. New York: Charles Scribner's Sons, 1960.

Larkin, Jack. *The Reshaping of Everyday Life, 1790–1840*. New York: Harper & Row, 1988.

Launius, Roger D. "Mormon Memory, Mormon Myth, and Mormon History." *Journal of Mormon History* 21 (Spring 1995): 1–24.

Leo, John. "Memory: The Unreliable Witness." *Time*, 5 January 1981, 89.

Lowenthal, David. *The Past Is a Foreign Country*. Cambridge: Cambridge Univ. Press, 1985.

Lowenthal, David. "The Timeless Past: Some Anglo-American Historical Preconceptions." *The Jnl. of American Hist.* 75 (March 1989): 1263–1280.

Ludlow, Daniel H., ed. *Encyclopedia of Mormonism*. 4 vols. New York: Macmillan Publ. Co., 1992.

McDannell, Colleen. *The Christian Home in Victorian America, 1840–1900*. Bloomington: Indiana Univ. Press, 1986.

McGavin, E. Cecil. *Nauvoo the Beautiful*. Salt Lake City: Stevens and Wallis, 1946.

Miller, David, and Della Miller. *Nauvoo: The City of Joseph*. Santa Barbara, CA: Peregrine Smith, 1974.

Milner, Clyde A. II. "The Shared Memory of Montana Pioneers." *Montana, The Magazine of Western History* 37 (Winter 1987): 2–13.

Milner, Clyde A. II. "The View from Wisdom: Region and Identity in the Minds of Four Westerners," *Montana, The Magazine of Western History* 41 (Summer 1991): 2–17.

Minnigerode, Meade. *The Fabulous Forties, 1840–1850: A Presentation of Private Life*. New York: G P. Putnam's Sons, 1924.

Mitchell, Sally. *Daily Life in Victorian England*. Westport, CT: Greenwood Press, 1996.

Montell, William Lynwood. *The Saga of Coe Ridge: A Study in Oral History*. Knoxville: Univ. of Tennessee Press, 1970.

Neisser, Ulric. *Memory Observed: Remembering in Natural Contexts*. San Francisco: W. H. Freeman and Co., 1982.

Newsome, David. *The Victorian World Picture*. New Brunswick, NJ: Rutgers Univ. Press, 1997.

Powell, Allan Kent, ed. *Utah Historical Encyclopedia*. Salt Lake City: Univ. of Utah Press, 1994.

Reed, John R. *Victorian Conventions*. Athens: Ohio Univ. Press, 1975.

Roberts, B. H. *A Comprehensive History of The Church of Jesus Christ of Latter-day Saints*. 6 vols. Salt Lake City: Deseret News Press, 1930.

Roberts, B. H. *The Rise and Fall of Nauvoo*. Salt Lake City: Bookcraft, 1965.

Rose, Steven. *The Making of Memory: From Molecules to Mind*. New York: Doubleday, 1992.

Rose, Steven. "Two Types of Truth: When Is a Memory Real, When Is It Not, and How Can Anyone Tell?" *New York Times Book Review*, 26 February 1995, 26.

Sansom, William. *Victorian Life in Photographs*. London: Thames and Hudson, 1974.

Thelen, David. "Memory and American History." *The Jnl. of American Hist.* 75 (March 1989): 1117–1129.

Thomas, Brook. *The New Historicism and Other Old-Fashioned Topics*. Princeton: Princeton Univ. Press, 1991.

Thrapp, Dan L. *Encyclopedia of Frontier Biography*. 3 vols. Glendale, CA: The Arthur H. Clark Co., 1988; Bison Book, 1991.

Tompkins, Jane. *Sensational Designs: The Cultural Work of American Fiction, 1790–1860*. New York: Oxford Univ. Press, Inc., 1985.

Veeser, H. Aram, ed. *The New Historicism*. New York: Routledge, 1989.

Welter, Barbara. "The Cult of True Womanhood, 1820–1860." In *The American Family in Social-Historical Perspective*, edited by Michael Gordon. New York: St. Martin's Press, 1973.

Index

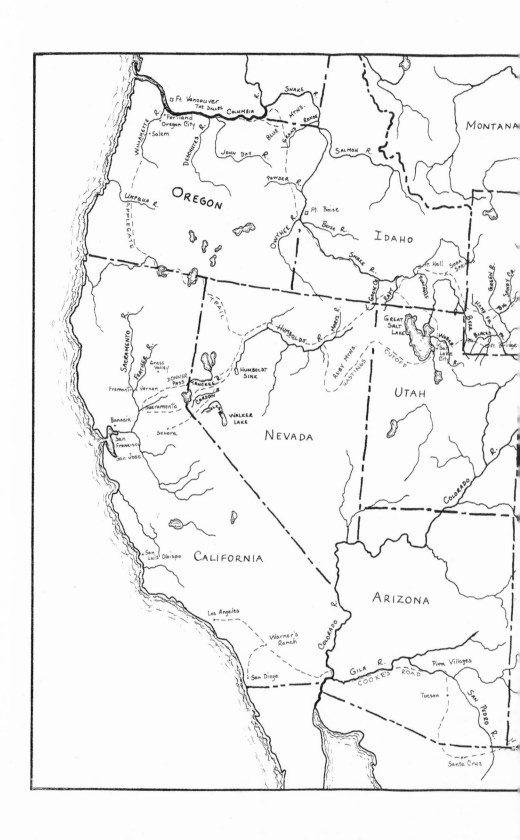